ADVANCE PRAISE FOR CAROL
FINDING MAGIC MOUNTAIN

"Carol Zapata-Whelan's informed and energetic account of her family's medical nightmare is interwoven with spiritual questions of universal significance. This true tale of a remarkably strong and mature young man on his way to medical school will leave readers inspired and humbled by Vincent's courage, his mother's perseverance, his father's steady faith, and the whole lively family's gift of hope." —MARGARITA ENGLE, author of *The Poet Slave of Cuba: A Biography of Juan Francisco Manzano*

"Carol Zapata-Whelan takes us on a powerful journey of the human spirit no one would ever choose." —MAS MASUMOTO, farmer and author of *Epitaph for a Peach*

"The study of rare genetic disorders can yield the most striking insights about everyday health. *Finding Magic Mountain* shares some of this process of discovery, but more importantly, it illustrates the lessons a mother learns about optimism, courage, and acceptance in the midst of battle with her son's rarest of rare genetic disorders, FOP. Anyone facing a rare disease, a common condition, or just a hard day, will find hope and solace in this mother's story." —HUGO W. MOSER, MD, director of the Neurogenetics Research Center at the Kennedy Krieger Institute, professor of Neurology and Pediatrics at Johns Hopkins University

"The example, the courage, and the testimony Zapata-Whelan and her family offer in this book are going to be a great help for many other patients and families. Don't give up, Carol! Your investment will pay off someday." —JOSÉ CARRERAS, award-winning opera singer

"At once inspiring and heartbreaking, Carol Zapata-Whelan's story probes the capacity of a family to deal with an inexorable enemy within. The family proves that enduring FOP with grace and courage is as important as prevailing. FOP offers 'no way out,' but Zapata-Whelan and her family carry on, fight back, and see the long term as well as the short in the face of what seem to be impossible odds. As a result, this is a book about humans functioning very near the top of their spiritual abilities." —GERALD HASLAM, author of *Haslam's Valley* and *Workin' Man Blues*

ABOUT THE AUTHOR

CAROL ZAPATA-WHELAN, PHD, is a lecturer in Spanish and Hispanic literature at California State University, Fresno, and the mother of five children. Her writing has appeared in *Newsweek*, Hispanic Link News Service (affiliated with the *Los Angeles Times* News Service), *Chicken Soup for the Latino Soul*, *The Rotarian*, *El Andar*, *Diario Uno*, and *Under the Fifth Sun: Latino Literature from California* (winner of an American Book Award in 2002). Her family has been featured in *USA Today*, the *San Francisco Chronicle*, and Radio Bilingüe. She lives with her husband and three youngest children in California's San Joaquin Valley.

FINDING MAGIC MOUNTAIN

Life with Five Glorious Kids
and a Rogue Gene Called FOP

CAROL ZAPATA-WHELAN

FOREWORD BY
Frederick S. Kaplan, MD

AFTERWORD BY
Michael Henrickson, MD

MARLOWE & COMPANY
New York

Finding Magic Mountain:
Life with Five Glorious Kids and a Rogue Gene Called FOP

Copyright © 2006 by Carol Zapata-Whelan
Foreword copyright © 2006 by Frederick S. Kaplan
Afterword copyright © 2006 by Michael Henrickson
"The FOP Laboratory Today" copyright © 2006 by Verena Dobnik

Published by
Marlowe & Company
An Imprint of Avalon Publishing Group, Incorporated
245 West 17th Street • 11th Floor
New York, NY 10011-5300

AVALON
publishing group inc.orporated

Library of Congress Cataloging-in-Publication Data
Zapata-Whelan, Carol, 1957–
Finding magic mountain : life with five glorious kids and a
rogue gene called FOP / Carol Zapata-Whelan ; foreword by
Frederick S. Kaplan ; afterword by Michael Henrickson.
p. cm.
ISBN 1-56924-400-6 (pbk.)
1. Fibrodysplasia ossificans progressiva—Popular works. I. Title.
RC931.F48Z37 2006
616.7′42—dc22
2006002615

ISBN-13: 978-1-56924-400-5

9 8 7 6 5 4 3 2 1

Designed by India Amos, Neuwirth & Associates, Inc.
Printed in the United States of America

Para mi queridísimo esposo, Walter
For my five glorious children
Para mis queridos padres

Sube a nacer conmigo, hermano.

No volverás a la profunda
zona de tu dolor diseminado.
No volverás del fondo de las rocas.
No volverás del tiempo subterráneo.
No volverá tu voz endurecida.

—PABLO NERUDA
"Alturas de Macchu Picchu,"
Canto general

Allons! whoever you are come travel with me!
Traveling with me you find what never tires.

The earth never tires,
The earth is rude, silent, incomprehensible at
    first, Nature is rude and incomprehensible
    at first,
Be not discouraged, keep on, there are divine
    things well envelop'd,
I swear to you there are divine things more
    beautiful than words can tell.

—WALT WHITMAN
"Song of the Open Road,"
Leaves of Grass

CONTENTS

FOREWORD

By Frederick S. Kaplan, MD

DISABLING CONDITIONS AFFECT not only the individuals who have them, but every member of the individual's family. That is the pretext, conveyed with humor, hope, and pathos, in Carol Zapata-Whelan's personal account of her family's struggle with fibrodysplasia ossificans progressiva (FOP). Zapata-Whelan's story is about a mother's determination to guide the life of her family around its collision course with one of the rarest and most disabling conditions known to man. The book takes its title from a roller coaster park called Magic Mountain, a name that also evokes the towering heights of Thomas Mann's epic work of the same name. Zapata-Whelan's son Vincent, and Mann's character Hans Castorp, find themselves in a transcendent world of ungodly challenges where the laws of nature subtend a slightly different reality. "It is like living in the Middle Ages," writes Zapata-Whelan. "And all of us follow the hidden path of FOP, though it is Vincent who lives with it in his bones with fortitude and grace."

Zapata-Whelan is at the artistic helm of a complex and creative family of five "glorious kids" and a husband-attorney. Now, add to that cosmopolitan mixture of frantic normalcy the single ingredient that her second son has one of the rarest conditions known to man, a condition affecting approximately one person in two million, and the wild card of a hair-raising ride on a Magic Mountain emerges. Zapata-Whelan, an efficient paradox who is always late, but whose roller-coaster life moves faster than the speed of thought, makes the world accelerate to observers in every frame of reference, but it is not fast enough for FOP—that unmagical and all-too-real disease that afflicts her son Vincent. Zapata-Whelan launches us into the dizzying world of anti-magical surrealism in which medical scooters and Radio Flyer wagons assault a new dimension of time, space, life, and medicine. Life with FOP as Zapata-Whelan describes it is "a race against time" and "an assault on the future."

FOP, however, is neither fiction nor imagery. It is no amusement park. Rather, it is a stark and sobering reality that transcends the imagination.

The childhood victims of FOP appear normal at birth except for telltale malformations of the great toes. But usually within the first decade of life, children succumb to progressive waves of renegade bone formation that, over time, transform the body's muscles and soft connective tissue into bone, leading to permanent loss of mobility. Any attempt to remove the extra bone leads to episodes of explosive new bone growth. At the present time, there is no effective prevention or treatment.

Although definitive treatments and cures are not yet available, the goals of FOP research are clear: to establish the genetic and molecular cause of FOP, and to use that knowledge to develop effective preventions, treatments, and a cure.

In the past decade, tremendous progress has been made in understanding the causes of this mysterious affliction, but much work remains to be done. Someday everything about this mystifying puzzle will be known—its genetic cause, its molecular origin, the nature of its pathways, the identity of its receptive cells and their downstream targets, the drugs to prevent it, and the therapies to cure it. That day is not yet at hand, but the journey and the climb toward the Magic Mountain continues, with insight and conviction.

The story of FOP has moved far beyond descriptive accounts that stir fear and anguish and into the laboratory that provides hope. Eventually, the work must return to the clinic with genuinely useful answers for the children. And it will. This work holds hope not only for those with FOP, but for those with more common disorders of bone formation as well, disorders like osteoporosis, osteoarthritis, and congenital malformations of the skeleton.

Finally, FOP may entangle the human body, but it does not warp the human spirit. This is evident in every page of Zapata-Whelan's compelling story, not only in the reflections of her own family, but also in those of other families whose stirring quotations illuminate the beginning of each chapter. As Connie Green, mother of nine-year-old Sophia, who battles FOP, states in the opening of chapter one: "[We] had been captured by this enemy and given a life sentence, having committed no crime." It is through such eloquent testimonies that Zapata-Whelan reaches toward hope: "FOP is no curse. It is, instead, a course, a path to ascent."

It is finally there, on an ascending path up Magic Mountain, where Zapata-Whelan starts and ends an account of this wild and dizzying journey. Recognizing her own son's courage in the eyes of others on the same difficult trek, she states with elegiac grace: "Maybe it is the look of the spirit that takes up spaces suffering leaves behind." It is precisely this equanimity and nobility of spirit that provide the inspiration for all of us who are privileged to participate in the FOP journey up Magic Mountain. As William Faulkner stated in his Nobel Prize speech in Stockholm on December 10, 1950, "*I believe that man will not merely endure, he will prevail. He is immortal, not because he alone among creatures has an inexhaustible voice, but because he has a soul, a spirit capable of compassion and sacrifice and endurance.*"

"A spirit capable of compassion and sacrifice and endurance"— that is exactly the spirit of Zapata-Whelan's message in *Finding Magic Mountain*.

FREDERICK S. KAPLAN, MD, is Isaac and Rose Nassau Professor of Orthopaedic Molecular Medicine at the University of Pennsylvania School of Medicine in Philadelphia.

PREFACE

*When my family held our first fund-raiser, after I was first
diagnosed, I felt uncomfortable talking about FOP and
refused to have my name in the paper. I just wanted to be
a teenager. FOP was so new to me, I wasn't comfortable
advertising to the world I had it . . . but this time around, at
our last family fund-raiser, my feelings drastically changed.
. . . I spoke in front of an audience of six hundred people
and told them how far I had come over the past eight years.
This was a monumental moment in my journey with FOP
because it showed I was no longer afraid to speak about
FOP. It also made me realize the reason I have this condition is to be a strong advocate on behalf of all my friends
with FOP and their families. . . . I am not afraid to fight
and make my voice heard until the day a treatment and a
cure is found.*

— HOLLY PULLANO, twenty-five, diagnosed
at age sixteen, North Haven, Connecticut

OUR LIFE IS a Magic Mountain. I realized this the day I was
in the California theme park's Gotham City, strapped to a giant
wheel—"The Grinder Gearworks"—revolving at atomic, perpen-
dicular, and paralyzing speeds. My then thirteen-year-old son,
Vincent, was enjoying the ride while I kept my eyes shut. "Are you

OK, Mom?" he yelled into space. All I could answer—after we had stopped spinning—was that I had been thinking about fainting. "Don't worry, Mom," Vincent told me. "If you had passed out, the centrifugal force would have kept you standing." This is the same force that operates in our home.

My husband, Walt, and I have five children. Life is a white-knuckled revolution around conflicting events, sudden trips to the doctor, lost homework, disappearing shoes, report cards signed at red lights, and backseat fights. I know of other mothers whose children never arrive anywhere short of breath, whose sons wear the same brand of shoe on each foot, whose daughters have real parts in their hair. Some might say I have a good excuse for the dizzied orbit of our life, but I know better. It has always been this way—even before everything got harder, nine years ago.

Ten years ago, our perfectly healthy son, Vincent, started limping. The limp persisted, confounding the finest doctors, white tunnels, and bone scans. Vincent was diagnosed with fibrodysplasia ossificans progressiva, FOP for short, a rare genetic disorder that turns muscle and connective tissues into bone, building a second skeleton that completely immobilizes the body over time.

Ten years ago, Vincent played soccer and baseball like his brothers Brian and Lucas; today, he cannot raise his arms high enough to comb his hair; he is unable to bend down low enough to tie his shoes. FOP is a monumental force that harrows the muscles at random with painful tumorlike swellings that rise, shift, and fall, leaving ridges of bone in their wake. And because even slight trauma can accelerate FOP's progress, Vincent must no longer play organized sports. A minor fall can have the consequences of a car accident.

Vincent has raged against FOP, but he adjusts to its sudden shifts with a determination and grace that catch me by the throat. He strove mightily in his high school marching band, and in his first year of high school won the title of "Most Courageous" as his band, combined with five other Central California ensembles, won first place in a competition parade in Hawaii. His courage is evident in an unusually generous spirit: Vincent is usually the one in the family who will patiently help friends with math, or follow our youngest around a playground. Though sidelined, he has rooted or played trumpet in band at his brothers' basketball games. And I have learned something vital, essential, in witnessing my son's spirit, in following this spirit to the small footholds of grace that appear along the way to right us.

One summer, on one of those infernal afternoons when windows get hot and asphalt softens in the San Joaquin Valley, I was leading our then six-year-old Isabel past parked cars, past a young woman fluttering around a raging infant. As Isabel peacefully sipped her Windex-colored ICEE, I wanted to say to the new mother, *It'll get better.* I wanted to say, *It'll get better* to the young woman. But I didn't. I didn't, because I knew I couldn't have stopped with a plain truism, even in the urgency of a hot parking lot. I would have had to let her know—by the way—that my nineteen-year-old, Brian, a former raging infant, had just called from San Francisco to announce, *Mom! This is the best day of my life!*

I would have gone on to explain that my college kid had the best day of his life because he had just had a hot dog. And he had had a hot dog because his jaw, wired shut for six weeks, had just been sprung. I would probably have gone on to describe the oral surgeon with a ponytail and the gorgeous name of Bloom who held my hand when I tried to talk and cry at the same time after Brian was attacked in a gym at UC Berkeley. And that story might have led me to say that our second son, Vincent, must never be hit, since even mild trauma can freeze his joints forever because of his rare condition.

I couldn't have said any of the above to a new mother on an infernal day of soft asphalt.

So I have written it here: what I've learned about struggle, light, faith, good days and bad, from my brave son Vincent, and also from his older brother, Brian, his younger brother, Lucas, and his little sisters, Celine and Isabel. I have learned more from my family, from the paths each member takes and crosses, than from all the books

I've read for a PhD in comparative literature. And all of us follow the hidden path of FOP, though it is Vincent who lives with it in his bones with fortitude and grace.

Vincent's FOP may be a catastrophe that strikes one in two million, but my son's struggle, our struggle, is not especially different from anyone else's efforts to stay standing despite the twists, turns, and breakneck falls that life can spring on us. Our family's particulars may be unique, but—as the truism goes—struggle is universal. And I think that when we see someone like Vincent move gracefully with a great burden, we take heart. So I offer here part of Vincent's story, our story, as an effort to share some courage and tell the world about our unusual path. And along the way in this testimony is an everyday life, tales of things gone right and wrong in a large family, fables of the twists and turns and little miracles that have led me, a recovering worrier, to trust in the universe.

I believe in a Divine Plan. I believe that part of this Plan is that my husband and I must guide our children through what I can only call "Magic Mountain," a dizzying, exhilarating, white-knuckling life. I, myself, may never master the details of the trip, but I believe I can manage the big shifts and still stand. It did not take me long to realize, the day I accompanied Vincent to the roller coaster park called Magic Mountain—on an eighth-grade graduation trip—to inspect rides, comfort white-faced kids, look in Lost and Founds, and ignore squabbles, why I felt no more fatigue than at the end of our "normal" days. I knew why my eager son never once blanched or balked on the harrowing roll of the tracks. It was because it all felt hauntingly familiar. And surmountable.

FINDING
MAGIC
MOUNTAIN

APRIL 1995

"GO, VINCENT! GO!"

A third grader with a proud look is running to first. He wears the sky blue uniform of the Dolphins, and he is moving with his usual zeal. It is a mild California evening in the San Joaquin Valley, and the navy blue mountains hide in the haze.

"You're late," says my husband, but he kisses me anyway, and turns to shout, jubilant, toward the baseball diamond.

I've made the trek from our new house, a dream home under construction, out in the middle of nowhere, far from this worn school field; that's my lateness excuse for today. But I'm just in time to hold up the video camera. And in the little black and white window, I see our son on his way to home.

He's still limping.

The familiar itch of worry. "Just a pulled muscle," said the pediatrician. Our doctor is used to waving my fears into the air. (The first word Vincent ever said as a baby, thanks to his mother, was *Uh-oh*.)

Well.

Vincent wouldn't want to be taped limping home. I let the camera drop to my side. We can wait for the next game.

ORANGE FLAME

When Sophia started her first body flare-up, I walked around contacting everyone who knew anything about medicine, FOP, Sophia, me. . . . During that time, I thought I was grounded in my body, but I was not present. Stress does things to us that we can hardly be prepared for. And FOP is such an unusual, isolating stressor, that my mind had gone into hyperdrive to find some of life's sweetness and normalcy to escape the pain and yet find a way to accept that Sophia and I had been captured by this enemy and given a life sentence, having committed no crime.

— CONNIE GREEN, mother of Sophia, eight, diagnosed at age fourteen months, Fort Lee, New Jersey

"MOM! IT'S FROM the Philippines!" Vincent, my eleven-year-old, his beautiful face round from steroids, his T-shirt distended by a swelling on his back, held out the receiver. It was near the end of summer, 1997, and we had written to a healer across the ocean. I had mailed her an old picture of Vincent, healthy and freckle-faced in his navy blue Catholic school uniform. I had sent a story, "Protein Builds Second Skeleton," from *Science* magazine, about a rare genetic disorder, fibrodysplasia ossificans progressiva, FOP for short, that ossifies muscles with strange swellings.

"Good morning," said a woman's voice when I took the phone. My husband, Walt, and our five kids—Brian, Vincent, Lucas, Celine, and baby Isabel—rounded the dinner table, opening white cartons of long brown noodles and glazed vegetables, framed in the dark reflection of the bay windows.

"Good—evening," I said.

"Your letter has been providential," said a woman's voice with an Asian accent. "A few days before it arrived, I dreamed about your son."

A spasm of hope—or panic—took my throat, and I had to put a finger to my ear to block out a fight for fortune cookies. "Two nights before I received your letter," the healer went on, "I saw a soul pass through an orange flame."

The competition for fortune cookies was getting louder. I needed to change phones.

But I couldn't move. "The next night," said the woman with the Asian voice, "I dreamed about a foreign boy—I had never seen his face. And then your picture came and I—"

Our one-year-old, Isabel, was pitching into a wail, unhappily waxing the high chair tray with her fists in a slick of apple juice. Our oldest, fourteen-year-old Brian, was loudly counting out fortune cookies.

"The boy in my dream was Vincent," I was able to hear.

This was not just a fly-by-night healer on the line. The woman on the other side of the ocean was a reputable practitioner, recommended by a trusted friend.

The baby's complaint and the fortune cookie fight were escalating over my husband's commands. It was time to change phones. But before I could excuse myself, the word *hex* filtered through.

"There has been," I heard, sitting in the dark of a different room, a room lined with books in Spanish and laundry baskets, "in the family of mother or father, a malediction—or sin—transmitted."

Wait a minute.

Hadn't Christ healed a blind man and exonerated his parents? The healer's explanation seemed extravagant, ignorant, archaic, and, on the other hand, very sensible. I tried to picture this healer, who, I had been told, was a nun: she would be young, with a scrubbed full face, coarse black hair hidden under blue linen.

The nun went on. Her diction was stilted, oracular. "The

malediction, the curse, is from a past generation. An evil suffering will purify."

Whose family bore the unpaid sin? It had to be my side, no doubt: Great-grandfather Tiburcio, slumped at a card table, gambling away the Zapata vineyards grape by grape. Or my mother's cousin, the one who fell off Manchita at full gallop and was never right again. What about my husband's roots? An angry Irishman? A British uncle who lost his manners? The most likely mischief would have to have come from the French branch, but with a name like Le Sage, it seemed impossible. Surely, the curse was in my bloodline, if for no other logic than by reason of maternal guilt.

I agreed with the nun about the extraordinary power of prayer, but began to feel a strange distaste for her kind voice. No matter what I asked, she seemed to be answering a different question—across the English language, the satellites, the sea, and the fifteen hours between us.

After setting down the phone, I sat in the dark, in that room full of laundry. I am a Latin, prone to magical realism (the strange is normal, the normal is strange); a mother, prone to guilt; and a literature PhD, prone to suspending disbelief. So the healer's words haunted me, they haunted me. Fibrodysplasia ossificans progressiva is an unreal condition, so unreal it is difficult to fit it in the imagination. When I first heard F—O—P, the letters, *it*, made no sense. And I felt the full force of César Vallejo's lines: "*There are blows in life, so hard . . . / Blows as if from something like God's hate.*"

The room full of laundry where I sat in the dark was in our old house, a blue two-story, with a field of wheat and sage behind it. From the front of our home you could see silver eucalyptus lining land that had held a fort in another century. And down the road were groves of walnut trees with their dark-skinned jackets on grafted white wood. And there were vineyards, rolling green, for acres and acres, beyond the wheat field. When we first saw the land around what would be our new neighborhood, before we broke ground to build, I felt like I was back in Mendoza, the agricultural province of my family in Argentina. And my husband felt less far from the olive ranch in Porterville, where he grew up taking care of the trees.

There was a great peace in the land. The sheltering eucalyptus seemed to promise it.

It was a false peace.

Through our years in the neighborhood of the blue two-story, I began to wonder what really happened on the land lined by the eucalyptus, the stretch of grass that had held a fort adjacent to us when California was a new state. I wondered if it was the site of something terrible, of a massacre. I wondered if a native shaman set a curse to it. Because our neighborhood was the site of unusual luck: of "blows in life so hard." One Christmas a young child was killed. Later, a young wife became very ill. One spring a boy fell from a tree and lost consciousness for days. Then a surveillance van kept watch over a family threatened with violence. Neighbors congenial in past lives fought through lawyers. Friends moved away without saying good-bye. And when we broke ground to build our house on the hardpan of that new development, our perfectly normal eight-year-old started limping.

The healer's words haunted me.

But there is no such thing as "God's hate." And while Vincent's condition, fibrodysplasia ossificans progressiva, is so hard to say it must be cut to three letters, so mythic it seems like a biblical punishment, I know in my bones—six years after the healer's call—that FOP is no curse. It is, instead, a *course*, a path to ascent.

That night as I sat in the room full of laundry and books, the hall light found a picture of Vincent holding a starfish, taken the summer before at a beach, during a failed experimental treatment. I like to think he is radiant in that portrait. And looking at the image of the boy and the star, I realized I knew nothing of the Filipina healer's religious order. A new vision of her came to me: it was not the profile of a young woman in the abbreviated blue of Catholic nuns. Instead, I saw a form almost erased in saffron robes, with crossed legs and dancer's hands, posed mirror image to the gold statue, shine muted in incense, eyes steeped in solitude.

I think the kind Asian voice that called me that night from the other side of the sea belonged to a Buddhist nun who dialed the wrong number.

LIKE MY MOTHER, who is an academic and a poet, I have always had trouble with the time/space continuum: I am chronically late and have trouble finding places. I like to think this problem stems from the possibility that I run on Latin time—in the wrong hemisphere. I should be living under the Southern Cross in my family's homeland of Argentina, where people stay put for centuries (so they never get lost), and where it is unfashionable to arrive punctually. As it stands, my missing sense of time leads friends to fit me with Zapata-adjusted invitations, prosthetic schedules. And nobody who knows me will ever think of asking me to give directions, or consider putting me in charge of anything with time/space coordinates. Once when a Mexican colleague suggested I might like to lead a Latino group at the university, I offered to assist, but warned him, "I'm a little absentminded."

"I know," he agreed.

"How?!" I thought—truly, I did—my absentmindedness was camouflaged in an academic setting.

"I read about it in the paper," said another instructor, lightly, looking through his mail.

It is not a good thing to be a mother of five who gets lost and arrives late everywhere.

I struggle with this problem, and the only advantage in it is it distracts me from my tendency to worry. Ironic, then, that someone dubbed "worrywart," or *preocupona* in Spanish as some of my students have called me, would be given something like FOP to add to her schedule. But life has a strange way of handing us challenges that are completely unsuitable.

JUNE 2003

TODAY VINCENT (a normally punctual person), who is now sixteen years old, and I are late—but not lost—in our hospital. We are in the elevator on the way to the ground floor, to Rheumatology. (I have

made this trip many times, and still find myself saying to Vincent,
Was it up or down? I ask myself this same question when I go to my
husband's law office, and always seem to end in front of a sign that
says FBI. My husband doesn't work for the FBI.)

Where we are, Children's Hospital Central California, is like a
medical facility made by magic. It is a fairy castle on a hill, a hop-
scotch of sunrise colors—where patients' rooms have ceilings full of
stars that light the dark. Children ride Radio Flyer wagons instead
of wheelchairs, and the staff is a force of real-life fairy godparents, as
jolly and kind as they are practiced at their magic. There is a Grape
Jellyfish Café, with bold walls of deep-sea life and real aquariums.
The lobby is a three-story rotunda, a map of the earth with all its
oceans and continents colored in on a big round rug.

Today Vincent has agreed to take part in a locally held University
of California, San Francisco, medical conference—"A low-key setting
with small groups rotating to different gurneys," Dr. Henrickson,
our rheumatologist, has explained. Vincent consented readily. He
knows the future of FOP patients depends on medical research. And
he also knows most health professionals have never seen a case of
his condition—and that what they don't know can impair other
FOP sufferers. Should any nurse, doctor, or X-ray technician decide
to "help" someone like Vincent by adjusting a limb, or by simply
tugging a shirt over stiff arms, the passive exercise could trigger a
domino effect of pain, cartilage formation from muscle, bone from
cartilage, and, finally, lost mobility.

After descending in the hospital's Blue Diamond tower, we follow Paula, our lovely dark-haired nurse, down a passage lined with
Crayola castles and finger paintings. We enter a lecture hall, where
Vincent and I find chairs at long tables. Dr. Henrickson, a luminous
soul with a patrician look, stands at the front taking questions from
people in lab coats. I notice a few gurneys along the walls set up for
the young patients with rare disorders. I see a small Asian boy with
his parents, and a Hispanic youth, but do not look long enough to
see why they might be here. Dr. Henrickson acknowledges us and
smiles, but I can feel Vincent's braced anticipation. Or maybe I'm
the one who's braced. In spite of the hospital's friendly decor, any

lecture hall looks forbidding when you have something to do with what's going on in the front.

Dr. Henrickson concludes his talk and some of the older physicians rise to go, while others trade greetings and comments. It looks like we have some time before the residents are ready for the individual gurney exams, so I tell Vincent I'll be right back, remind him to tell doctors to *not push his limbs past capacity*, and rush off to find a restroom.

When I get back, I see Vincent already seated on a gurney, near the far front corner of the lecture hall, facing a team of young residents chatting with him amiably. I scold myself for believing I had more time, and my only thought as I charge toward the doctors—who look to be about fifteen years old—is that I have to announce: *Do not push his limbs past capacity*. No doubt, Dr. Henrickson has given a similar warning, but I like to compensate for my no-sense-of-time fault with a talent for persistence I've had to pick up over the years. With all that, I must appear grim to the residents, who turn serious as I arrive.

Dr. Henrickson is rounding the gurneys, giving instructions, and he intervenes pleasantly, introduces us, and tells Vincent to offer no information beyond the questions posed, as the assignment is to diagnose his condition from clinical findings.

Two young men and three young women: they look harmless enough, and one of the men, teddy-bearish, with a mustache and glasses, seems the friendliest. I give them all The Warning—as hastily as possible—"Do not push his limbs past capacity": my son's arms, neck, legs must not go past their "give," no passive exercise; *"please be careful."* Their intelligent eyes are all on me. They, Vincent—I—are all much too serious. So in conclusion, it occurs to me to add, "Or I'll kill you."

Even the teddy-bearish resident looks over a little sharply, unsure what to make of the last bit. Fortunately, Vincent breaks into a smile, showing his retainer, and the least tired looking of the group laugh. The ice is broken. So for the rest of the hour, I will hear myself repeating amiably to each team in rotation, "If you try to move his limbs past capacity, I'll kill you." A nurse accompanying one of the groups greets me cheerfully: "I heard you telling people you were going to kill them—so I was waiting to find out what not to do!"

I watch the new doctors ask Vincent questions. A young Asian woman palpates his hands, asks to see his fingernails. Normal. *Do you have rashes?* No. *Trouble sleeping?* asks another. No. *Digestive problems?* No. *You seem to be sitting very straight, a little stiff,* notes a young woman with blue eyes and curly brown hair. *Does your back hurt?* No. (Not now.) *May I feel your back?* asks a young Indian woman. *Carefully,* I warn. The young Indian is gentle, and she feels, no doubt, the topography of bone, the ridges and hills of ossification that have formed over time, the wing of bone on one of Vincent's shoulder blades that keeps him from leaning back into wooden chairs and taking off his T-shirt when he goes swimming with friends. The residents—proceeding as most top specialists in the world have proceeded—are far from posing any question that might help them diagnose their first case of FOP.

"Why don't you ask when it started?" I prompt. When he was almost nine years old, Vincent tells them. "Why don't you ask him what makes it worse?" I suggest. *Trauma,* Vincent explains, *any kind: falls, bumps, especially medical injections. But it can get worse without any trauma at all.*

Do you have something progressive? they ask. *Will it get worse over time?* Vincent answers matter-of-factly: *Yes,* but explains that his condition affects different patients differently—some worsen faster than others. My son, who first began to limp nearing the age of nine, has been one of the "lucky" ones, as FOP symptoms typically arrive in toddlerhood. (Try to keep a two-year-old from falling or bumping into things.) I feel an odd relief that Vincent can answer the questions he is given so easily, without a trace of unnaturalness in his voice. This boy has accepted FOP in ways that I have not.

"Has anyone asked Vincent to walk?" says Dr. Henrickson as he makes his rounds through the room. No one has asked my son to move about. You can't know if someone limps when he's dangling his legs from a gurney. FOP has not interfered with Vincent's growth. The round-faced boy has grown into a handsome youth with brown eyes full of light that are sometimes too sober. He is tall and lean, a poplar in the wind. But the FOP has created a winding vine of bone around his ribs, like a corset, so he cannot arch his back or bend far or raise his arms high enough to comb his hair. And the disease has taken hip flexion year by year. Without FOP, I know he would have been a natural athlete like his father and brothers, and it is this unused gift that allows him to adjust his balance to the surprise attacks of the disorder. Though he can no longer swing his arms back and forth as he walks, his hands hold an invisible balance, and he moves with his own precise grace, with an up-and-down gait that exalts every flexion. Not long ago a physical therapist and I stood watching Vincent move. "It's a miracle how he walks so well with all the hip ossification I've measured," said the therapist. "Technically, you would think he wouldn't be able to balance that way." Vincent's balance, his miracle, is spirit and will.

Vincent obliges the residents' request to walk, limping with distinction, like a war hero. The young doctors study his movements thoughtfully, and then he returns to the gurney. They continue their rheumatologic questions, still far off the mark, and I decide to play "hot" and "cold." (They are, after all, "kid doctors.") My son gives his accomplice a smile as he and I call out "cold, cold" when the doctors ask him to extend an arm that he can raise no higher than shoulder height, or turn his neck, for which he needs a special mirror when he drives to see peripheral traffic. They are nowhere near "warm," near the simple clue that is FOP's defining feature, one that requires no lab test or X-ray. I begin to forget that the residents are not my own students and improvise a lesson. I don't know if we are breaking the rules of their assignment, but everyone is caught up in this medical game of Clue, and the young doctors appear as intrigued as Vincent is amused. They continue in the dark.

Finally, I say it: "Why don't you ask Vincent to take off his shoes?"

Because of the bone growth up and down his back, Vincent can no longer bend down low enough to remove his shoes with his hands. But he is able to shuck off his Nikes, toe to heel, with a practiced motion. Same with the athletic socks. The young doctors stand in a semicircle looking down at his bare feet. Puzzled.

"Is it because his feet are long?" offers the pretty young resident with curly brown hair. I can tell Vincent likes her. My son shakes his head no.

"Why don't you check Vincent's toes," I say.

The young doctor gets down on her haunches, feels carefully with her thumb and index finger. She looks up with light in her eyes. "He's missing a joint in his big toe," she says quietly. She is the first of the teams to note this anomaly with such conviction. No one, no one at all—not even Vincent's mother—would make this discovery for nine years, not until Dr. Henrickson carried out that first exam in the fall of 1995. I see the same illumination in the face of every resident who palpates Vincent's big toe. With something as rare as FOP, it is the patient who must teach the doctor.

We are fortunate to be at this UCSF conference at our hospital for a reason even more urgent than the need to advance FOP education. Vincent is fighting a new flare-up in his hip joint—pain and stiffness from an overnight stay at a leadership camp—and we must see if this fresh threat to mobility warrants an experimental treatment. The only FOP laboratory in the country, led by Dr. Fred Kaplan and Dr. Eileen Shore at the University of Pennsylvania, has just begun to study FOP and pamidronate, a treatment for osteogenesis imperfecta, "brittle bone disease," where bone fails to remold—the polar opposite of Vincent's condition. Fibrodysplasia ossificans progressiva creates robust calcification and builds, in fact, a second skeleton that immobilizes the body with *too much* bone. In theory, pamidronate should accelerate FOP's process—and no one knows for sure if it works—but three baffling successes in Italy, Israel, and England have led researchers at the University of Pennsylvania to consider the drug to combat FOP.

Once the residents have gone, Dr. Henrickson examines Vincent. The hip pain has lessened, responding, it seems, to the cocktail of medications we've mixed through trial and error over time. The new treatment is unwarranted, Dr. Henrickson decides. I do not gently insist or wonder otherwise out loud. (Vincent's kind doctors are indulgent with my persistence faculty.) I do not insist, because pamidronate is different from anything we've ever tried. Its common side effect is high fever, and the drug requires hours of an IV drip over the course of several days of returning to the hospital. I am, frankly, relieved.

Vincent and I leave the fairy castle of Children's, pleased with ourselves and the UCSF medical conference. Ironically, UCSF just rejected Vincent, who lends himself to science as few others can, for a high school biomed summer internship in our town. I've reacted in dogged persistence mode, making phone calls, writing pleas to local directors, to distant administrators, to university colleagues, to anyone who might find a medical mentor for a future doctor with a 4.67 GPA, stellar recommendations, and a race against time. But I've finally gotten a response, thanks to the medical school chancellor's office. The director of the program would like to see letters and documents. So I dig through boxes and boxes in our new house and fax and fax every pertinent piece of paper I can find. *Enough is enough*, says my husband. Walt is a trial lawyer and knows a lost cause when he sees one. *We'll see about that.*

)

JUNE TURNS OUT to be what I call "Bone Month." The bad luck of Vincent's hip flare-up is "counterbalanced" when our nineteen-year-old, Brian, has wires removed from his jaw, metal that has clamped shut his mandible fractured in an attack at Berkeley. (In an argument over basketball points the day before Easter, a nonstudent using university facilities took a running start from behind Brian, swung, and fled the scene.) But the bad-luck pendulum swings again.

I will describe now what happens exactly one week after Brian has "the best day of my life" eating a hot dog, ending six weeks of liquid food through a dental cage.

I am in our brand-new master bedroom, with bay windows looking out to giant cedars and a front yard of earth Brian and his friends have furrowed for sprinklers. I feel the ease of our new home in the country, a white wood one-story with a shaded porch wide enough for a bench swing. I am at my desk, basking in the glow of letters of recommendation for Vincent faxed to UCSF, when I hear crying, distant crying, growing louder, coming down the hall, aiming toward my room. I do not know, until that moment, that our new house is soundproof, virtually from one end to the other, and that we should have added this feature to my worry list. Fourteen-year-old Lucas is calling: "Isabel got hurt." I expect to see scuffed knees or a bump that will need some ice. Instead, six-year-old Isabel appears, her freckled face red, her brown hair wild, left arm hanging limply at her side—buckled and distorted above the elbow. It is all I can do to keep from passing out.

OK—OK—OK. Let's get to the hospital. OK—OK—OK.

Eleven-year-old Celine is at our entryway, crying in sympathy, and Vincent emerges from his room, groggy from a nap. Lucas ushers his little sister past them out the door, while I grab keys and purse in a trance. Impossible for me to understand exactly how this accident happened. All I can absorb between accounts is that Isabel was on some kind of seat that moved and nobody could get to it in time. I make sure Lucas has his sister standing in the minivan so her arm doesn't bend. As we drive off, I give our new porch swing a glance. It looks back innocently. We are too far away from Children's. But there is a good hospital two streets down, and this will be our first trip there since our move to the new house.

Lucas, who knows more about Vincent's private struggles than I ever will, calmly holds his little sister, reassures her, keeps the arm steady. I, on the other hand, while decent at dogged persistence, am at my very worst trying to locate places in panic gear. I aim the car in the general direction of the hospital; pass murky canals, orange groves, a helicopter landing pad, parking lots; and flag down a human figure. "How—where—which—do I get to the ER?!" Lucas absorbs the human figure's instructions.

Once in the ER lobby, I shout to anyone who will listen: "*She broke her arm!*"

"It's broken?" Poor Isabel cries, surprised, even more alarmed.

"Well, maybe not," I say, hopefully. No X-ray is needed to see the bones are not in logical sequence.

I have a vague impression of pale linoleum and double doors, and Isabel is seen immediately. (Our first ER without a waiting room wait.) But we are spooked in triage by the unshaven male nurse with a snaggletooth who says the four-letter word *SHOT* so profanely my child and I both start and her wails escalate. *Where are the doctors?*

Must get specialist.

I'll call Dr. Henrickson.

As the mother of five kids, I know exactly how emergency rooms operate. You wait in a front room. You wait at a little window where you are given a plastic bracelet or a sticker with information. You wait at a nurse's station. You wait in a waiting room. You wait in an examining room. You wait more. You wait for another nurse. You wait for a doctor. You wait. You wait for a second doctor. You wait more.

But for this problem *I'm* getting the second doctor. Myself. Now. Even though we have progressed to a gurney in a long room with heavy curtain partitions. I have a cell phone.

"This is the Exchange," says a young male voice.

"Is Dr. Henrickson on call?"

"Dr. Wright is taking his calls."

"That's fine!" I give the young man from the Exchange my full name and spell it.

"Patient's name?"

"She's not really a patient. Her brother Vincent is a patient. He has a rare genetic disorder."

"I can't put you through if she's not a patient."

"Dr. Wright knows who I am. It's an emergency!"

"Well, if the child's not a patient—"

"Just get me Dr. Wright!"

"I'm sorry, but I can't do that, Carol." The young man from the Exchange is calling me Carol. I look over at my little girl's arm. It's swelling. I think of all the nerves that run through those delicate bones snapped in two. By now I've learned she fell off a revolving office chair, not the porch swing I suspected. Whatever the cause, she needs more intervention than this small hospital is set up to give—and she needs it *fast*, I know that much. I give the young man from the Exchange my number and tell him to *get me Dr. Wright.*

"What's the problem, Carol?" asks the young man, reasonably enough.

"It's none of your concern!" I don't have time for explanations. He does, though, and starts to launch into one, trying to call me Carol again.

"What is *your* name?" I cut the poor kid short.

"Brian," he says amiably. My daughter is looking terribly pale. *Where are the doctors?*

"Brian what?" Same name as my firstborn. I will remember this.

"Everyone knows me as Brian."

Lucas is walking in, hesitant. It is a comfort to see my tall, steady lad, exactly half-Irish, half-Latin, in this drab hall partitioned into three sections by heavy curtains. *Where are the doctors?*

"Well, Brian: *Thank you* for *being no help at all!*" I punch off.

"Why did you talk to Brian that way?" asks Lucas.

"It's not *our* Brian!" My son's dark eyes give me a quizzical look. And suddenly I know something else: the simple fact of Lucas's presence makes up my mind about it.

On the second or third ring a teenage voice answers.

"Is this John?" It is. "This is Lucas's mom. Is your dad on call?" John gets his mother, who is also a doctor. A *doctor*.

John was Lucas's classmate. His father is an orthopedist. Not just any orthopedist. He is a world-class surgeon, and before Lucas ever met John, John's father was one of the specialists who saw Vincent when he began to limp. And Dr. Joseph Gerardi, the best orthopedic surgeon in the world, had the humility to admit he could not find the trouble behind a mild limp. But he sent us to someone he thought would, and did, *in one visit, a speed unheard-of in the annals of FOP.* And unlike every other specialist stumped by the disorder, Dr. Gerardi tried no complex surgeries, ordered no invasive tests that could have locked Vincent's leg. I have met children with necks frozen forward from biopsies; one girl permanently genuflecting, scar tracks down her thigh; a young woman whose arm was amputated—unnecessarily. Our son is walking today because of Dr. Joe Gerardi. And I was hoping to avoid bothering him during dinner.

"Ma'am?" I hear a man's voice from the other side of a curtain. "You're not allowed to use cell phones in the hospital."

Uh-oh.

I forgot about cell phones and magnetic waves and hospital machines. I lean through the curtain apologetically and just as quickly step back. It is the attending physician, a handsome fellow with white hair, quietly stitching a massive wound on a youth's face. "And we contact the specialists from the hospital ourselves," he calls through the curtain.

But I still don't know if Dr. Gerardi is free. John's mother is going to try to find him. Maybe I can go use a pay phone and call Brian at the Exchange—again. Maybe not.

Just when I am plotting how to use a pay phone by a gurney, Lucas ushers in his father, thank God, Walt, my redheaded Braveheart, looking strong as he glances at our daughter's swelling arm. (Everything in life is easier with Walt along, and he has a keen sense of direction and a good watch.) Isabel has just been in X-ray, down the hall, and I cannot look at the film of white shadows and gray a technician has slapped on the lighted panel.

And suddenly a spry, blue-eyed man appears in the room with the partitioned curtains: *Dr. Gerardi!* Dr. Gerardi reads the dark films on the lighted panel, says, "OK," reassuringly, and pats Isabel, who is looking very brave. She needs surgery and a pin in her elbow, he explains. Now. We can go to the fairy castle by ambulance or take her ourselves. He will meet us at the OR.

"Thank you." I give Dr. Gerardi a hug and Walt shakes his hand. "Were you on call?" It is dinnertime.

"No, but I'm honored you thought of me."

The attending physician is splinting our daughter's arm for the trip to Children's, giving me a bemused look that seems to say, *Anything I can do for you, now that you have your diagnosis, your surgeon, your OR? Coffee, maybe?*

"Our sons are friends," I offer. I don't tell him that in strange, roundabout ways Isabel's arm has been saved by her brother's FOP.

"I heard," he says, carefully looping the stretchy flesh-colored material.

"Mom!" Lucas's handsome face again: he has opened the examining room's door. "Dr. Wright's on the phone."

Brian from the Exchange. His mother named him well.

And from the time Isabel falls from a spinning chair to the time Dr. Gerardi tells us to say a prayer, to the time he emerges from the OR announcing the surgery went perfectly, only four hours go by. *A speed unheard-of in the annals of the ER.*

LOCKED GLASS

*I thought that we were coming out of this flare-up but now
he has another lump in his neck. Does this ever stop for a
while??? I feel so bad for him, not being able to tell us that he
hurts. He is taking this pain soooooo good for a three-year-
old, but then I think pain is all he knows. He is coping very
well in adapting to getting into cars differently, getting into
chairs differently, and just about doing everything a little
differently now.*

—DEE WHITMORE, mother of Lucas, three,
diagnosed at age two, Albany, Illinois

I OFTEN GIVE MY students the French writer André Breton's
famous definition of surrealism: the chance encounter of an
umbrella and a sewing machine on a dissecting table. This unlikely
conjunction reflects, in part, the peculiar chaos of a twentieth-
century world between world wars. But the metaphor could also
reflect my living room, or our life with FOP between its diagnosis
and future cure. Writing about FOP, a newspaper reporter in the Bay
Area told me that when Dr. Kaplan reached her from Philadelphia,
she was emerging from a YWCA with her gym bag and had to duck
into a post office to conduct her interview. "Not the usual way,"
she said. Around FOP nothing much happens in the usual way.
My friend FOP mother Connie Green, who sings opera, has had
to assert herself in an ER while still in costume, and Dr. Kaplan,
Chief of the Division of Metabolic Bone Diseases at the University
of Pennsylvania, has examined Vincent in an Elks Club lodge with

a moose head mounted on the wall behind him, trophies overhead, and a sawhorse with a saddle in a corner.

Sometimes I get carried away with the surreal, and it is Vincent who directs me to proven orders. Not long ago, in the space of two weeks, our refrigerator broke down, lights went out, the microwave caught fire, the house alarm went wild, and our water pump stopped. "Maybe that's related to my writing about FOP," I wondered out loud. "If the brain is electrical, why not?" *Could be,* said our builder, who liked my explanation. But Vincent is a scientist. "Electricity needs a pathway," he said. "What would the electrical pathways be between your brain and the appliances?"

As for the surrealism of FOP itself, I will start where it *really* begins, on one hot summer night in July 1996, long after the actual diagnosis, right after Isabel was born:

It was during the bedtime hour push, downstairs in our family room, when I noticed something unusual. "Did you hurt your back, Vincent?" I asked our nine-year-old, who had his shirt off. I had seen—for the very first time—a strange bump in a strange place. The bump was the size of an apricot pit and it was high up on my son's back, alongside his spine. Vincent shook his head no to my question.

The next day we went to see our pediatrician, Dr. Weinberg, who carefully palpated the knot. "Did you hurt your back?" he asked. Again, the answer was no. The little bump didn't look too bad. Maybe it was the FOP showing itself, Dr. Weinberg and I considered—but maybe not.

Still, that night, concerned, I called my mother in the Bay Area. "I think it's starting," I told her, talking low, trying not to wake our newborn. I was in the upstairs alcove, which had been built for a study off the master bedroom but had ended up as a nursery. The little room with glass doors had a grand view of gold wheat fields, and it still had my books gathering dust. But all I saw at that moment was a black window and its reflection of a frizzy-haired woman in her thirties with a deflated look: me.

"What's starting?" my mother asked. She would be in her own upstairs, in a satin robe, a book in her lap, in her extraordinary condo, the one with a floor-to-ceiling window framing the Santa Cruz hills. Roland, our children's adopted grandfather, would be downstairs, making her a cup of chamomile tea and paging through an ancient manuscript.

"That—condition." I still couldn't say the words, and I still didn't know any of what we would learn in the coming weeks, months, or years. I was worried—a little beyond my usual default level—but had I known what was coming, I would have been breathing into a brown paper bag. "The F—O—P," I said, making out the shadowy farmland through my reflection.

"But nothing has actually happened, has it?" said my mother, after I described the strange bump. She reminded me of all the knots, swellings, stitches, and scrapes that had come and gone in our household. She was right: *nothing had happened.* After the diagnosis, FOP hadn't done a thing. It hadn't progressed. Vincent was just a kid with a mild limp. "Use the Ultracur," she advised. My mother liked to push this magic ointment from Argentina, one that was thick and white and cod-livery, and was supposed to work on everything from diaper rash to rattlesnake attack. "You're not using it, are you?" she said. "And the holy water?"

I told my mother that I had, in fact, taken water from a special bottle she had brought from Lourdes and sprinkled it on Vincent's back. The water came in a translucent little statue and we handled it respectfully, sparingly. "How much?" asked my mother. "How much holy water are you using?"

"God doesn't—*Mamá*—that's ridiculous—" I stopped myself. My mother, it seemed, was more concerned than she was letting on. "We've been applying five cc's every four hours." My mother laughed. Everything would be fine if your mother was laughing.

She was, no doubt, right about the FOP: nothing had actually *happened.* And if my mother had anything to do with it, nothing would dare happen. This is a woman with an old-world authority and glamour that makes people suck in their stomachs and mind their grammar. Once, when we were watching Sophia Loren put Johnny Carson in his place, Walt said, *She reminds me of your mom.* And when Julie Andrews plays a queen in San Francisco, calling to a cable car of enchanted riders: *Good-bye, trolley people!*, my daughters will say, *She's just like Miti!*

But FOP defies mortal authority—even my mother's. Over the next few weeks, the apricot pit on Vincent's back shifted positions, moving down his spine, swelling to the size of a massive hump on his right side. At different times during this period we visited the pediatrician and he prescribed painkillers. He—we—realized that this was the first real visitation of FOP. Up until then, Vincent's symptoms had been atypical, and that fact had given us hope that the condition might never progress.

But it did.

"Mom, my arm hurts," Vincent would say, walking with a hand held out as if it were suspended by an invisible string. I couldn't bear to look at my son's swollen back. And all I knew to give him were the painkillers.

The hump disappeared. But it left behind bone crossing Vincent's back and ribs, drastically limiting his right arm motion. He had to reach for glasses in the cupboard and volunteer in class with his left hand.

In 1996, there was not even an anecdotally effective treatment— let alone anything clinically proven—to stall FOP. *It's like living in the Middle Ages*, I cried to friends. I had been so proud to be able to solve any childhood ache or illness with a trip to the doctor: antibiotics for an ear infection, antivirals for the flu, antispasmodics for stomach aches—but there was no *anti-anything* for FOP. That kind of modern-day helplessness was disorienting. How would I, a dyed-in-the-wool worrier, find my bearings? How would I stay standing?

JULY 2003

OUR OLDEST, BRIAN, has left for study in Chile, not long after getting the wires cut that set his broken jaw. The week he arrives on the other side of the Andes from Argentina, on the gray streets of a city gloomy with winter, he sees Augusto Pinochet getting into a car in Santiago. Pinochet, as the world well knows, was one of Latin

America's most brutal dictators, behind tens of thousands of dead and disappeared, a violent "secret" history shared with Argentina, which includes a family friend who sued an Argentine general in San Francisco.

It was another, an earlier, a different totalitarian ruler in Latin America, Juan Domingo Perón, who was indirectly behind my own family's expatriation to a better life. We often returned to try and live in the family's province, Mendoza, "land of the sun and good wine," and I grew up hearing how everything was Perón's fault, Perón, whose wife, Evita, showed up in a café after one siesta, before my grandmother slammed down a teacup and told her daughters to ignore the tart with the bleached chignon.

Not living in Argentina was an exile of sorts, so my father made sure I could play tangos on the guitar, and he had my brother, Martín, recite the epic gaucho poem *Martín Fierro* every morning before breakfast. My beloved father, an engineer, made certain we knew that anything Latin is better: public transit, soccer, food, writers, kiosks, dogs, cafés, bidets, and bullfights. Only technology is better in the United States, but that is offset by Spanish being a better language than English, since you can say more and be more respectful in it (this is very true).

My mother dealt with her own nostalgia by writing poetry. She wrote so much of it she started to confuse poems with grocery lists. She would write *soy sauce*, for example, which, if you pronounce it in Spanish, means "I am a willow." Her poems had much better luck than her grocery lists.

My mother's poems held inside them what had been left behind, what a string of bad rulers kept us from recuperating as they led Argentina into altered and tragic states. Decades ago, my Buenos Aires cousins and I ducked into theaters on the Calle Florida to watch John Travolta dance over Spanish subtitles without knowing people were "disappeared" into detention centers or drugged and thrown from planes into the Atlantic. Today old Argentine generals roam free. And today Pinochet wanders—with supporters—through a reestablished democracy whose legacy is a collective angst. Brian's sighting of this old villain going about daily life makes me wonder if worrying has *some* purpose: to worry over a Pinochet, unseen but *somewhere*, or to worry over a cruel foe like FOP, which appears and disappears. Can worry keep us, sometimes, from falling asleep when we need to stay awake? (Maybe the word is not "*worry*," maybe I mean "*vigilance*" . . .)

I try to read life the way the Mexican poet Sor Juana Inés de la Cruz read the world—as if it were a book—or the way I read poems to my classes, trying to find what isn't *there*. And for someone who is always lost or late, it is ironic, but I look for some kind of hidden schedule or invisible signposts along the way.

As far as schedules go, Isabel gets her blue cast removed in time for her birthday. She turns seven on July 9, Argentina's Independence Day, a good date to celebrate freedom of movement. We are in an examining room in Orthopedics: speckled floors, walls lined with flags of the world—China, Seychelles, Saint Vincent. Vincent has to be the only kid to visit this hospital who knows that Seychelles is in the Indian Ocean. And I would be surprised if anyone else has noticed a mistake in the flags. *Maybe the orange faded to yellow,* said Walt the time our son remarked the error for Ireland. *Faded to the exact same color as yellow in all the other flags?* said Vincent. *You've got a scientific mind on you,* admitted his father fondly.

An orthopedic nurse totes in a machine that looks like a canister vacuum cleaner with a little buzz saw on one end and Isabel watches suspiciously. The nurse helps her lie sideways over the white sheet on the examining table, and the loud grind of the machine starts up. "I'm *scared*," says Isabel, eyes wide. I'm a little nervous myself when I see the blade start spinning. But she holds still, and as the metal teeth sink into the white fluff under the shell, her sobs turn to giggling. "It tickles!" she cries. The buzz splits the cast, a mold that has just made a new arm. Isabel examines her elbow: a little stiff, but perfectly shaped.

"Would you like to keep this?" the nurse asks, holding up the blue shell. Isabel shakes her head no. I feel the same way.

Dr. Gerardi enters with pliers, or whatever they call the tool to extract the metal pin looping out of Isabel's elbow. "That looks like something we have in the garage," says Isabel doubtfully, her freckles standing out on her beautiful little face.

Dr. Gerardi clamps the loop, tugs the pin, as routine as removing a piece of jewelry. "Your X-rays look fantastic," he says to Isabel, who smiles proudly, and we see the films of mended bone. "But you have to be careful for a while," he warns. "No roller skating. No running on concrete." No falls. Dr. Gerardi knows I know too well about preventing trauma. Luckily, the elbow will regain full motion with normal activity. "No need for physical therapy," he advises.

Isabel and I leave the hospital, the Disney castle. At home we have the best cure for a fixed arm: a hot dog, a buddy, a gummy-worm kit. Vincent organizes the project, helping Isabel and her friend Rachel measure sugar crystals and gels, set up molds, time the candy. He is the only one in the family with the patience to decipher instructions.

)

A FEW WEEKS into July, Vincent appears to be losing some hip mobility after spending the night on a hard bunk in a Rotary leadership camp at a Sequoia park. Walt went up the mountain to bring him down early because of the narrow cot that hurt his hip. I'm angry. I'm angry at myself—*for not worrying enough*—for not making sure he had the right kind of bed. "Why didn't you say *something* to *someone?*" I ask my son, handing him an ice bag.

Vincent has never been one to call attention to himself. He will have to learn to bother people. He needs this skill for college—for life.

The new FOP flare-up, its pain, the medication side effects, and having to come home early from camp have subdued my son. So I'm still faxing, calling, e-mailing about the missed UCSF internship because this project is one he can carry out near home. I'm not alone in trying: other parents whose sons or daughters didn't make the cut have contacted the program. But I will probably bother more personnel—for longer. I tell my students when they want something important: *keep at it; if one person says no, ask another—then ask again.* Does my plan to wear down UCSF work? I can only answer that question with a story, one that starts on the day before Vincent applied for a slot:

One late afternoon in winter, Vincent, Celine, Isabel, and I left Children's Physical Therapy, the satellite office. I had my keys out, ready to go, and we found our silver minivan in the parking lot right off. But the moment I put my hands on the wheel, I realized I had to run back into the building. Vincent stayed with the girls in the car while I rushed into the office and asked for directions to the facilities.

When I emerged from the restroom, the office was dark, the front door was locked from the outside, and everyone had gone home.

I used the office phone system to call Vincent in our car and contacted the hospital, a freeway drive away from its satellite Physical Therapy site. Twenty-five minutes later, a gentleman in a uniform arrived with his heavy key ring on the other side of the glass door, let himself in, and greeted me with a puzzled look.

"Don't you use the door down the hall to get out when you leave work?" he asked. I told him I was just a patient's mother. "Follow me," he said, and we walked ten feet down the darkened hallway and into a room full of rubber balls and jungle gym equipment I knew very well, with a door—completely unlocked—in one corner.

"I didn't remember this door," I said, feeling ridiculous. The man smiled and let me out, and that was that.

I was reminded of the locked-entry episode the day before yesterday by a receptionist at the PT office who said, "Everyone knows about you!" while a young man arranging medical files behind her smiled to himself. But something that happened *after* I was reminiscing with the receptionist over getting trapped in her building helped me understand what's really going on when we're pushing into locked doors without realizing there's an exit a few feet away, one we've seen but don't remember, and to which—if we're patient—someone might show up to lead us:

It was back in February that Vincent applied for the high school summer biomed internship with UCSF. Like I said, the UCSF internship—in Fresno—was perfect for Vincent, who loves science and math and wants to be a doctor. His grades were stellar and so were his letters of recommendation.

So when a formula rejection from the program came in the mail a few months later, explaining it had been "difficult" choosing twelve out of seventy-five outstanding applicants, I knew there had to be a mistake.

I called the internship administrative assistant. The poor woman had been busy with similar calls from parents all day, and could only give out statistics and pious explanations. I gave every good reason why a mistake had been made.

"It's—a—lost—cause," she enunciated.

I wrote an appeal to the program's local directors. *Twelve out of seventy-five is nothing,* I pointed out. "Vincent battles a rare disorder like FOP daily for an A+ in trigonometry and a 4.67 GPA—and he is one in two million!" No one answered.

I called the administrative assistant—again—who happened to mention that a biologist at my university was one of the program's mentors. I faxed this colleague, phoned, e-mailed. She agreed to look into the possibility of adding Vincent to her team—but never got back to me.

I appealed to a UCSF oncologist who had diagnosed a toddler with Vincent's condition. On his own initiative, this doctor called the local UCSF program to intercede. He was dismissed with the same explanation I was given: seventy-five qualified candidates, twelve slots. This doctor offered to mentor Vincent himself, but because he practices in San Francisco, the plan was impossible at the time. So I appealed to yet another physician, a local UCSF orthopedist, one who had seen Lucas when he broke a finger in freshman PE. The orthopedist responded immediately. He would be honored to mentor Vincent if his partner returned soon from overseas. The partner did not return in time.

Still frustrated that the directors at the local UCSF Medical Education office hadn't responded to my appeals, I wrote to the Chancellor of the University of California San Francisco School of Medicine.

The chancellor forwarded my plea to the San Francisco director of the Medical Education Program, whose office contacted me, sympathetic. But skeptical of success at that point, I asked what—exactly—the director might do. "What she says, goes," I heard, which I took to mean some kind of favorable arrangement might be made for my son, a boy who—as I stressed—must race time, and whose accomplishments are the equivalent of an Olympic runner winning marathons wearing weights.

After lots more e-mails and lots of faxing, the results I got from my plea to the medical school chancellor's office were—nil. After two months of appeals, all I achieved was an apology from the local program director—no internship. I thanked her, and asked one last question: how many of the selected students had a physical disability? That response was prompt: she—the program director—did not know.

So that was that. I gave up, annoyed with myself for all the windmill tilting and wheel spinning.

But the story doesn't end yet. And here I come to the open door down the hall, like the unlocked door in the PT office that had been there all along, and all I had to do was sit and wait for someone to lead me to it.

Not long after all the calls and letters, my oldest friend in the Valley, Julie Olguín Molina, a medical social worker, called to say a friend was desperate for help with a new software program. "Since Vincent is a genius with computers, can he help?" Julie asked.

Vincent called Julie's friend, who was, of all things: a Faculty Research Fellow for the Latino Center for Medical Education and Research for the University of California, San Francisco. Julie's friend, Phyllis Preciado, was a physician (who would later appear in *Time*), and she was implementing a diabetes education program, mentoring a team of high school students. She asked if Vincent would like to join her group to study diabetes, develop a medical education project, and implement it not only for the summer, but throughout the school year.

I was stunned.

After Vincent spoke to Dr. Preciado I told her that her mentorship was exactly what I had been banging my fists against locked doors over for months. I had appealed to offices of every stripe up the state, when all I had to do was wait for my *comadre* Julie to call. So there was the open door that had been there all along, and my oldest friend in my own town was the one who showed up to lead me to it.

I think that all the *effort* and *energy* and *passion* we put out in the universe for a noble cause, banging against locked doors, God sends back to us on those days when all we have to do is sit and wait for the one with the key ring to arrive on the other side of the locked glass.

BLACKTOP

AUGUST–SEPTEMBER 2003

*She is six years old and doesn't understand why she can't
play on the monkey bars at school and doesn't know what
to say to her friends when they ask her why she can't.
She says she doesn't want to be like this forever and then
says, "Mommy, if I had my old arms, could I go on the
monkey bars?"*

*I just sit there trying to find the words to tell her, to
comfort her, and I just don't know what to say. I feel so
powerless, and that is ripping me apart. I know we have no
control over what will happen, how FOP will progress. I
guess I should say "if and when" it progresses.*

*The fortunate thing is, Erin has the best attitude. She
is constantly smiling and figuring out a way to get it done,
whatever it is, in her own way. That's where I find my
smiles.*

—LORI DANZER, mother of Erin, six, diagnosed
at age ten months, Oceanside, California

I AM IN OUR small town, an outpost of Fresno, with its historic
sign, GATEWAY TO THE SIERRAS, strung in green, yellow, and
white neon across the main avenue. When we first came, almost
two decades ago, the town was slightly closer to its cowboy origins
of hitching posts and dirt streets, with wooden structures of vertical planks, wide porches, and flat roofs, down the street from the
rodeo grounds. Over the years it has all been renovated, built up,
and Walt calls it Disneyland-ish, but I like the theatrical Western

look. I like the grand yellow and white hotel named after the town's founder, which went up across from our friends' family restaurant, DiCicco's, and its aromas of garlic pizza and baking bread. And I don't mind the turn-of-the-century brick facades, or the green or red clapboard storefronts with striped awnings, or the faux cobblestone circle where families congregate on Farmer's Market nights in summer. There, by card tables loaded with tomatoes and peaches under little tents, Vincent danced up a storm on that cobblestone circle one Friday when he was three. As he jumped and shimmied in the warm summer dusk, we laughed with a grandmother standing nearby. "Somebody's been watching TV!" she exclaimed. My dad's *Sábado Gigante*, we knew, as our quiet little son improvised his salsa rhythms to a country fiddle.

I THINK THE confusing nature of FOP, visible one day, gone another, mobility there, but not there, has made it difficult for our other children to articulate its impact. When our oldest, Brian, was in eighth grade, and we had lived with FOP for two years, the school principal asked if he would like to say something about his brother's condition to the class. Brian stood up, but no speech came—and Brian has never been at a loss for words. Celine, on the other hand, has been the most verbal in her reaction to FOP. She was four when her brother began to limp, old enough to see something was wrong and young enough to address it directly. She has said what my sons have never actually put into words and what Isabel, as our youngest, who has never known life *without* FOP, might not feel as pressed to articulate: *I'm sad that Vincent has FOP.*

Celine's sensitivity to her brother's battle and her greater awareness of disability in general took an original turn one day. It was an afternoon I had retreated to take a nap (*la siesta*, as my father points out, a better tradition from *over there*). I had fallen asleep with a book on my chest when I heard a knock.

"Mom! There's a boy selling candy at the door." Celine had poked her head in through my doorway.

"We don't need any."

"But, Mom—" Celine leaned in further to say in a loud whisper, "the little boy is blind."

My daughter's sea-colored eyes had turned dark. If the child had a disability, we couldn't just send him away. "Go get some change," I said, swinging my legs over the side of the bed.

Celine found a handful of quarters and I took them to the front door. Standing on our porch was a boy with red hair and freckles, about nine or ten, Celine's age.

On Rollerblades.

"We're selling candy for our soccer team," said the boy, one hand gripping the cardboard handle of a See's box, the other wrapped in the leash of a tiny terrier. He was wearing a sports jersey, number 10, and an older boy stood a few feet behind.

I bought a couple of chocolate-almond bars; the boy thanked me and rolled down our driveway, trailed by the little dog.

"What made you think he was blind?" I asked Celine, who was at the kitchen table, head down over a propped book.

My daughter looked up at me, disconcerted. "Because he stared straight at a window the whole time he was talking," she said. "It looked like he couldn't see!"

It was no mystery to me. Celine could not know that a boy of nine or ten might be unable to look too directly at a girl of nine or ten with gold hair and sea-colored eyes. But her equally lovely heart was in the right place.

WE EXPLAINED AS well as we could to Vincent when he was nine that FOP *could grow another bone in your muscles, if you get hurt.* He understood this surreal possibility as well as anyone his age could, and because there is such a thing as *too much information,* we refrained from giving more detail. Our son knew: no more Rollerblades or skateboards or two-wheel bikes or contact sports. He had already been a careful soul since birth, one not likely to jump from jungle gyms or bunk beds—favorite activities of our firstborn. But the restrictions still had to be imposed and they were still painful. Vincent raged, *Why me?* when friends went off on bike rides with his brothers. We bought a three-wheeler, which Vincent pedaled on minimart trips without enthusiasm. We went to see a child psychologist, as we were as much at a loss as he was to understand it all. (*And here is my personal, nonprofessional advice in that direction: see a counselor who likes upbeat or bold décor—not one who hangs sad pastels; find someone with common sense and Old World wisdom and convictions—not an overtrained professional with modern doubts; look for an energetic, optimistic soul—not anyone muted, harried, or haunted. Find someone who hands out tangible tools—expressions to use, stories to read, exercises to do, a deck of cards naming feelings to shuffle—in short, someone trained in cognitive behavior modification therapy, someone not aiming for an ad nauseam course of help.*)

I've heard from some FOP adults that the younger children are when diagnosed with FOP, the less torturous the restrictions, because the life they lead is the only one they've known. In those cases, they say, the greatest pain is for parents. It is hard for anyone, no matter the age, but I must admit that Vincent was at that middle childhood stage where he suddenly had to stop playing as he had been playing for no good *apparent* reason. When he was nine, his restrictions were mainly preventative. I tried to take my lead from the head of the International FOP Association, a formidable woman who told us, "My parents never treated me like there was anything wrong with me." (She fondly recalled sliding down banisters when nobody knew much about the disease process.)

After the first massive flare-up, in July 1996, when FOP stopped being an abstract prohibition and when Vincent was nearing the age of ten, we understood—agonizingly so—that he would need more information. Before that our conditions and explanations had been rudimentary. So Walt and Vincent had a father–son talk. It was a tough conversation, though Walt did not have to add too much because FOP had taught its own brutal lessons. Vincent wondered why he had been singled out in such a way, and of course, there was no answer. "God will take care of everything," Walt told him. "And there's a lot of hope, people working on a cure at Doctor Kaplan's lab. There's a chance it might advance—but it might not." So while taking pains to protect our child from the worst, we would expect the best.

We also took heart, and advice, from another FOP mother in California, Susan Williams, whose son, Shay, had graduated from UC Berkeley. "I've had very few dark nights of the soul," Susan assured me on the phone one morning. I have always held on to those words, and today Susan, who went on to finish a PhD in psychology, assists countless families and helps men and women with disabilities live fully independent lives.

FOP seemed to take almost an entire year off after it struck Vincent in 1996 on his right side, limiting arm motion, but leaving him with enough range that he could function without special adjustments in school. No one could tell there was anything wrong if he didn't try to raise his right hand in class.

My plan to introduce the world to FOP involved going discreetly from classroom to classroom, raising a photo of my fifth grader, addressing what children could understand. But before I had gotten my speech ready, our principal, an enthusiastic soul, got on the public-address system one day and explained everything thoroughly. She warned the whole school, her voice carrying over the playground, through hallways and into classrooms, to be careful around Vincent: *no pushing, tripping, hitting, bumping.* "And if you're playing basketball and Vincent needs to go by, stop the game!" she ordered. *She meant well.*

I did not know the principal had put Vincent and FOP out in public until a friend of Brian's informed me when I arrived that day at school to pick everyone up. "If I were Vincent, I would be *so embarrassed,*" said the friend, appalled as only an eighth grader can be appalled.

What do I say to Vincent?

As the rest of the school let out Vincent and Lucas and Brian making their way out of the pale stucco buildings, over the painted boundaries of the blacktop, past clusters of parents and kids in blue and plaid, past the sisters in their white or navy habits, I waited in our station wagon, with Celine quietly clutching a scrolled watercolor and Isabel asleep in her baby carrier. No matter how I turned over what I had just learned, I could not figure out how to address it. My brain had become one of those 8 *Balls* you shake for answers, and all I could do was wait for an inky liquid to clear over my message.

No message appeared. All I could think to say to my son when he tossed his backpack in the backseat was, "What did you think about the principal's announcement?"

Vincent's intelligent brown eyes looked blank for a moment. But then he remembered. "I couldn't hear anything she was saying." The parochial school loudspeakers were famously fuzzy, and Vincent has always had a mild hearing loss, related—we now know—to FOP. *Things have their own funny way of working out,* I keep having to remind myself.

It was in the summer and fall of 1997 that Vincent continued to struggle with his second major flare-up, which struck him almost a year to the day in July from when FOP first reared.

Through all the worry and fear and pain from FOP's second major assault, Vincent was to have a guardian angel: his sixth-grade teacher, Sister Paulina, small and dark haired with kind brown eyes, always ready to second any idea we proposed. All of Vincent's teachers have been important advocates, and he also holds particular affection for Mrs. Carter, who sparked his love for science, and for Mrs. Clopton, his seventh-grade teacher, who calls Vincent *one of the people I most admire on this earth.* But during our first efforts to cope with FOP at school, we formed a special alliance with Sister Paulina because she had witnessed an immobilizing disease in her own sister, back in Spain.

Sister Paulina herself sat for Vincent's oral homework and exams when his arm was hurting. "He's so intelligent, he doesn't even need the tests!" she would say. She welcomed occupational therapists and school district personnel, and we all congregated regularly in the principal's office. These experts brought in adaptive PE equipment, ideas, solutions, and gave us catalogues and names and numbers. The people Sister Paulina invited into her classroom were formidably resourceful and deeply caring, though Vincent often resisted their intervention. And when the special equipment didn't suit our son, Sister devised a makeshift book lectern, brought in a padded swivel chair, and dragged in a little table.

Sister Paulina wrote to all manner of religious and political dignitaries, to the pastor of the church, the bishop of our diocese, the president of our country. She asked them all to take up a collection for FOP research at the only lab of its kind in the world, at Penn.

Sister Paulina became the ally of Vincent's adaptive PE instructor, Lisa Keller, from our public school district, who made it her mission to improve recess. Lisa brought Nerf balls and scarf games and foam toys and taught new sports that could include everyone but that would protect our son from trauma. It was blessed Lisa Keller who saved Vincent from fighting pain and solitude on a bench for more recesses than necessary. It was also Lisa Keller who saved him from just sitting at PE. *That's like eating candy in front of a person on a diet,* said my father, indignant, the morning he saw Vincent's gym class on one of his trips to drop off a lunch bag (and to remind the nuns to speak in Spanish to his grandkids).

Sister Paulina often chose Vincent to stand at the lectern for the school's Friday Masses. One of those times we made it there late, and as I rushed through the vestibule with Vincent, dipping my hand in the holy water font, I noticed the cowlick that resisted an arcing combing tool Vincent himself was resisting. (After Vincent lost reach in both arms, we ordered catalogue devices to help with a few routines, but he, we, ended up burying the devices in a cupboard.) We had no comb, no Dep, no water. I looked back at the double doors, at the little font I had just reached into. I reached in again.

There was, and always has been, something, a certain grace in Vincent's voice when he is reading or praying in public. In grade school, everyone always seemed to pay special attention whenever his quiet tones carried through the church or over the intercom saying the Our Father or reading a biblical passage as vice president of the school. That day after Friday Mass, Sister Paulina came up, as usual, to compliment my son's aplomb.

"Thank you, Sister," I said, but I was feeling funny. "Sister? I used holy water to fix Vincent's hair."

"God bless him from head to toe!" said Sister Paulina, waving her arms up and down in dismissal.

I suppose something like FOP entitles you to a few shortcuts in church. During that time in sixth grade, I remember one Saturday morning Vincent and Walt were leaning against the rough rock walls of a chapel, waiting in a Confession line that was snaking too slowly around the bank of blue candles. My line from across the way was twice as long, but moving twice as fast, since the shortest wait is always behind the most people: everyone knows which priests are quick. I was about to give Vincent my spot to keep him from standing so much. But Walt had a better idea. He marched over to the confessional's middle door, flanked by the entrances for penitents, and rapped on it sharply. The door flew open. "Can you hurry it up in there?" said Walt. From where I stood, I saw an astonished priest in his black shirt and white collar. The door closed. The line picked up speed.

People reacted kindly when Vincent had to stay home during the course of that sixth-grade year, which was the worst of the first period of FOP's attacks. Friends brought food over, children from our school and the schools of friends designed scores of elaborate get-well cards with paint and crayons and construction paper. I did have to censor the children's messages, as they were likely to express well-meaning sentiments like, "I hope you don't die." You never know what will show up on some of these heartfelt *Get Wells*. When Isabel's first-grade class sent cards to Brian, recuperating from the broken jaw, one little boy made a crayon portrait of Isabel's oldest brother under a basketball hoop and wrote, "I hope what happened to you doesn't happen to me!" Another little girl put down, "I'm sorry you lost your job."

For a preteen with a condition that is not temporary but chronic, I found people's kind intentions sometimes had the opposite of the intended effect. In sixth grade Vincent was suddenly facing not only the drastic physical changes of FOP but those first shifts toward adolescence and its particular rules of decorum. I knew my son did not want his name announced on the school intercom for prayer. And I knew that he fidgeted uncomfortably when people told us in front of his friends that they were saying the rosary for him. One time during Lent, two well-meaning mothers asked permission to gather children to give up a recess and pray for my son. "Think of all those little souls fluttering up to heaven because of Vincent," said one mother, her fingers fluttering up. The dear women meant well, truly they did. But I couldn't imagine what kid would want to be the beneficiary of another kid giving up recess. And what kid would want to believe that he might be in pain so another kid could make it into heaven? I was grateful—and miffed. I thanked the mothers and passed on the offer.

Sister Paulina's spiritual support, on the other hand, was nothing if not human. "If ten of us are planning on going to heaven," she asked me one afternoon, eyes pained behind her spectacles, palms out, "why does one of us have to suffer so much more than the other nine to get there?" Neither of us could think of any answer, but standing there by the school's orange picnic tables with the question between us helped shift something forward.

Part of what shifted forward when Sister Paulina asked her unanswerable question was a realization that came after mothers offered to have children sacrifice recess. I realized—and this took a while—that when people are faced with something like FOP secondhand, no one is sure how to act or what to say. Some, not wanting to offend, say nothing. Others, like the mothers offering to organize recess prayer, risk offense. There were times during Vincent's sixth-grade year when nobody around me could do or say anything right. There were days I felt neglected if no one asked how my son was doing, and there were days I felt invaded if anyone did. I learned, eventually, to accept the kind intentions behind concern, whatever perfect or imperfect gestures resulted.

Walt joined the IFOPA board of directors to advance the FOP battle, and closer to home he found every other avenue open to Vincent to make up for what our other children have taken for granted: sports.

Walt was a gifted athlete in high school and would have gone on to play basketball in college if his course hadn't been diverted by a sports injury. And all of our children have inherited his athletic abilities. So FOP hit especially hard in this direction. Walt was the one who found music lessons, a piano, a trumpet, keyboards, recitals, songbooks, and teachers. I remember Vincent at a baby grand piano in a church recital, proudly playing his first five-note song. And in one of his school essays he wrote, "I owe my love of music to my father."

When baseball season came around, Walt found a Boy Scout troop and made balsa-wood cars, even though he had never joined Boy Scouts in his own youth, occupied as he was suckering trees, tractoring, and irrigating on the family farm. When Vincent joined band in high school, Walt went along as band parent, getting up at 3:00 A M for faraway parades, pulling Radio Flyer wagons of water bottles, and jogging along marching routes to adjust someone's hat or instrument. And it was Walt who supervised overnight field trips and took Vincent for altar boy practice. (It was my father who made sure to sign up and coach his grandson as a lector for the Spanish Mass.)

AUGUST–SEPTEMBER 2003

LATE AUGUST, EARLY September is harvest season for our pistachios, not far from Children's, along a narrow stretch of highway divided by broken yellow lines and flanked by orange groves and nut orchards. My father is walking the furrows, wearing a baseball cap over his gray hair against the rising heat. He is carrying a half-empty Pepsi box, handing out sodas to the Mexican workers, who also bring big-ribbed thermoses. At the edge of the orchard, along the canal, the pistachios pour out in a golden stream from bins hoisted up by a little forklift. They make hills in a long truck with the packing-house logo. A few of the slatted bins lie strewn alongside the canal and its dark waters.

I learned years ago that pistachios are not picked by hand.

They are harvested by machine, noisy grinding equipment that grips the trees to shake the nuts loose in just three days. There are trays attached to vehicles that stop at each tree, and the pods rain down on slanted slats and into receptacles. It is a strange sensation, watching leaves and branches convulse in the dusty light. Walt tells me there is an art to shaking, and the men practice it right now in goggles and dust masks, sweatshirt hoods pulled on to filter out debris. Walt follows the trail of the machine and Luis and Juan, to whom my father has introduced me, walk another furrow, signaling trees that can bear one more shake. "If you rattle a tree too many times, no more fruit, right?" I say to them in Spanish. They nod. "Same as for people," I tell them, and they smile knowingly. (Men like Luis and Juan are the reason Walt took Spanish years ago during law school, and he gives of his time to help Latino immigrants with legal issues.)

I still feel rattled, fruitless, after "Bone Month": Isabel's arm, Brian's jaw, Vincent's leg. I cannot shake a feeling of disorientation and I move idly through the dusty orchard, idly through our dusty house still full of unpacked boxes. Meanwhile, Walt is a dynamo. More than ever, it is plain my husband grew up on the healthy labor of farming—and I didn't. After the harvest he is busy in our backyard of dirt, laying irrigation pipe, digging flower beds with the boys: Vincent, overseeing, Brian, Lucas, and their friends Rafael, Dimitri, and the Storelli brothers, manning an augur, making back-and-forth trips with muddy wheelbarrows, planting young bushes with waxy leaves and bougainvilleas at the foot of a fence, fixing a path of sapling redwoods, pouring, raking, moving, setting. Later on, they will start a vegetable garden with the girls, a little vineyard, and an orchard with all the fruits under the sun, even Buddha's hands, Pluots, pomegranates, and quince.

The pistachio harvest is done and the backyard is under way by the time the two-week stretch of September birthdays for our boys arrives. I relive those three births every September, and today recall scores of chocolate and vanilla cupcakes baked for classmates and our crowd celebrations over the years.

It is hard to have Brian on the other side of the world for his twentieth birthday. He has made the trek up to Machu Picchu, with a fifty-pound backpack and altitude sickness, meeting a Quechua guide with the name *Condenado,* "condemned to the mountain." Condenado is a brother to the poverty that complicates FOP in Latin America. There are patients in Brazil without wheelchairs, carried in relatives' arms. There is a São Paulo doctor, Patricia Delai, who trekked where cars cannot go to take an air mattress to a boy with a pallet for a bed. There was María Claudia in Peru, Isabel's age, tied to an oxygen tank because her fused ribs kept her lungs from filling with air. There is Josseling, Celine's age, whose family must rely on a less disadvantaged family to transmit medical messages. (Thomas Jefferson University Memorial Hospital in Philadelphia has generously helped with the effort to assist Latin American patients.)

"LET'S TALK," SAYS Isabel companionably, interrupting me as I am struggling to print a handout on time for my Spanish composition class. "OK," I say.

She looks at me expectantly. "So—" I start.

"Ask me how my day went," she prompts.

"How did your day go?"

"*BAD.*"

"Bad?"

"Bad!"

"Why?"

"Sentences."

"What kind of sentences?"

Without a word, she produces a sheet of drab writing paper with broken lines and solid lines: *I will try not to be tardy. I will try not to be tardy. I will try not to be tardy. I will try not to be tardy.*

And she had to stay in at PE.

"Well, you don't like PE much, anyway," I say by way of apology.

Isabel's baby face looks stern—and then she makes an impish, jack-o'-lantern smile with her missing bottom teeth.

Poor Isabel was tardy because of her mother—as usual—and though things worked out in the end, it was no thanks to me. As I've said, I've always been this way to one degree or another, but giving birth to five kids has compounded it to the fifth power. So I have a reputation at my children's school: late with children, late with myself, late with proper forms: *I don't have it; she won't have it,* says our secretary to any new room mother who asks optimistically if I turned in documentation on time to drive on field trips to the Saroyan Theatre or the Pumpkin Patch. (I do always end up running through parking lots with the forms.)

And my kids and I fare well enough when those in charge of dates and papers are game enough to chase me with a clipboard or just roll their eyes. I'm also lucky to have best friends in the same boat, and we pool information. These are mothers I've met over the years standing in line for tardy slips or replacement forms. They, too, get a deer-in-the-headlights look when you ask, *Is the science project due tomorrow?* or, *Is today early dismissal?* None of us has been able to break the specially engineered code of communications used by mothers who arrive early and know when everything is happening. But we do have our own organization with its own secret sign (palm to the forehead) and we call ourselves The Late Club.

I am the mascot for The Late Club, so when I run into a "rules-is-rules" person, things can go from bad to worse. This happens at the beginning of school this year, and I let it ruin my day, my week, and maybe even my relationship with Vincent, when I say to a rules-is-rules mother who wants or doesn't want something from me: *I have a lot of balls in the air. We all do,* she says. *But I have five kids, and one has a rare genetic disorder,* I say back. Vincent is standing next to me, and objects: *Don't use me as an excuse!* He is right, of course.

It is a rules-is-rules person—I will call her Mrs. X—who is partially responsible for Isabel crying into her meat loaf at dinner this evening. Mrs. X has told our seven-year-old at the soccer Ice

Cream Social that she will be on a team different from the one we had picked for sharing rides with a Late Club friend.

"I'm sure we can work it out," Walt tells Isabel, dialing up Mrs. X. But I'm not so sure.

After Walt states his purpose, I can hear a voice rising and falling through the receiver. My husband explains that there is, after all, room on the team, makes consenting sounds on and off, and finally hangs up. "She wishes you had told her earlier that we needed that team," he says. "Rules is rules."

"But I did tell her earlier!" I remember this point because when I get anything done ahead of time it is branded in my brain. "What if I call?" I'm asking him as my lawyer.

"Give it a shot."

In the grand scheme of things, this is a blip, but it is *of utmost importance exactly now*: no carpool, no soccer, no world peace. I reach Mrs. X, who lists all her good reasons before I can list my one good reason, and she concludes cordially, "I wish you had told me earlier."

"I *did*, Mrs. X! I did tell you *earlier*." I can hear my voice straining, like I'm driving it into the wrong gear.

Mrs. X will not take my word for it. But she seems used to having *her* word taken for it, because she teaches at a college—which can lend a certain authority in the world of rules-is-rules. "Well, I have a master's," she counters, "and my memory isn't perfect, but—"

For once in my life I am able to trump someone who is never late and who never needs replacement forms. Who can blame me for seizing the moment? Under these conditions.

"Well, *I* have a *PhD!*" I spout. *"And I have a near-perfect memory for dialogue!"*

Having a PhD is no guarantee of a near-perfect memory, but my comeback is so sterling, it seems to me that Mrs. X can't help but falter (respectfully) and offer to pass the matter on to a higher authority.

I like to think that after our conversation Mrs. X will treat everyone as if he or she has a PhD. And if a PhD in literature can get my second grader into soccer, then it's worth a lot more than I thought.

WHITE TUNNEL

SEPTEMBER–OCTOBER 2003

Rachel first got flare-ups at nineteen months and had ten months' chemo; she was diagnosed with having aggressive fibromatosis, after the ten months all the lumps on her back seemed to disappear, and she was fine until she was nine years, when she banged her back on a swing and the lumps came up again. After more chemo and also radiotherapy the lumps calcified and she lost movement in her arms.

We still thought she had aggressive fibromatosis at that time; they were just about to do radiotherapy on lumps on her chest when another doctor came in to see her and he explained to me that her chest would not develop properly if she had the treatment. So he said we could go away and think about whether we wanted the treatment or not. To our amazement the lumps went down on their own. Rachel had no more treatment after that.

Then at the age of twelve years she was rightly diagnosed with FOP.

—JULIE HOPWOOD, mother of Rachel, twenty, diagnosed at age twelve, Manchester, England

"I HATE IT WHEN people tell you, 'I want to say yes.' If they want to say yes, they can just go ahead and *say yes.*" Walt is frowning at a memory. We are in the car, waiting for a light to turn green. "What is this 'want to'? Just say it or don't say it."

I am agreeing with my husband over things that get in the way of answers, and notice, at the same time, a very blue sky over a building made of mirrors. "At least it's a beautiful day today."

"*I want to say* it's a beautiful day," Lucas echoes, palms out. "No, *I think I'm going to just go ahead and say it*: it's a beautiful day." Lucas is a master at tweaking *received ideas*. He has that straight-man's look in his Latin eyes, and I can picture him leaving his high school gym flanked by boys getting ready to laugh.

"And the next time anyone asks me, 'What color is your shirt?'" Lucas goes on, "I'll say something like, 'Green! Does that answer your question!'"

"What's so funny about that?" says Isabel. The rest of us are laughing.

"It just makes an answer confrontational, like when a witness doesn't want to release a fact." Walt gives another example of the frustrations of getting at answers.

Through the summer and fall of 1995, we were dealing with the frustrations of trying to get answers to the questions raised by Vincent's mysterious limp. FOP was not about to yield information easily. At the time I was taking my then eight-year-old to our original children's hospital, a sprawling mishmash of buildings in an older section of town. Despite its modest appearance, Valley Children's, as it was named back then, was one of the finest facilities you could visit, its staff trained, in part, by the sheer numbers of children in the area.

In 1995, Valley Children's did not have its own magnetic resonance imaging unit, so we made appointments around the equipment's traveling schedule, and it arrived in a trailer, the white tunnel situated on one side, technicians behind glass on the other. To exit you had to walk past the bank of monitors with their images of oily rainbows, which I gave up trying to read because they made me uneasy.

I remember sitting in our first MRI trailer, promising to buy Vincent his favorite toy, LEGOs, at the Target on Shields, if he could lie very still. Children were often sedated for the test, but you could get away without that step if you had a calm kid like Vincent. So I sat in a chair in a corner, my watch removed so it couldn't get sucked off my arm into a white tunnel. I had *Leaves of Grass* in my lap to read, but mostly I talked to distract us in between the times Vincent was told over a loudspeaker to go ahead and move. Every now and then a pretty blond technician would open the trailer divider door, poke her head in, and ask, "You OK, bud?" The white tunnel sounded like a clothes dryer with a watch or a belt rattling around in it, not like the MRIs today, which sound like a jackhammer.

The results of the MRI tests were baffling. They showed a persistent lesion in the left sartorius muscle. ("Sartorial," my father explained, "like *sastres* in Spanish—tailors, who held their pincushions on their thighs.") "We'll keep an eye on it," said our orthopedist, Dr. Gerardi. The lesion could be caused by nothing at all, a muscle pull—or by anything at all, whatever medical nightmare you didn't want to have to ever even think about for one second. Dr. Gerardi monitored the lesion closely, with more X-rays and another MRI, regularly watching Vincent walk down the well-lighted hall of Orthopedics. The limp wasn't getting worse.

It wasn't getting better.

Dr. Gerardi, I had noticed, had a tendency to look down at the floor while he was talking and thinking. But that one day in particular, when we were in the old Orthopedics building, separate from the hospital, with pale walls, pale floors, pale kids wearing blue or pink Day-Glo casts, packing the waiting room, he looked directly at me and said, "I don't know what this is." *God bless Dr. Joseph Gerardi for his forthrightness—and for his intuition, which spared Vincent's leg a biopsy.* "But I'll send you to someone who will."

)

"WE NEED TO take another X-ray," said the voice on the phone. Before we had our first appointment with the rheumatologist to whom Dr. Gerardi was sending us, we contacted a specialist at Stanford. I was on the line with the Stanford doctor on a day our house was filled with the yogurt smell of fresh paint, and there were tarps everywhere left by a band of enthusiastic painters we called Mel and his Merry Men. Everywhere you looked were stacked boxes, stuffed trashbags, china wrapped in newspaper, Ninja Turtles and Polly Pockets fighting willy-nilly with odds and ends. We were moving to our new two-story by the bank of eucalyptus trees, the wheat field, and the old fort land.

"Another X-ray?" It seemed to me we already had *another X-ray*. We had taken all those *other* X-rays, the regular ones, leg and body, and a bone scan, with dye and radioactive isotopes, waiting ages for the dye to "take," then standing over Vincent bent over hospital water fountains, making him drink gallons and gallons to flush out every last isotope. And then, of course, there was the white tunnel.

"We're looking for calcium," said the new specialist. "If there's calcium in the lesion, it's a benign process." I knew the flip side of the word *benign*, and it didn't take a worrier to jump to conclusions. Every fiber in my body froze.

"Isn't muscle cancer—like—a *zebra?*" I asked, familiar at that point with the medical maxim *If you hear galloping hooves outside your window, think of common causes first: horses, not zebras.* With the "noises" of most diseases, the sensible course is to consider the more ordinary beast before you start worrying about anything exotic.

"It happens," said the Stanford doctor quietly. *Zebras happen. Zebras happen. Zebras happen.*

It had to be the worst day under the August sun to be moving. There are still things in boxes I packed that morning that I have never seen again.

"And if there's no calcium?"

"We biopsy."

Biopsy: until then no one had thrown that grenade of a word at us. And it was miraculous, too, because we now know that a biopsy is often one of the first tests ordered in the face of FOP symptoms. And, of course, for a child with undiagnosed FOP, a biopsy is the worst possible kind of test, as it can damage muscle fibers permanently, setting off explosive bone formation and prematurely limiting precious mobility. *Biopsy* is the word that has triggered needless surgeries, invasive procedures, useless chemotherapies, radiation, and one unnecessary amputation. Ironically, the word that might be the first step in a process of healing for one disease is an agent of disaster in FOP.

But I didn't know any of all that and had the usual reasons to fear the word.

)

SYNCHRONICITY, TIMING, COINCIDENCE have a special significance when you deal with a disease in which time is a crucial component. Life with FOP is a race against time. But the period of our diagnosis quest, a time during which our son neither worsened nor improved under the watchful eyes of his Fresno doctors, *was exactly what spared his leg.*

The X-ray the Stanford specialist recommended was ordered locally by our pediatrician. Again, Vincent and I waited in a crowded Radiology for the white X-ray eye. And all that time we had an unimaginable zebra, one the Stanford specialist himself had, most likely, never imagined: a zebra of zebras.

Vincent lay, once again, on a long table, the big white apparatus hovering, the lead pad draped around him, me watching from the corner in a heavy gray apron. "You're not pregnant, are you?" technicians routinely asked. (This was a question I got outside X-ray rooms often enough.)

The day the results for that X-ray were ready I was as nervous as—if not more nervous than—I had ever been in my life, with a warm soupy feeling in my solar plexus as I approached a reception window. "Dr. Weinberg, please?" I said, hearing my tongue stick to the roof of my mouth. I did not have to wait. Dr. Weinberg appeared in his familiar white lab coat and yellow duck tie, took my arm, and sat in the waiting room chair next to me.

"It's full of calcium!" he said, with his German accent, joy in his blue eyes. I can still hear those exact words.

I hugged Dr. Weinberg, let out all the air I had. "Now what?"

"We watch it." And that was the best possible advice in the course of an undiagnosed case of FOP.

THE UNIVERSE WAS taking care of us in its own unfathomable
fashion, like the story of the fairy tale princess cursed by a witch
at birth, but blessed by a godmother with some kind of simple
antidote. The prolonged quest for the diagnosis—though short as
FOP diagnoses go—was exactly as it should have been. And it was
the timing of the last X-ray that was crucial. It was early enough in
the lesion's development that it would provide important information to the next specialist we saw, but late enough in the lesion's
life that the site had calcified. Had there been no calcium in the
lesion—and there would not have been, earlier—another doctor,
one less intuitive than those Vincent had had, would have ordered
a biopsy. And had the biopsy been taken at an early stage in the
lesion's development, it could have robbed our son of leg motion
and tricked pathologists into diagnosing cancer.

I don't know why circumstances unfolded as they did, why we
were blessed with doctors who spared us the agonies of a misdiag-
nosis. I don't know. Looking back, I wonder if it had anything to
do with saving us for another major surprise, one that came at the
end of October.

But Vincent continued to limp. And in early October 1995 he
and I were in a little pastel examining room, waiting to see Dr.
Henrickson for the first time, in another stucco one-story across
the street from Valley Children's. The cheery main waiting room
had the usual baskets of toys, and there were pamphlets on juvenile
arthritis I glanced at but would not read: they looked worrisome
enough with their lists of symptoms and support groups.

I remember that first visit, when a young nurse weighed my son
on a regular vertical scale, not the high-tech platform Rheumatology
has now. And we measured Vincent's nine-year-old height with a
calibrated giraffe stick. In the hallway hung a boy's drawing of the
human body with the heart and bones, all the internal organs, all
in relief. (No doubt that picture was one child's way of drawing out
a weariness of X-rays.)

That visit was the first time we saw Dr. Henrickson, tall,

luminous, genteel, with a trace of the East Coast and maybe even his native New Zealand in his speech. He gave Vincent a careful rheumatologic exam, measuring his flexions with a plastic ruled instrument that looked like a compass, protractor, and ruler in one, recording his geometry of movement. Dr. Henrickson placed his hands on Vincent's feet. "His ankles don't pronate," he observed, and I wasn't sure what that meant, but I felt that pronating must be something you wanted ankles to do. It didn't take me long to understand, however, that what we were learning—for the first time—was that Vincent had stiff ankles.

That was not all.

Astonished, I realized—also for the first time—why it was that my second son always pulled his school uniform shirt away from his breastbone for buttoning. I thought it was a personal quirk. And maybe Vincent figured it was simply the way he was, that his hands reached just shy of his collarbone. I also discovered in that little examining room that when my son raised his arms and bent them at the elbow, as if in calisthenics, his hands reached an inch shy of his shoulders. Recently Vincent remembered those days, pre-FOP: "When I was seven and they told you to touch your shoulders and I couldn't, I just thought, 'Oh, well,' and crisscrossed them over my chest—since I could reach my shoulders that way." *Good attitude!* said Vincent's best friend, Peter, admiringly.

And during that first Rheumatology visit, Dr. Henrickson noted that Vincent's neck was slightly stiff, something we had always known, an anomaly one ear, nose, and throat specialist had remarked in passing, without giving it importance. But it suddenly became clear that all of the above had to be tied, somehow, to the mysterious limp.

We were to take one more set of X-rays to come to a diagnosis. "And a blood test to rule out juvenile arthritis," said Dr. Henrickson. Having seen the pamphlets down the hall, arthritis would be my worry of the week. But we seemed closer to uncovering answers, I could tell that much from the startlingly simple revelations in that little examining room.

(We will always be grateful to Dr. Henrickson and to the doctors

before him, who spared Vincent the trauma of invasive tests, spared his leg.)

As Vincent and I left the little Rheumatology building, I felt some relief that his set of symptoms couldn't portend the *worst*. My biggest fear at that moment was that the limp might mean juvenile arthritis.

"The X-rays and blood test results are in," said Dr. Henrickson over the phone a few days later. He went on to tell me that there was to be a geneticist from UCSF making rounds at the hospital, and would we mind coming in when she visited his clinic, that she might confirm a tentative diagnosis? "I think I know what it might be," he said. At least the blood tests told us it wasn't arthritis, thank God.

I made our next appointment with Rheumatology and stopped worrying—proving, in retrospect, that worrying is no good way to figure out the future—in this case, a future so surreal, no amount of fretting could have made it less unfamiliar. *Maybe those of us who worry so much are trying to trump the future by creating it ahead of time—all on our own.*

In October 1995, I checked Vincent out of school early, and we met Walt at the old Rheumatology clinic. Dr. Henrickson was accompanied by a blond resident in a lab coat and a tall woman with an Australian accent. The tall woman was the visiting geneticist, and she shook my husband's hand, but did not see mine outstretched. I don't know if the senior doctor appeared in a white lab coat. I remember her as very tall, in what was possibly a green outfit that gave her a pine-tree look—part of a surreal memory, I realize, some of which I've retained with perfect clarity, and some of which stretches and distorts like images in a fun house mirror.

I don't know what Dr. X—I'll call the geneticist that—was really wearing, because I only remember her in green, whether she wore that color or not. I will always remember her looming over my boy, who was dangling his legs from the child-size examining table, its covering making crinkly white-paper noises. She put Vincent through the old paces: "Can you touch your hands to your shoulders?" she asked. "Most children can." He tried to oblige, and she continued to examine him with an air of vague disapproval, as if he were failing a test for which he hadn't studied.

The diagnosis, when it was finally arrived at that afternoon, was anticlimactic. It didn't affect us like a thunderbolt or a cataclysm: it was more like a formality or an official certificate. This was because the disorder was so remote, so unknown to doctors, patient, parents, and medical resident in that little room that it was like an abstract concept, nothing *real*. It wasn't a condition any of us had heard a friend or a neighbor complain about. It wasn't even something we might have seen on television or read about in the newspaper. So the words we were given were more like an expression you might learn in a foreign language: random, opaque, innocent of associations. Our diagnosis felt like a made-up lingo, like what in Spanish you could call *jerigonza*.

Something was wrong, we all knew that, but I think nobody standing in that little examining room that October afternoon in 1995 putting a name to it could really know *how* wrong.

Vincent sat innocently, still swinging his legs, a child, and, like anyone in a similar predicament, not fathoming the explanations Dr. X directed at my husband.

"It's genetic," said Dr. X. "It's progressive. There's no treatment yet." She looked at Walt: "He can't have trauma." She looked at Vincent: "You could take up track instead of football." How could she—we—know back then that such advice was dangerous?

We had been taking Vincent to physical therapy to stretch the leg with the limp. Dr. X recommended we continue.

"He doesn't like it very much," I offered.

"Well, it's like homework," she said to Vincent and me in the sweetened voice adults use when they expect resistance in a child. "You just think of it that way, and do it!"

Again, this physician could not know, nor could we, that she was endorsing passive exercise, forbidden to FOP patients. And she was a clinical professor at a major medical institution. No reason to doubt her. No reason to doubt what she said and did next, either.

Dr. X suddenly noticed me in the tiny room and took my right arm to twist it behind my back. "Not very flexible," she said in the tone of voice she had used to examine Vincent.

"Why don't you try *him*," I said, pointing to my husband, seated on an acrylic chair to my right.

"Men aren't flexible," she said dismissively. "Hold up your hands," she instructed me instead.

I spread my fingers out and held up them up, as if to surrender or ward off a blow.

"Your thumb's too short," she reprimanded. My thumb had made the mistake of not reaching the middle joint of my index finger. "The gene's probably from your side," she said.

Just like that.

All of us in the room stared at my hands, which I lamely kept in the air.

"Let's see *his* fingers!" I said finally, looking at poor Walt, who was still sitting quietly.

Walt held up his freckled hands.

"He's fine," said the doctor mildly, noting my husband's thumb normalcy and proper extension. His was, no question, a good thumb, especially next to my stubby digit, which had seemed perfectly fine—until then.

All of us in the tiny room held up our hands. The resident with long blond hair raised perfect pianist's fingers. I was starting to resent her silent presence.

There was a little more discussion about the disorder, about carrying on with a normal life. The Australian doctor talked about having the ossification in the sartorius muscle removed surgically if it became a bother. It was later, of course, when we learned that surgery qualified as major trauma in FOP.

"There was a young man with this who had a piece of bone removed from his buttocks," said Dr. X. It would not have occurred to me at the time to ask how things had gone for the young man *after* such a surgery.

Maybe it was that numbness that suffuses you in the wake of news like the news we were given, or maybe it was something else, I don't know. Because—worrier that I am—I felt an unusual calm, an irrational sense that everything would work out as I looked up at the October sky over the drab little building that held Rheumatology. I had taken a rosary in my pocket and felt strangely protected. But I must say that what I felt was, in many ways, a false calm, produced by what went from a mystery with no name to a mystery we had named—and the name meant nothing.

SEPTEMBER–OCTOBER 2003

THE NEW CHILDREN'S opened in the fall of 1998, and all the Valley saw it rising on its hill. The Corn Maze, a labyrinth in a cornfield, was there a couple of years later, planted for Halloweens. We would go, all of us, in still-warm Octobers, into the fine dust, calling kids through green stalks, swatting leaves with black smudges, trying to race each other out. But as time in the maze wore on, the novelty wore off, the baby in the stroller grew impatient, the sun turned on us, kids disappeared, and parents squeezed through thickets to grab an arm or a shoulder, calling, panicked.

The boys always found their way out and we could hear their voices from the sides of the green cage. *What if someone fainted or fell in the maze*, I would think. Ironic, with a hospital right there, but nobody to find you in the convolutions, no way to see a body—if you were prone—from the wooden bridges raised in the labyrinth. In the end, it seemed, we always took the easy way out, tired and hot, ducking out the edges of the maze like the baseball players in *Field of Dreams*.

The maze gives me a good metaphor, not so much for FOP, because FOP has, as yet, no sideways exit, no way out. But in my opinion, the reason the maze never lasted in front of the hospital was because it was too much a reminder for worried parents about the twists and turns, diagnoses and procedures, the mysterious labyrinths that can make up a path to getting a child out of even the nicest of hospitals.

October is a month of organized sports, and we make our rounds like most families. Isabel got into the right soccer team after my exchange with Mrs. X, but it wasn't because I wrote a doctoral dissertation. It was because another kid dropped out, leaving a space of exactly the right dimensions. This month Brian tells me from Argentina about a more high- powered soccer game he watched in Buenos Aires, with my uncle Jorge, between River and Chicago. "It was crazy!" says Brian, happily. "The fans were throwing chairs!" The stadium in La Boca was let out in shifts to tamp down emotions. "And Jorge and I are taking tango lessons," Brian concludes. Tango lessons seem safe enough. I try not to worry more than necessary about Brian.

Today we are watching another sport, volleyball. It is a mild autumn afternoon, and we are at one of the Catholic schools, a school with long green fields and lovely girls I will see laughing in groups with Celine when she transfers here. But today she is playing volleyball on the other side, and I see girls in navy or royal blue with ponytails and kneepads tensed to spring as the ball makes an arc. Celine is especially intense, powerful in her motions, fist under the volleyball. She is a gifted athlete.

Vincent and Isabel are with me, watching from picnic tables. Isabel, in her blue plaid uniform, sits near her brother, pressing one cheek against his arm, and we are chatting with a team father, an amiable redhead with the gift of paying attention. He is listening reverently to Vincent talk about the Stanford application process.

I hear my name called, and an old friend I have not seen in a while sits with us, glad to find Vincent so well. "How are you?" I ask my friend, who doesn't answer right away.

When people see you cope with a cruel unknown like FOP, they are more likely to tell you how they really are: my friend's eyes get teary. Her husband has a chronic disease that has turned acute, and may require an organ transplant. I give her a few words of sympathy and she says to me, "You're so strong." Of course, I am not "so strong," no stronger than anyone else. I've only learned that when your equilibrium is routinely challenged, you look for footholds. And you take each foothold as you find it, one at a time, one day at a time, one prayer at a time, one volleyball serve at a time. I can say all that to a friend more convincingly than I can say it to myself.

But it is when I say it to a friend that I understand it to be true. Like teaching a class: sometimes you learn what you know when you stand behind a podium.

When we get home from the game, Vincent remembers a teacher's recommendation for Stanford. It is sealed in a white envelope, not for him, but for his parents to see. I am afraid to look at the letter, and hand it to Walt, who is on the couch with the kids, watching a TV movie, *Rudy*, about a boy whose impossible dream is to make it into an elite college. Because Vincent works so hard to conceal his effort and avoid attention, I worry that others might miss his gifts, and I am not up for a generic recommendation. When I ask Walt if the letter is good, he just says, "Mm-hm" without taking his eyes from it. But once I start reading, I know why Walt could not say more. Vincent's calculus teacher's heartrending praise makes me suppress a sob.

BLIND STAR

I just want to share a little story. Six years ago I read an interview with a famous Swedish girl named Kristin. At that moment she was pregnant and she got the question, "Are you worried about if your child is having an illness in some way?"

Kristin answered: "Once an old vise woman said to me, 'If you get a child with a disease, you will have that child because you have got the strength to handle that.'"

And those words I had in my head when I was pregnant with Hugo. And when we got the diagnosis two years ago, I had the feeling that I must be a very strong and special person, who gets a child with a disease like FOP. There must be something meant for me to do. And I have the same feelings about Hugo. Even if life feels like sheat (sorry about the expression) sometimes, too.

—MARIE HALBERT, mother of Hugo, six,
diagnosed at age four, Eskilstuna, Sweden

ONE SATURDAY WHEN Isabel had just turned three, the seven of us were having lunch at a Boston Market, with the usual discussions over who got the leg or the breast, with corn bread or wheat bread, who would gag over string beans and who had stuck someone else's plastic spoon in the wrong mashed potatoes, and *That's disgusting*, and whose order was wrong, and who started drinking from *my* straw, ad nauseam. Isabel—I remember her well that day, in a hot-pink shift, her tea-colored hair short and curly—had recited her order with aplomb before the usual confusion of elbows and utensils and ruckus, and it was lucky the restaurant was empty. While the chatter and discussions continued, none of us noticed that Isabel took a napkin, placed it on the table behind us; took a fork, placed it on the other table; took a drink and did likewise; and finally carried off her plate of food to seat herself all alone, her back to the family. "Isabel, what are you doing?" we started asking.

Isabel looked over her shoulder, calmly swallowed a mouthful of mashed potatoes and said, "There's too much people in the family." She put a napkin to her mouth and went on to have her own peaceful lunch, off from the fray.

I will never forget Isabel's three-year-old instinct for self-preservation as the youngest in a large, noisy family. I suspect that whether FOP came into our lives or not, she would have found a way to stake out a small—if temporary—space for herself. In some ways, Isabel was doing what I decided to do not long after FOP turned into an assault on the future. I had to remove myself temporarily, stake out a space.

)

IT WAS IN the fall of 1995, and I was upstairs in our new blue house, sitting on the bed, looking through the window at the rough earth of an empty lot, talking on the phone with our pediatrician. "Do you know anything about this disease?" I asked.

"I saw a case in New York forty years ago," said Dr. Weinberg. "You know me," he added, "I'm a minimalist: leave the kid alone and let him enjoy life." Our doctor knew every one of our children inside and out.

I had never doubted our pediatrician, the grandfather of pediatricians, the author of a book on child care, and what he said made sense: just go on as if nothing has changed. Fundamentally, it was excellent advice, but then again, neither he nor I could fathom FOP.

"I'll check the hospital data banks for you," said Dr. Weinberg. This model doctor had always been there for us, had always guided us through any crisis, had always waved my vain worries into the air. Every anxious question about ear infections, stomach flu, fevers, rashes, falls, bumps, and stitches got the best diagnostician's instructions.

One fall afternoon I found a manila envelope in our brand-new brick mailbox. I knew what was in the envelope and tossed it on the kitchen counter to open later. I might as well have been leaving a nuclear warhead in the breakfast nook, as what was in that envelope would rock our foundations. But of course, I couldn't know that just by looking at a peach-toned packet with our pediatrician's return address on it. As I said before, we had walked out of our diagnosis session with Dr. X feeling calm enough, relieved that a mysterious limp had nothing to do with the worst of the zebras. We knew the disorder was untreatable, something to be reckoned with, but so what if Vincent had to "take up track instead of football," as Dr. X had recommended?

That night, after we had seen everyone to bed—twelve-year-old Brian, nine-year-old Vincent, seven-year-old Lucas, and three-year-old Celine—Walt and I sat on our old blue sofas incongruous in a house with white walls innocent of crayons and nails. I brought the manila envelope to the family room, took out a stack of papers in murky black and white, and divided it between my husband and me.

What had taken place at our rheumatologist's office after Dr. X's pronouncement—bewilderment and resignation vis-à-vis a remote unknown—was nothing like what would occur in our new family room that night.

I learned that night in October 1995 that cold and fire blast through you with the initial jolt of unthinkable news. And then there is a strange calm, a sense of unreality I suspect people get when they are in a war zone and the order of things as they know it is undone before their eyes. To this day, I can't remember the exact words of the texts in my hands because I later ripped them to shreds. I recall snatches: "corset of bone," "stone man," "frozen jaw," "pitchfork." I remember the word *pitchfork* because one of the faceless subjects in the study was the son of a farmer, and he had become immobilized forever after an accident with a pitchfork.

As my husband and I sat in the family room that night, absorbing the words on those Xeroxed pages, it was as if all sound and motion had stopped, and that white room with blue couches was a bell jar, or a frozen frame in a film, or even that instant when the electricity goes and you suddenly hear the silence under ordinary life. And when I was able to look up from the pages in my hands, everything looked different—the white walls of the new house, the blue sofas on which we sat.

I don't know if it was right away or after an eternity of this sudden difference I felt around me, but all at once everything unfroze; it was like the electricity surging back, putting a hum in the air again. And I felt something coursing through me. I don't know what to name it, but it allowed me to speak, to push ordinary words into a void: "This is absurd!" I said to Walt, who was still on the other blue sofa, suspended over his stack of studies. "We don't even know if this is actually what he has! And the names, they're all different"—which was it? Myositis? Fibrodysplasia? Ossificans? And the word *progressiva* appeared in one study, but not in another.

I seized on nomenclature as proof that none of what we had in our hands matched our child's symptoms. For one thing, the papers described strange swellings we had never seen, and even Dr. X hadn't mentioned any of that when she was blaming my thumb. Since I admired and trusted Dr. Henrickson, I had to think his hunch was right. But since I *didn't like Dr. X* and her confirmation—or the studies we were reading—I had to conclude that all our son had was a limp.

Walt and I moved into a place in the house with more privacy than the family room, with its cathedral ceiling. We sat on the floor in our new guest room downstairs, where there was a bookshelf of portraits of our four happy children, some candid, others posed at JCPenney. They all served to reassure that nothing had changed, that this was all a big mix-up; and shame on our pediatrician for sending that plain manila envelope with no warning on it. On the other hand—would it have made a difference if he had stamped it flammable, or stuck on one of those yellow decals with black triangles that warn away people in hospitals? Or maybe he should have called ahead of time and said, *Make sure you're sitting down when you read this,* knowing, of course, that most people sit down to go over medical studies—but then again, the metaphorical meaning would not have been lost on us. *Make sure you sit down* would mean: *you might faint or something when you read this, so don't be too far away from the ground.* But in the end, it would have made little difference.

So as Walt and I sat in that downstairs guest room, we asked each other, "What do we say to Vincent?" What could you tell a nine-year-old about something that his parents couldn't fathom? What we decided to say was nothing, at least until we could get what would amount to a third or fourth opinion.

Through that cold fall night, Walt and I both lay awake, on and off, in the dark. "I'll never be happy again," I said, staring at the shadows in the ceiling.

"That's an insult to God," said Walt quietly.

I could almost hear myself crying back, *But God started it!*

My faith has always been a natural part of my life, from the years when I was too young to understand it through the time when people start to question belief. My beliefs have deepened, but they remain essentially as they were in the days I held my grandmother's hand at Mass in the Spanish church with wooden kneelers where my parents married. Outside of church, my grandmother usually had knitting needles and yarn in her lap to make blankets for mothers in need, out of some promise or other she had made to God for family favors. My grandmother's regular blanket making was proof enough that God came through if you knew how to knit. And I knew, that night after reading the FOP studies, that if I wanted results like my grandmother's, I would have to ask God for more than my share of favors.

So Walt's words braced me. And since my husband and I have always been competitive, I thought: *if he can see happiness ahead, then I can, too.* I guess.

But before making an effort to sleep, I got up, went downstairs to the kitchen, and wrote a furious letter, not to God, but to our beloved pediatrician.

)

"*PROGRESSIVA*," SAID DR. Baldwin, my Stanford obstetrician, the one who delivered Vincent. "Sounds like a soup." He meant that Italian brand of broths and minestrones. I had known Dr. Baldwin since high school, and his irreverence in the face of danger had always calmed me. I told him we were hoping for one more opinion because I didn't want to believe someone like Dr. X could be right.

Dr. Baldwin gave us another name at Stanford. In the meantime, my mother had talked to the Bay Area pediatric group that had cared for my brother, Martín, and me, and she was told that one of the doctors had once seen a case of FOP. "It never progressed," my mother reported. That gave us more hope.

Throughout those days in the fall of 1995 denial was working on and off like a painkiller. There were moments when the black and white columns of words in the studies Dr. Weinberg sent would flash in my memory as on a magic lantern. What if, after all, it was all true? What if our child's future was told in those lines, like so many lines on an opened palm? And then, mercifully, denial would kick in, until I felt hardy enough for the next round of mental acrobatics, exercising my *what-ifs* in loops and circles.

Not long after reading the medical studies, I went to a psychologist for help with my fear/denial/fear/denial dynamic. I saw a very nice grandfatherly man who handed me a box of Kleenex that ended up wadded to a pulp at the close of our session. I went there during a fear cycle: *it was all true, most likely*, and I told the psychologist the world looked sinister, the blue sky looked sinister, everything I looked at looked sinister. As the mother of four children, I told him, I was *used* to things going wrong: premature labor; trips to the ER; teachers giving you "the look"; playmates who turned; even watching a newborn taken off for surgery—but there had always been a happy ending. The bogeyman had always shrugged and left, letting everyone convalesce on Popsicles and Disney videos. But this was different. The bogeyman had moved into our brand-new house—forever, by all accounts.

The psychologist sympathized and agreed that my thumbs did not look at all responsible for such a catastrophe. "Your hands look fine to me," he said when I held them up.

"What do we say to Vincent?" I asked. "What do we say to everyone?"

It seemed we could say little to our son until we had definitively confirmed the diagnosis, the psychologist agreed. And as for everyone else, it was none of their concern. The psychologist and I decided that the last thing we wanted was for Vincent to feel like a victim.

Of course, with our limited knowledge of the disease, the impossibility of knowing what trauma actually *meant* in something like FOP, neither the psychologist nor I, nor any of our doctors, could know that the advice to tell no one was a potentially dangerous mistake.

Before I left, the psychologist glanced at the paste of Kleenex in my hands and told me he would prescribe some Valium.

"I'd prefer not to," I said. And that was a time when worry actually worked like a charm, but for a very important reason that would not reveal itself until the end of the month.

A week after I was talking to the psychologist, my husband and I were at Sacred Heart seeing a priest we had always liked, a pastor with a radio announcer's voice, a keen faith, and a good way of linking both to real issues: Father Chuck, who battled his own chronic condition, diabetes, and who would also offer me a box of Kleenex that day.

I had arrived late, since I was pulled over for going too fast on the way to Celine's preschool. I had cried under the police officer's nose, but instead of Kleenex, he handed me a yellow carbon copy.

So when I entered the little rectory of the elegant old church with Gothic ceilings and stained glass, I found Walt and Father Chuck deep in dialogue. Father Chuck's usually jovial face was sober, but he stood and gave me a great bear hug, as he was a bear-sized man of the cloth.

"I don't know why the Bible says, 'My yoke is light,' I said to Father Chuck, making another paste out of Kleenex. "How can that be? How can something this terrible be called *light*?"

Father Chuck nodded in agreement, and I thought he might give us a pious explanation of the mysteries of suffering. Instead, he looked at me and said simply, "The original Hebrew says, 'My yoke fits well.'"

Huh.

But still, that version did not explain why suffering can ruin people.

I had to suspend my ongoing mental acrobatics—fear/denial/fear/denial—to stop and think. And thinking about Father Chuck's Hebrew translation that day, and through the months to come, I came up with something helpful for myself, which has made me feel a little better ever since.

There is a well-known saying in Spanish: "God squeezes, but he doesn't hang." The saying's reference to something around the neck—a noose, not a yoke—is typical Latin fatalism: if you can just tough out forces beyond your control, the saying promises, you can make it. But considering the Hebrew version, I began to see the yoke in contrast to the Spanish maxim's noose. A noose means death, but a yoke drives a plow to ready fields for seeding. And if "my" yoke means God's property, then suffering links us to transcendent work: we do not just skirt death, but cultivate life. I say nothing new, but it helps me to visualize it all that way.

I've relayed Father Chuck's Hebrew translation over the years to friends facing crises. And they always have an *aha!* look in their eyes when they hear it. *My yoke fits well*, they repeat to themselves.

That morning that Walt and I sat with Father Chuck, I recalled how on Vincent's birthday, not long before the diagnosis, I had relived the day of his arrival, as I do for every for one of our children's birthdays—September being the busiest season, as our boys are all from the ninth month. And I explained that after "infertility" was

scrawled across my chart on a doctor's visit in 1985, every time I
discovered I was pregnant, it was like getting a tap from God on the
arm. It was that sense of personal attention from God that Father
Chuck encouraged me to hold on to during this time.

I did my best.

Once, when I was driving the kids between schools and soccer and piano lessons, accelerating through a yellow light, Celine,
who was nine at the time, asked, "Mom, when I'm a grown-up, will
I have a mustache?"

"Of course not."

"Because Lucas said mustaches are hereditary," Celine explained.
"And you have one."

I glanced involuntarily in the rearview mirror.

Celine's worry was not without some foundation (I guess), but
it helps illustrate for me one reason why worrying over what *could*
happen is a waste of energy, because it is no preparation for the good,
bad, or indifferent things that actually do take place. The day Walt
and I were talking to Father Chuck about fears and memories and
taps on the arm from God, I was in no way worried about something
that would happen a week later, near the end of October.

Exactly a week after our visit to the priest, I was standing at the
bathroom sink, holding up a little white wand. I had to check the
back of the wand's box again, because the kits were all maddeningly
different: plain white sticks, wands with windows, tiny beakers,
different colors: pink or blue, or numbers of lines: one or two. My
plastic wand had a single blue slash in a little felt window. But was
I supposed to see one line or two? It was all a formality, I was out of
whack from stress, and—*on the off chance*—wanted to make sure
I could have a margarita that night. My father, who had moved to
the Valley to live near us, had already arrived to watch our kids; I
could hear the salsa rhythms on *Sábado Gigante* and don Francisco's
Chilean accent rising from the television downstairs.

The back of the little box in my hand said that one blue line meant—. My solar plexus got soupy. There was the tap on the arm from God. *But this time, the tap was terrifying.* Hadn't that geneticist from UCSF, Dr. X, said—

I met Walt in the hallway, near the upstairs bridge that looked down onto our family room of sea blue carpet. I handed him the wand. We hugged and stood together for a while. And I knew we were both thinking the same thing: *What are the odds that our fifth child will have FOP? And what are the odds of conceiving under these circumstances?*

I thought it was best to get the news out as fast as possible to all the women in my family. Everyone reacted with strained congratulations, and my mother, with frank alarm: "Right at the time of such a diagnosis!"

And suddenly my father was upstairs in the hallway, asking if he could make tacos, and I stopped him with the look on my face. "Don't be upset," I warned. My father was sober for a moment, his gray eyes dark behind his engineer's glasses.

But the moment I had finished giving the news, my father hugged me joyfully, as if there were not a single thing wrong in this world. "Why would I be upset?" he said. "Just like *mi mamá*! She had five!" And I will never forget my father's simple confidence and the strength it gave me that night.

That evening, Walt and I went to one of those theme restaurants decorated with barbershop spirals, turn-of-the-century inventions, bicycles, ferns, servers in straw hats, and it was all too much like a strange dream. I had no margarita. And neither Walt nor I said a word about the FOP gene and my thumb. But I was able to recognize a sign then and there—and it was a good one: I had refused the Valium the psychologist was going to prescribe the week before, *and that time worry was a very good thing.*

In November 1995, I was stopping our blue station wagon in bike lanes, hanging out my window, and running out of produce aisles. I had been queasy with other pregnancies and had had my share of morning sickness, but the nausea in this pregnancy was an entity unto itself, coloring everything, even colors. A red sports car on the freeway could set things off. A heavy-metal tune on a yellow radio could make me lose a day. The nausea—and its usual conclusion—was relentless, hollowing me out. And it took my mind off everything—even FOP. There is a Spanish saying (*They have one for everything*, my husband likes to say): "One nail removes another."

NOVEMBER 2003

IN THE STREET that runs parallel to ours, backyards jut up to the canal and its orange groves. Along that street are giant cedars and pines, a weeping willow, and trees colored like apples in the fall. I jog past these every morning; their peace and the rhythm of the running helps me to think. Today I am considering Brian in Santiago. *Why did you have to run past a riot?* I asked him over the phone yesterday. *I didn't know La Chile students were burning a Pinochet effigy*, said Brian. *I'm fine! The tear gas just stung a little bit in one eye.*

I decide not to worry, and focus on the quiet of the trees instead.

But a California redwood I pass, mascot of the Stanford Cardinals, reminds me that the deadline for Vincent's application is looming. An Early Action application means the school is Vincent's first choice. The postmark must, at its latest, read November 1, 2003, or the manila envelope holding pages of blanks filled in, essays, and a special photograph will not count. We will go to Kinko's to make a color copy of this photograph, one of Vincent and me that appeared in *Newsweek*, and the thought of it suddenly brings back a memory of what happened exactly three years ago:

In November 2000, Walt, Vincent, and I were on our way to an airport van, riding down the escalator of the Wyndham in Philadelphia. This was the hotel where the Third International FOP Symposium took place, with scientists and FOP families from around the world. That morning, there was the usual coffee brew perking up the air, the usual clinks of breakfast china coming from the lobby restaurant—but something was different. The place was full of police, men in uniform seated on lobby chairs, standing, wearing or holding helmets, black-and-white motorcycles visible through the glass entrance of the hotel. "Guess who spent the night here?" said Walt.

I couldn't imagine.

"Al Gore."

The symposium took place just before the presidential election, with its ballot recounts, hanging chads, and chaos in Florida flip-flopping our nation between Al Gore and George W. Bush. But before all that, Al Gore arrived at our hotel for one of his last campaign stops.

As we checked out at the front desk, I noticed that, in addition to the police, there were also men in suits with earpieces, the kind you see in movies. And I was thinking: *The Vice President of the United States—maybe the next president—slept under the same roof with us last night and we have to leave before I can get a message about FOP to him* When would I ever get another chance like this to appeal to a prominent political figure for attention to research funding for a rare disorder? But our airport van was already idling outside the lobby's glass atrium, sending plumes of exhaust into the cold morning air.

We loaded our luggage and climbed into the van. And after a second or so of waiting for another passenger, I couldn't stand it anymore. "I'll be right back," I said to the driver, who gave me an unhappy look. "We have to get the *Newsweek* article to Al Gore," I said to Walt, not checking his reaction before I jumped out. (Walt always thinks I might make us miss something important, like a plane.)

I knew where copies of the *Newsweek* article with Vincent's picture were: on the floor directly above the lobby in a stack on a counter. That floor was visible from the lobby, like a balcony, sharing the same high-tech ceiling of pipes and skylights.

I ran like a maniac up the escalators, grabbed a copy of the article, wrote a note to the vice president, and bounded down again. Halfway to the ground floor, I suddenly noticed all the policemen in the lobby had their necks craned, eyes on me. I smiled back, hoping to keep them at their stations, and ran over to one of the tall men in suits. I pushed my *Newsweek* piece at the man: "Please give this to Al Gore."

The man in the suit with the earpiece hesitated. "Please!" I almost grabbed him by the lapels. "It's about a rare genetic disorder. My son has it!" I pointed at the photo of Vincent and me with the balloons and the giraffe.

The man in the suit gave the picture a bland look. *See: I'm her, that's me in* Newsweek, I wanted to say—*but not for being a dangerous maniac,* I didn't want to say. Some of the police were watching, but the rest had gone back to doing whatever it is police do when a vice president is out of range. No doubt the airport van had already left.

"I'm not one of his people," said the man in the suit, flatly. He was no help. And I didn't like his lack of facial expression, either. "You need to give it to one of Gore's people."

"You aren't—I don't—I don't have time to—" I scanned the lobby. What did Gore People look like? Hopefully they looked friendlier. I glanced back at the hotel's glass entrance. The orange airport van was still idling, exhaust going, Walt and Vincent inside, waiting. I wouldn't have time to find out who was or wasn't a Gore person. Time to go. But as I made to dash off, I turned right into Marilyn Hair, mother of Sarah, who had brought a room to tears telling of the pencils she sold for research funds, the Spanish she studied, the university where she would live independently, all from a reclining wheelchair, mostly just her fingers mobile. "I may not have had experiences most people my age have," Sarah had said. "But there are lots of things I *can* do."

I handed Sarah's mother the *Newsweek* article. "Please give this to Gore's people!" I said. Marilyn, a minister and FOP activist who has done much more than I ever could in a million years to advance our battle, nodded and hugged me good-bye. Then I ran past the police, pushed through the revolving door, and jumped in the airport van.

The next day, Walt looked up from his *Fresno Bee.* "Guess who was across the street from our hotel visiting the Archbishop of Philadelphia yesterday morning?"

"Al Gore?'

"George Bush."

No wonder. The man in the suit with the earpiece, yards away from the Archbishop of Philadelphia at the Gothic stone church, wouldn't help me because he wasn't one of Gore's people, he was—*he had to be*—one of Bush's people.

Marilyn Hair passed on my note to Gore's people, and during the following weeks of election 2000, I sent one letter to Al Gore and one to George Bush. And because at the time nobody knew how things would turn out, I used the same salutation for both: "Dear Mr. President."

TWO DAYS BEFORE Stanford's mailing deadline, Vincent brings home a sealed copy (for parents only) of another important letter, one from the high school principal, a charismatic Dominican who is taken with Vincent's resolve. Usually the guidance counselor assumes college letter-writing tasks, but because of my son's spiritual bond with the priest, I have told Vincent to choose him instead. Did I mention *this letter is extremely important?*

I am holding the recommendation in my hand; it has the school's mission bell tower at the top. But before I can even read the text I know something is wrong. The letter is too short.

The recommendation is kindly, but so generic I am ready to cry. The principal is new; he has known my son for only two months, and the letter makes this plain. *What was I thinking?* I know Stanford places great weight on these recommendations, and judges them not only by their content, but by who authors them.

It is not just because Stanford is Vincent's "dream school" that it is so important we move heaven and earth to insure his chances of acceptance. It is because at Stanford all the ideal qualities for a student with Vincent's challenges intersect: topography: a campus with level ground; geography: only three hours from home; medical facilities: a world-class teaching hospital. For Vincent, these are crucial features that do not congregate at any other college, and the fact that the university ranks with the Ivy Leagues means it would open doors for a boy whose talents are his particular ticket to defeating FOP.

It is already past dinnertime, and we have just hours before the application mailing deadline. *Impossible to include the principal's letter.* I call a friend who teaches at the high school. She wrote a case study with recommendations on Vincent's special needs for a university course and got an A on it. "I'll never ask you for anything else, ever, ever, ever," I plead.

My friend has the flu.

I send a midnight fax begging the guidance counselor for *the fastest and finest letter you've ever written.* She'll help, she has to.

Usually everything looks better when the sun comes up, but in the morning everything looks worse: Lucas is ill; my midnight fax never made it; the printer has no ink for another Stanford form, and when I bring home a cartridge the printer actually breaks down. Today is the first cold snap in a warm fall and our new country house has *no heat.*

Vincent has exactly one day to get his application in the mail. Today is Halloween.

By the time I call the doctor for Lucas, fax the guidance counselor, and find out no one can install a vital component we need for normal temperatures until after the weekend, it is already afternoon. The guidance counselor still hasn't called back. How could I expect her to drop everything to write a brilliant letter in three minutes?

I drive to the school. And when I get to the guidance counselor's office, I see my last fax made it by the message on her face: it is a steely *no way.*

"I can't," she says, before I open my mouth. The counselor is a pretty woman, blond and resolute. Normally, I like her. She has a plane to catch, other recommendations to finish, more deadlines. I make a motion of getting on my knees. "I can't," she repeats, her eyes softening to a pained look. I explain, beg, plead, refute, bargain. *She can't. She can't. She can't.* But she kindly agrees to send a letter the following week, after the deadline: *I'd be delighted,* she tells me. If Stanford is a rules-is-rules place, the letter will be moot. But I'm betting it will help. *It has to.*

The counselor suggests I go check with the principal to make sure he has all the right forms, and when I reach the main office, as if on cue, the principal himself emerges, ebullient, with his white robe and fringe of white hair—as if I had an appointment: "Mrs. Whelan!" he says. "I have a seat just for you!" He motions me into his cluttered office with its bank of windows, rows of books, and stacks of papers on a large mahogany desk. He removes a stack from a seat he waves me to, takes his chair, and announces: "I just realized I left a lot of things out of my letter for your son!"

It is as if the principal himself got the midnight fax that never arrived. "I'm going to rewrite!" he says with a hand flourish. I thank this wise man profusely, relieved, relieved, *amazed.* "And I have only one hour to do it." *One hour is exactly right.*

At home I find that Lucas has no fever, that an electrician is on the way, and that we can have heat this weekend. So on Halloween night, Walt and I go trick-or-treating with the goddess Athena and the Blue Fairy and company.

Stanford, here we come.

)

WE RECEIVE A letter from Stanford's Dean of Admission. It is addressed to Walt, as a Stanford alumnus, and it says:

> Ever since Leland and Jane Stanford founded this university in honor of their son in 1891, familial ties have played an important campus role. . . . Your Stanford ties may come into play when we are making incredibly fine distinctions between your son's application and our many other exceptionally talented applicants.

"That sounds good!" I say.

We are in our room, with its windows looking out on the new

rose garden Walt and his brother Chris and the boys are setting up in circles around a tiered fountain. The harsh stalks in pots bear no resemblance to the illustrations tagged on them, but I know these roses will exceed the tags' promises. "They want money," says Walt, looking up from the letter.

Over the years you learn that anyone who writes to you from a college mentioning ties is asking for a donation. Still, the letter looks encouraging, even though I am positive Vincent's grades, scores, and talents can get him in—with or without a Stanford legacy.

I commend my son to the *Nuestra Señora de Guadalupe* and place our Stanford letter next to her likeness, a sepia-toned statue Brian brought from Mexico one summer. The letter will share space with candles and water from Lourdes and family photos.

IN NOVEMBER, THE Italian tenor Andrea Bocelli is the first star to appear at the new Save Mart Center built at the edge of the college where I teach, a pretty campus of green stretches, old maples, and mission styles mixed in with modern structures. This center will draw all manner of major artists, but tonight's star will shine more brilliantly than any other to appear.

Bocelli's music is the kind that can mend you inside, and near the end of the night he sings "Time to Say Good-bye." When Bocelli sustains those notes of yearning and loss, it is as if his voice and the music had always already existed together, but it is the first time we are allowed to hear them. Bocelli sings, beatific, eyes closed, in his spotlight, the tips of his black shoes lining up to a mark on the edge of the stage. There is a dark-haired soprano at his arm, lovely and accomplished, but she is like an Olympian running alongside someone who can fly.

I have followed Vincent up the narrow tiers of the center to get here, holding my breath as he navigates the precipices of the upper levels. And while Bocelli sings, I see my son's profile in the dark, his rod-straight posture, the way he sits to spare the wings of bone on his back from the hard seats. And he is so still, between

his grandmother and father, and so quiet, listening, I am convinced
he hears something I cannot.

Andrea Bocelli, the blind star, shines with the redemption of
his music.

SILVER TRUMPET

*A few days before Christmas, there, at the hospital, was
Teresa, the mother of another child with undiagnosed FOP,
whose name, coincidentally, was also Claudia. Teresa told
me her doctor had found information about this disease
and had sent our records to the U.S. to verify if this strange
disease had the name of FOP.*

*Four days before Christmas, they halted my three-year-
old's chemotherapy, which was a great relief, even though I
didn't know then what it was we would be facing.*

*In November of 2000 we came to Philadelphia for the
symposium and I took the risk of staying in the U.S. to give
my daughter a better life, leaving behind my family and a
good job. It was difficult at first, and we lived with another
family and slept on the floor. But all the medical, moral,
social, and educational support I have found for Claudia, I
wouldn't trade for all the gold in the world.*

—MARI FUENTES BARRANTES, mother of
Claudia, eight, diagnosed at age three, Lima, Peru

IN NOVEMBER 1995 Walt took Vincent to Stanford University
Medical Center in the hopes of disproving what Dr. X had told
us. I was too stranded by morning sickness to make the three-hour
trip, which was just as well, as the news Walt was given would not
have made me feel any better.

Vincent was born at Stanford University Medical Center on a
morning with royal blue skies, after a long labor, but without a single

complication. No one could have known on September 10, 1986, that a warning sign for something like FOP was in our newborn's feet. No reason for anyone to think of counting joints in perfectly normal-looking toes.

And I will forever be glad nobody did.

If the young pediatrician who held up our eight-pound son like a trophy had known to palpate his big toe, Vincent's mother might never have allowed her second child to learn to Rollerblade, or try a skateboard, or fall off a bike, or get his clavicle fractured playing football in the backyard. When the Stanford pediatrician said, "You have a perfect baby!" his pronouncement was absolutely, irrevocably, and eternally correct.

Nine years after we celebrated Vincent's birth at Stanford, in a room full of relatives, with a Super 8 camera, Walt learned in another room at Stanford that Vincent did, indeed, have something called fibrodysplasia ossificans progressiva, though the disorder seemed to go by other names and acronyms, which made it less mysterious, but more confusing.

"Maybe it won't progress," reported Walt when he and Vincent were back home. "The doctor said it looks like a mild case." My husband and I were alone in the same downstairs room with all the happy portraits on the shelves. "And if it gets worse, he said they could surgically remove the calcification and radiate."

"Radiate?"

"To prevent it from calcifying again."

I repeat: if you try to remove FOP ossification, you court explosive bone growth and loss of movement. But because the disease is so rare, a top geneticist from UCSF had not heard that caveat and neither had a top orthopedist from Stanford, who did not seem to have the name of the top researcher for the condition. And if radiation prevented FOP bone growth, the story I have to tell here might be a very different one.

One day near the end of 1995, I drove Celine to her little preschool across town. I could barely manage to shuttle kids and carry on teaching part-time at the university. I worried I would have to suddenly stop talking about labyrinths in Borges or gypsies in García Márquez and burst out of a classroom with one hand over my mouth. (I will always be grateful for the phenomenal students that semester, who kept me standing.)

The little school to which I drove Celine every day was run by Blanche Nosworthy, a luminous octogenarian with Katharine Hepburn cheekbones, blue eyes, and fine white hair in a bun. Blanche was a Valley icon, one of the original Dust Bowl immigrants, and she had reared generations of preschoolers. In her light-filled kitchen looking out to a garden where children rode tricycles and made mud pies, you could find a poet having tea and meet a farmer, a singer, or a bank president. Some of these people had been Blanche's students, and others were current parents. Her little school was "an enchanted place for childhood," as the *Bee* once called it. She had a tire swing and a Tarzan rope; honeysuckle vines and pomegranate trees for juice; a wooden playhouse; a sandbox; ivy everywhere; swings, a slide, rabbits, and a porch with easels. Inside were books and music, silkworms living on mulberry leaves, and a trunk filled with homemade costumes. A giant oak extended its branches over the yard, and as my father once said in Spanish, Blanche's had *a certain angel.* Her home brought me back to my grandparents' house at the foot of the Andes.

I had known Blanche for a long time, long enough for her to have said to me one day, "I love you, but you're always late!" That was a statement, coming from Blanche, because patience was her philosophy. So was: *It will work out.* Even so, it took me a while to tell Blanche about FOP. I persisted in a fuzzy trimester of nausea and denial, thinking that if I didn't tell anyone, especially someone like Blanche, then my boy's diagnosis wouldn't be real.

But the fears kept popping up: *What about FOP? What about FOP and this baby? What about FOP and my children's children? What about me? How will I do this?*

One cool November morning after greeting Blanche and not talking about FOP, I led three-year-old Celine through the garden to the swings to help her get going in the air, her mermaid's hair flowing up with each push. I stopped my little daughter for a hug, for her soft cheeks and her laugh. I couldn't leave her, and took a walk through Blanche's neighborhood instead, listening for the sounds of the children in her yard. As I went, I reached in my coat pocket for a rosary made from wood, keeping my fingers on the cold beads until they warmed. I walked and prayed, down streets protected by ancient oaks and marbled eucalyptus trees. And bead by bead, step by step, something inside me began to ease.

In the mornings my strolls helped, but at night it was all I could do to run hot water full blast in a tub, soak my feet, fight nausea, and sob. Still, what I understood almost immediately into my fifth pregnancy was that worry was too expensive a luxury; I had learned this lesson years before, when I discovered how emotions can affect your reproductive tract.

When I was an unmarried graduate student in comparative literature at UCLA, I was hired as a bilingual interviewer for a study called "The Birth Project," conducted by the School of Public Health and the Department of Anthropology. The study was an effort to learn how the American medical establishment, as a subculture, impacted childbirth for Hispanic women, another subculture. The study would check stress-hormone levels through late pregnancy and correlate them with childbirth experiences.

During my summer as an interviewer, I traveled to clinics throughout Southern California, interviewing pregnant Latinas, listening to some of their stories, collecting urine samples, and learning what to write in spaces next to terms like "Estimated Date of Confinement (EDC)," "Gravida," and "Multiparous." It never occurred to me as I filled in blanks by those medical terms that my future saved multiple spaces for me in their categories. I learned back then that I am now a "multip"—a "multiparous" woman, a mother who has given birth more than once—in my case in much more than one way. What was posited theoretically in that study—that stress may not exactly help when you are having a baby—I learned later on, firsthand, as a stressed-out pregnant graduate student:

The last thing I remember before my first baby was born—after we rattled down Santa Monica Boulevard one warm September night in our

blue Beetle; after my belly was gelled, bound, and connected by cable
to a machine that made sounds of horses galloping under water; after a
green lagoon gushed out from under me; after my husband turned the
color of the lagoon and was replaced by a jogging pediatrician (I wish
we could have met under different circumstances, I said to the young
doctor trying to shake my hand and run)—the last thing I remember,
having counted into the anesthesia mask, is someone asking, Does
anyone know how to—

Brian arrived a day after his due date at Santa Monica Community
Medical Center dressed and swaddled, his hair parted and combed. It
took a crash C-section to spring him into the world, though it was not
due to his lack of effort. Brian, who has never liked being in one place
for long, had done just about everything in his unborn power to get
going two months ahead of schedule. And when the time finally came,
he pushed urgently enough on his umbilical cord to set off alarms on all
the internal, external, and eternal monitors in charge of our fate.

I had spent most of my summer in our student apartment by UCLA,
with my belly—large enough for twins, doctors thought—beached on an
egg-crate mattress on the sofa bed in the living room, reading Redbook
and García Márquez and watching Bewitched reruns, allowed to budge
only for the bathroom and nonstress tests on a fetal monitor. The slightest
movement I could make was a labor cue, and my belly would seize.

Just as the bed rest came to a close at the thirty-seventh week, I was
sent back to our sofa to lie on my left side, while UCLA friends ripped
and reripped a Velcro blood-pressure cuff to practice readings. If my
blood pressure did not return to normal, doctors told me, the baby would
be oxygen-deprived and labor would be induced (induced!). To check
kidney function, I was sent home with plastic gallon jugs to fill. As for
this particular test, I didn't recall anyone saying that every jug, every
drop, counted. So when I returned one tightly capped gallon container
sloshing discreetly, an alarmed obstetrician decided I would be hospital-
ized immediately—until I mentioned I had flushed the rest.

I never got the chance to do any of the third-trimester pregnancy
exercises in my Jane Fonda Workout Book for Pregnancy, Birth, and
Recovery. (I hadn't done the first two trimester exercises, either, but
was planning on it.) The book, at least, helped illustrate what it might

*have been like to have been conscious when my baby was delivered,
since my doctor, a pleasant young woman with long dark hair everyone
called Patty, appeared in a labor photo. The exercise book also had a
shot of Brian's new pediatrician, the one to give him the first of many
high scores in life, a 9/10 Apgar, and who looked more like himself in the
book's illustrations than he did running alongside my gurney.*

Those past life months of bed rest, ritodrine for contractions, lab
tests, fetal monitors, blood pressure readings, and rosaries with my
mother and Walt evolved under an invisible pressure front: it was
as if the entire weight of Nature had come to bear down directly on
my belly and my unborn child. But the instant I woke from my first
childbirth surgery in a green recovery room, smelling medicinal,
my voice thick and raspy, I saw a perfect head of brown hair in the
crook of my husband's arm and felt a relief and exhilaration I had
never known before in my life—and that has come with the birth
of each of my children.

What I didn't want to experience again, though, was everything
that had led up to Brian's birth. *You have a 50 percent chance of some
of this happening again,* Patty, my doctor, had warned. Since, years
later, by 1995, I hadn't had problems with my other pregnancies, I
worried that the odds were no longer in my favor. So for the sake
of my fifth child—as well as children numbers one, two, three, and
four—I knew I had to stay standing. I had to have faith.

Around the time I worried that I had to stop worrying, a well-
meaning friend sent me an article on FOP, one stating that the
disease could cause mental retardation. I stayed up all night after
reading it and got sick. So as a defense against worry, I decided I
would protect myself from too much information. I would put FOP
on hold for three trimesters.

"You're going to have to be the one who thinks about FOP," I told
Walt one dark afternoon in November. "I'm not going to research
it. I'm not going to think about it until the baby gets here."

Walt consented. He would be the designated FOP thinker.

One cool autumn morning, after dropping Celine off at preschool,
I went to Barnes & Noble, which happened to be a good walking
distance from Blanche's. Maybe it was the proximity to the school's

"certain angel," but something a little miraculous took place at that bookstore—in the original building on Blackstone, the one with wood paneling, an elevator, and a Starbucks upstairs.

It was at that Barnes & Noble where I found a book that changed the course of things. This book was one of the most important volumes I have ever picked up. And I do not even remember the title or who wrote it.

I do seem to remember that on that morning at Barnes & Noble, there was a little half-moon of children and mothers sitting cross-legged on the colored carpet, strollers parked along a bookshelf, everyone listening noisily to a young woman probably reading something like *The Terrible, Horrible, No Good, Very Bad Day*. I had attended my share of story hours, but that day I was several rows down from the children's zone, in the Self-Help section.

I chose a book in Self-Help because *I needed help* and because I saw on one particular spine something about coping with a child's medical condition—something written by a mother. As I said, I cannot remember the title or the author, which is especially embarrassing for someone who gets after students for MLA-style bibliographies. But at that time, I still couldn't believe my son had a "medical condition," so I couldn't very well take the book home. Instead, I stood where I found it, skimming pages furtively, the same way I might have leaned into the fridge as a girl, snatching spoonfuls of flan. I could not install myself in an overstuffed love seat near story hour, and I certainly couldn't take reading material upstairs to Starbucks, where the bitter smell of coffee would have gagged me.

I remember the book explained that when you deal with any chronic condition in a child, you develop "emotional calluses," you become less sensitive to pain that seems overwhelming at the start. I can say that this metaphor was not only hope-giving for anyone at the beginning of a journey like ours, but very accurate: as you go, you get more durable. The book was exactly right. Even so, I couldn't actually process its advice for what I couldn't accept, know, or imagine. Impossible to will myself to it. I might as well have told my stomach to stop resisting even the idea of food.

So why was that book so life-changing? It was crucial because I picked it up in 1995, before the telepathy of the Internet, at a time when most of us were still finding things out on paper or by phone. Even my pediatrician was copying his articles from hospital data banks, and for something like FOP, which was not even in medical encyclopedias at my university, you had to count on serendipity.

"You need to track down the top researcher for this orphan disease," had said Dr. Baldwin, who delivered Vincent. I had never even had occasion to say *orphan disease* out loud. So the next step—since I had suspended thinking about FOP during pregnancy—was for Walt to ask Dr. Henrickson for leads. I, personally, wasn't looking for any more doctors that morning at Barnes & Noble. And I wasn't trying to learn a single thing about FOP. Even if I had been, I knew you didn't go into a bookstore during story hour to hunt for an *orphan disease*. This was a search complicated by the fact that FOP has gone under different names, acronyms, and diagnoses through the years. In 1995 I would have been hard-pressed to track down the leading expert for such a disorder, even at a library like Stanford's. *Had I been trying, which I wasn't.*

So that book written by another mother I picked up at Barnes & Noble had nothing to do with FOP. I was looking for self-help, not more science.

I didn't know it at the time, but in that book was a key to what I needed to find—just when I had decided not to look. The key was in another unfamiliar acronym, NORD, the National Organization for Rare Disorders. I noted down N—O—R—D and its number in pen on my palm. I put the book back in its slot on the Self-Help shelf—and never opened it again.

"NORD" was still on my palm by the time I got home, but it washed off before I dialed its number.

ONE DAY I brought up FOP to Blanche. It was a typical school morning, when we had launched ourselves in the usual frenzy, with backpacks bouncing, lunch bags swinging, and shoes under people's arms. I always intended to leave the house with leeway for morning sickness, but I never did.

It was on one such day that I told Blanche about FOP, and it's possible it might also have been the day Celine and I arrived first on the porch of her little brick house. We had dropped the boys off in time for them to outrace the second bell, and there we were, my little girl and I, holding hands—*early*—our backs to the ivy arch and a fence draped in orange honeysuckle. I should have felt proud. Instead, I was ready to pull my hair out. "How can we not have your *shoes*," I asked Celine, looking down at her bare feet. It was an unseasonably warm day, but even so . . . We had always had backup items collecting in the station wagon—Pull-Ups, sandals, T-shirts, snow boots—but they had dwindled, and at the last major spill, the only thing I had for Celine to change into was someone's baseball uniform.

I could see Blanche through the little window in her school entrance, which always held Scotch-taped announcements for the arts or babysitting or holiday schedules, and she opened the door to us with her usual glad welcome, smiling down at Celine, one hand on the inside knob. I explained, embarrassed, about the bare feet.

"We don't require shoes here," said Blanche matter-of-factly, raising her chin. And that was that.

If Blanche dismissed the little things, she took the big things seriously. So the day I told Blanche about FOP, I didn't want to make it *too* big. Celine had danced off to make mud pies, and Raffi was singing, "An Elephant Sat on You." A little batman was flapping around the playroom, and a party of preschoolers with crayons was busy at the child-size picnic table made of oak. I motioned Blanche into her hallway, where she had a row of theater seats. Before I could pull one open or she could invite me into her kitchen for tea, I rattled it all off and waited for something like absolution.

"I'm so sorry," said Blanche. And her blue eyes looked hurt. She asked what she could do.

Blanche did something. She hosted Playday for FOP to raise funds for the lab at Penn. And it was our first experience with a public effort for something that affected us so intimately.

THE DAY I dialed NORD it was a wintry morning and the fig trees, pale and gnarled, were like sorrowing souls. But I wasn't seeing those trees or the Tule fog erasing them while I listened for a dial tone.

A woman answered after just one ring. I explained my son's diagnosis. "And we're expecting another baby," I said, relaying what Dr. X had told me about my thumb. "What are the chances of passing on the gene?"

"The chances are—" I can't remember the NORD woman's full answer or the numbers she gave out after she said we could, indeed, pass the gene on to another child. I think she quoted some statistics. That's all I remember, because the shock factor kicked in so hard it quelled my stomach.

No doubt the professional-sounding woman with whom I spoke has assisted thousands, and she ultimately helped me more than she will ever know. But her cordial tones and the casual way she handed out sharp, cold facts told me she had "emotional calluses," while I did not. As I asked and she answered, I stared at the off-white tiles and off-white grout in our new kitchen, where I was filing my off-white fingernails.

"And you and your children should see a genetic counselor," I was told, after asking if my other kids could pass on the FOP gene. They could transmit the gene, I was warned. As for seeing a genetic counselor, I wondered if having met Dr. X, the geneticist, counted. Hopefully it did, because visiting a genetic counselor sounded as scary as going into that pink house off Highway 99, the one with a hand lined in neon over the roof and someone probably called Madame Sophia inside.

The grout between the off-white tiles was starting to crumble a little. Even though my stomach was subdued, I was afraid I was going to have to lurch to the sink before we were done, so I thanked the NORD woman hastily and told her good-bye.

"Would you like the number for a support group?" she asked before I could excuse myself. *Sure, why not, any number without percentages, fine.* I don't remember exactly what I answered at that point, but it had to have been in the affirmative, and I had to have written something on my palm, as usual, before transferring it to paper—who knows? Somehow, the number got saved in our odds and ends drawer, where we kept pens and staples and rubber bands and batteries and film.

For some reason, I can't remember if I called the number NORD gave me that same morning before going back for Celine at preschool, or if I fished it out of the odds and ends drawer a week, or an eternity, later.

WHEN MUSIC REPLACED sports for Vincent and he joined band in high school, he began to save for a silver trumpet. We all saw catalogue versions of the instrument: sterling, sleek, with a promise of silvery notes. It was also extravagantly expensive. So Vincent began to save up birthday money, chore money, gardening dollars, gifts from grandparents and aunts and uncles. The silver trumpet, everyone knew, was one of those goals Vincent was legendary for setting his heart on and quietly achieving in unusual and persistent ways. The most famous example was the golden birdcage he brought home one day when he was seven. We had nixed a parakeet for some good reason or other, so the domed cage hung vacant for weeks. Then one afternoon, there it was, a nervous blue bird under the dome, perched on the tiny trapeze. (Vincent's accomplice was his Tata, my father.)

As for the silver trumpet, there was no doubt it would materialize. It was just a matter of when, though it would likely take a while. But one day Celine figured out a shortcut: Santa Claus.

"Impossible," said Walt. He was right. Walt was forging his solo legal practice, and my part-time teaching brought in little. Work as a lone practitioner allowed more flexibility for family than Walt's partnership in a large firm had, but it meant that when cases were pending or pro bono, we were stretched tight. In 2000 we had moved to a smaller house, a gray one-story, to save money and protect Vincent from stairs. At the time, Walt was representing a single mother in a sexual harassment case that would go to an endless jury trial.

The case would take years to resolve, in favor of the single mother, with Walt as one lawyer on loans up against a team of attorneys on steady incomes. A silver trumpet was out of the question.

One night in early December, Celine handed me a letter she had written in careful cursive on binder paper. It said:

> Dear Santa Claus,
>
> I am writing for Isabel and me. We want a lot of things this year but you probably won't be able to get all of it. Isabel wants a bike (a two-wheeler, she can ride one now). . . . Together we want. . . . If we don't deserve this stuff then don't get it. But this is the thing I want most: a Silver Trumpet wrapped up in wrapping paper for Vincent. He really wants one but he doesn't have enough money to buy a Silver Trumpet, and it would really make me happy to see my brother happy. . . . I also want people all around the world who don't believe to believe in you. . . . Thank you, Santa Claus.
>
> Love,
> Celine (and Isabel)

I mailed the original off to the North Pole.

"Do you think Santa will bring Vincent the silver trumpet?" Celine would ask me every now and then, her palms pressed together, her blue green eyes, colored like the sea, so hopeful. She was ten, and it would be her last season of wanting to believe.

"I don't know," I would say lightly—a little less lightly each day she asked.

On December 23, I couldn't stand it any longer. Santa would need help. As I was driving under the freeway leading to Vincent's high school I was thinking of some way Santa Claus might swing it with the funds Vincent had already saved up. That's when the name came to me: Stevan Fabela, Vincent's high school band director, the man who lived for his musicians. I called him. I explained. I mentioned Celine's Santa letter.

"I'll do my best," said Mr. Fabela.

Silver trumpets are not exactly everywhere, and we had two days to go until Christmas, so I knew our chances were not good. Mr. Fabela called back. He had tried most of the local places he knew. No silver trumpet. No silver trumpet. The last store he called: no silver trumpet.

"Then the owner said, 'Hold on, there's one more place in the back—'" Mr. Fabela told me.

It was not the best time to be asking Mr. Fabela to go on a musician's scavenger hunt. He was busy preparing for a band trip to London to play for the prime minister. But this man was a teacher who taught music for free, made tamales for fund-raisers, earned a license to drive the school bus, hooked up wiring for Drama, never went home, and rigged a device so a student without full use of her arms could shine turning letters at halftime. So, the night before Christmas Eve, Mr. Fabela was there, in his band room, shuffling sheet music, packing instruments, confirming flights—and tracking down a silver trumpet.

Late on December 23, Mr. Fabela found the last silver trumpet in the Valley. And he convinced the music-store owner to slash its price. That night I went to pick it up in the high school band room—the only classroom on campus with all its lights burning. Mr. Fabela handed me my treasure, gleaming sterling on blue velvet, in a case made of fabric, light as air (so light, in fact, Vincent later revealed he first thought his Christmas present was a trumpet case).

It took me a moment to find my voice, which could only come out as a movie line: "How can we ever repay you?"

"All I want is a picture of Vincent opening it on Christmas morning," said Mr. Fabela.

Vincent discovered his silver trumpet wrapped in silver paper with the girls at some time between 3:00 AM and 4:00 AM on December 25. I wasn't awake to get a picture of the actual opening, but the look on his face and on the girls' faces in the morning was Christmas itself.

DECEMBER 2003

BRIAN COMES HOME from Santiago for Christmas: he arrives at SFO, his auburn hair dyed black to fit in among the Chilean students. He is jet-lagged, his brown eyes dark after failing, via embassies and letters and a plane ticket he bought, to bring along his Chilean roommate of modest means—*mi hermano*—with little future in his country. Brian has used his summer earnings from construction work in the Owens Valley for these trips, and there are more: next semester he will study in Italy.

VINCENT AND I are in Rheumatology at Children's, and Barb, a lovely mom-nurse, scrupulously follows the instructions Dr. Henrickson has left in Vincent's chart.

"So you're a senior," says Barb, handing Vincent a bag of ice to put on his arm before he gets the flu vaccine, subdermal, as instructed. "College next year?"

"I want to go to Stanford," he says.

"That's his dream school," I add, not looking at the syringe in Barb's latex-gloved hand.

Our nurse is carrying the last dose of vaccine available in Rheumatology (there is a national vaccine shortage), saved for Vincent this morning. It is nine years since Vincent has had any kind of injection, nine years since we learned that intramuscular inoculations are the worst thing for a child with FOP. "He's going to be a doctor!" I say.

Barb regards my son with admiration. "You must be really smart to have the grades to apply to a place like Stanford," she says, twisting one of those high-tech ice packs with a chemical that freezes, handing it to us for the road. I say a few prayers silently as Barb carefully slips a minuscule needle in under his skin—almost vertical, nowhere near the muscle.

The decision to get the vaccine has been a difficult one, leading to this under-the-wire dash for the last ampoule in Rheumatology's fridge. We had to consider the University of Pennsylvania's recent study linking FOP flare-ups to the flu; consider the risk of the vaccine itself, the danger of needles; consider the "safer" live vaccine nasal spray, which has no trauma risk, but which has landed a little boy with FOP in the hospital this season.

But Vincent looks good. The hardest part is safely over with, and we exchange Merry Christmases with Barb on our way out.

"How are you doing?" I ask Vincent as we pull out of the hospital parking lot. Dusk is falling, muting the patchwork colors of Children's. Vincent is holding the travel pack of ice on his upper left arm.

"Fine," he says, clipped. He knows I will ask too often.

We drive over the freeways and reach Old Town, which has started twinkling for Christmas. There are big Victorian bows on the streets' faux gas lamps, white icicle lights everywhere, and we can hear the clop-clops of a horse-drawn carriage that takes children to Santa's Workshop. I am here to deposit my paycheck in the bank before December 25.

Vincent is the one who orchestrates holiday lights and ornaments at our house. Every winter, it is Vincent who finds the strings of icicles and goes through them carefully for shot bulbs. Every winter, he is the one who replaces anything broken, with his own saved money when necessary. Last year Vincent bought a deer made of gold lights to drink from a stream of blue icicles on our front lawn.

I am relieved the vaccine is behind us, and I am so happy Vincent looks fine. Old Town is merry with lights and bows and holiday shoppers, and we are on our way to the bank with money.

As I pull into a stall in the Bank of America parking lot, the cell phone rings in the jaunty French tune Vincent has just programmed for me. It is Brian: "Mom? The letter from Stanford came."

"Oh," is all I say. This is the decision for the Early Action

application. *We have our answer.* I glance over at Vincent. He is
looking in the direction of a steakhouse that used to have a life-size
plastic cow on the edge of its Western roof. (I remember Lucas giving
the cow, which looked poised to jump, a caption: *I'll do anything to
be a part of your meal!*)

But there is something I don't want to hear in Brian's tone. Like
any former college applicant, he knows: fat envelope, good; skinny
envelope, bad. In Brian's voice I hear a skinny envelope. I thank
my oldest and hang up, worried that if this is bad news, it arrives on
an especially delicate day. Vincent has just had the vaccine—with
a needle. He is still under observation for twenty-four hours, still
vulnerable. I think of the little boy with FOP in the hospital from
a vaccine reaction. Here is an instance where the truth will have
to be delayed, I decide.

Vincent stays in the car while I go into the bank. I find a short
line near a wall where the B of A logo is burned into a panel of
old lumber and a branding iron hangs over the polished wings of
a bull's horns.

I dial home on my cell with a plan. Isabel answers, her little girl's
voice always so much younger over phones. She may be only seven,
but it's not for nothing that seven is called the age of reason. Isabel
knows how many cartons of soda I must contribute for a carnival,
where I put my keys, who left the milk out on the table, and how
many cats we have staying in our yard at any given time.

"Isabel, can you find the letter from Stanford?"

Isabel finds it.

"Is it skinny or fat?" The question sounds ordinary enough for a
cell phone conversation in a line at Bank of America.

Not having much experience with correspondence, Isabel
is—uncharacteristically—hesitant, but after a few seconds, she
reports, "Skinny!"

"Sweetie, go get Lucas." I am holding down some kind of emotion rising like bile.

I remain in line waiting for a teller, having one of those urgent
and private conversations we all seem to be having in public these
days, trying to speak in code or just letting it all hang out. Behind

me is a paunchy middle-aged cowboy on his own phone, and in front of me is a Latina grandmother laughing with a little grandson in her arms. Neither seems particularly interested in my life. And any minute, I will find myself at the window of a friendly teller, pantomiming numbers, and Vincent will grow tired of waiting and show up, and my little plan will be blown.

"Lucas," I say with urgency as my fifteen-year-old's calm, deep voice comes on the line. "The letter from Stanford. It's skinny, right?" Lucas gives an affirmative. "Listen carefully," I say. "A skinny letter is usually a no." I'm not positive, anymore, though. You hear rumors. *Now they're getting tricky,* said Vincent's friend Peter the other day. Thin envelopes have been known to arrive and refer lucky winners to the Internet.

"Lucas, you need to put the letter in the wooden picture box on top of my dresser." I have to talk fast because the grandmother is zipping her purse at the teller window. "It could be bad news. Right after the flu vaccine I don't want to give bad news." If the news is good, it won't change by Monday. If it's bad, today, Friday, it could hurt. I explain quickly because my teller is waving me over. Lucas understands.

At home, at night, I feel like a character in a TV sitcom. If the news is, indeed, good, and Stanford is being "tricky," then there's no sense in postponing anything. So after dinner I go to the master bedroom, lock the door, and find the letter in my cherrywood photo box full of memories. The envelope is extremely skinny—emaciated. I take the thing over to my night table and move it around over the bedside lamp's bulb, trying to see, trying to discern a "We regret" . . . Nothing: just a jumble of symbols. After a while of checking vertically, backwards, upside down, I am able to make out the word *April. April* must mean a date for a deferred decision—I'm sure of it. *This isn't so bad! It's not a no.* Of course it isn't so good, either. No predicting whether Vincent will see this answer as a glass half full or half empty. If this were my skinny letter, I would take it as a big fat no. At any rate, it is a maybe. No hurry to tell Vincent either way. I don't feel right withholding this news, but it turns out to be a good thing that I do.

The first twenty-four-hour vigil after the vaccine passes uneventfully, with Vincent following instructions to ice the vaccine site, which looks innocent enough, no symptoms of any sort.

But Monday Vincent wakes with a pain under the vaccine arm. We are between a rock and a hard place. If the pain was caused by the injection, either by the introduction of a flu virus or a needle, then our first line of defense, prednisone, presents a particular conundrum. Start prednisone to avoid loss of mobility in the arm? But if we use the drug now, it also nullifies the vaccine. Dr. Henrickson points out that a real flare-up, not future flu immunity, is our most pressing concern. We decide to compromise: instead of jumping in with the steroid—the best way to boost prednisone's efficacy—we will wait and watch for one day. In the meantime, we ice the site.

The next day, *thank God*, my son is perfectly fine. And he is out of the danger period for a vaccine reaction.

Our correspondence arrives in the rural red Jeep, and Vincent goes to our green mailbox for *the letter*, which is, of course, in a cherrywood photo box in the master bedroom.

I feel guilty.

My son retreats to his room to gather books and papers, but before he can move to the dining room's mission table to start on homework, I stand in his doorway and produce *the letter* from behind my back, without a word. Vincent's face falls when he sees its dimensions.

"It might not be bad," I offer, as he runs a finger under the envelope lip. *Maybe this wasn't a good idea; maybe I should have waited until we were absolutely sure about the arm.*

"It came earlier," I confess. "When you got your vaccine—" He's not listening.

My son sits on the bed in a posture of grief. Clearly, he is his mother's son in this regard: this glass is not half full, it is empty to the second power. He has taken a deferred decision as a no. He lets the letter fall.

I give my best pep talk. I am waved out of the room. *But there is still hope, Vincent.* And when I relay to Dr. Henrickson that Vincent's arm is better and Stanford has a sent a maybe, Dr. Henrickson gives us back the glass half full: "You've come this far, your spirit has carried you this far," he tells my son.

CHRISTMAS FUTURE 2004

THE FIG TREE outside my window is pale and bare. It looks like a chandelier, branches bowed over, ends curling up for candles. There is a weird elegance in its look.

I am rejoicing that Vincent is better from his last flare-up; his arm pain is down to a one and we will continue a ten-day taper-down on prednisone.

Isabel learned all about an "Elf Calendar" today at her friend Shelby's. The calendar is a decorative wall hanging with a slot behind each date in December, magically filled with gifts by *elves*. This is the first I've heard of such a thing and have no inclination to look for one anywhere. But we are at the end display of a cereal aisle at Vons, and I am sizing up my eight-year-old with her Span-ish eyes lit up. She has spotted such a calendar at the display. It is made of green felt, with little pockets and numbers stitched for the twelfth month, a stuffed elfin face smiling merrily at the top. "Can we *please* get it and see if the elves come by?" Isabel asks, hands clasped together under her chin. Maybe to make up for our flakey tooth fairy, but mainly because of the look of hope on my little girl's face, I give in and purchase one "Elf Calendar."

Isabel is very excited on her way to bed: "*I can't wait*," she keeps repeating, wondering what the elves might leave, hoping they will actually take the bait of the calendar. "Do you think they'll make it?" she asks.

"I hope so!" I'm not sure myself. I rummage through the pantry to come up with a gift small enough to fit in a December 14 slot in case the elves don't arrive. I find a tiny holiday bag and put some coins in, but it is too bulky to wiggle into the tiny pocket. So I wedge three quarters in, and consider Isabel will be as pleased as she is when the tooth fairy remembers to do her job.

The next morning Isabel is on the couch jingling coins. She has a wry look on her face. "Mom?" she says. "Were you the one who put three quarters in the Elf Calendar?" This is a trick question.

It takes me a moment, but I decide to answer honestly, affirmatively: "I was worried the elves might not show up." Isabel's sweet freckled face says, *I knew it.*

That's that: all it takes is one more deductive step—and our last season of belief.

Then Isabel says: "Elves don't leave money!" Any fool should know that much about the elfin world.

"Oh." I'm not sure how to respond. "Well, maybe they'll actually make it tonight." I'm not sure what the workings in the elf world are for no-show elves, or for elves expected to arrive all of a sudden in the middle of their calendar cycle, so I offer: "You could write them a letter."

"OK!" A letter under her pillow has worked, after all, when the tooth fairy blows it three nights in a row.

So tonight Celine finds me at the computer in Brian's room and silently hands me a homemade card, drawn in red magic marker, with an elf traced carefully on the front. Celine will place it under Isabel's pillow, and it reads:

> *Dear Elves (Kindly say YES or NO to answer. Circle yes or no),*
>
> *Yesterday we bought a decoration that was spose to have you either bring a paper to find a present or get candy. So can you do that for us? We have the decoration in our kitchen.*
>
> *Love,*
> *Isabel Whelan your friend*
> *And a Merry Christmas to You Elves Out There!!*

The day after the elf letter, Isabel is happy to find a peppermint lollipop, which she twirls and holds up for me, observing its uniqueness and admiring its Tootsie Roll filling. All's well that ends well.

But fifteen minutes don't go by before Isabel gives me a suspicious look. "Mom?" she says. "Were you the one who circled the 'Yes' on the letter to the elves? I recognized your handwriting."

"No?" She stares at me. "Well—yes. Yes, I did." I don't want to lie. "I didn't think the elves would take the trouble—so—"

"*Did you leave the candy?*"

I can look at my daughter honestly and say: "No. I did not leave the candy. I did not leave it." I repeat myself a few more times before Isabel is satisfied and we leave it at that.

Subsequently, the elves mess up and skip one or two nights. Isabel makes no mention of her disappointment, and I consider it is because she has figured something out. She has, but not as I might think.

I make a photocopy of the letter to Santa that Isabel will go off to mail with Vincent.

"Isabel," I say. "Can you give me that letter you wrote to the elves?"

Isabel refuses. "I figured out that when I don't put it under my pillow, they don't come," she explains. "So I'm keeping it!"

This season, Isabel has achieved the right balance between the Christmas spirit and the scientific method.

ACONCAGUA

I was asked one time why Nick's parents allowed him to do such things as play soccer, do the 110-mile bike marathon, bungee jump, play golf, and many other things that most parents wouldn't even let a "normal" child do. His upper body was frozen by the time he was twelve, but he was still able to walk and run, as his lower body had not yet become imprisoned by FOP. No one knows when or how much a body is going to be affected. And you never know how your life is going to turn out. Now Nick is twenty-eight and he has wonderful memories of his childhood and the things he was able to experience before his body "froze."

He refuses to be slowed down by FOP. He is the vice president of our 1994–1996 Impala SS club, and he is now a licensed mortgage broker in the state of Texas in the #1 producing branch for the entire company of 612 loan officers. He was named one of the Texas Businessmen of the Year for 2004. He sometimes has a down moment, but his zest for life, I think, keeps him focusing on what he can do, not what he can't. His philosophy is, "Ya can't change it, so adapt . . ."

—LORI MAHER, wife of Nick, twenty-eight,
diagnosed at age eighteen months, Wylie, Texas

ONE MORNING IN December 1995, standing at our kitchen counter, I ate a few Saltines to steady my stomach and dialed an important number in Florida. I stood because I knew I was about to have the type of conversation you can't really have sitting down—at least I can't: I had to brace myself against something cold and hard, like a kitchen counter. Someone answered at the other end.

"Hi-I-was-given-your-number-by-NORD," I said without taking a breath. "My nine-year-old's been diagnosed with myositis ossificans—or fibrodysplasia ossificans progress—progressiva." Long *i*? Short *i* in the last word? I wasn't sure how you pronounced it.

The voice at the other end of the line was a woman's, kind, friendly—and mercifully skeptical after I described Vincent's symptoms. "That's not how FOP usually starts," I heard, after explaining all my son really had was a limp. Of course, he also couldn't touch his hands to his collarbone or shoulders, as we had discovered during that first visit to Dr. Henrickson, but maybe that wasn't important information, so I didn't mention it. "Is his big toe malformed?" I was asked.

"Not really." This was not exactly true, but it was *sort of true*. From the outside Vincent's toe looks perfectly fine. You can't tell it's missing a joint.

"A lot of people call here thinking they have FOP and they don't," said the woman's voice encouragingly. My heart lightened. But still, two doctors, three, had said—

"They did tell us his big toe showed something from the X-ray," I admitted. I was just going to have to go ahead and have this conversation as if my child *did have* what he *simply couldn't have*. Outside the sky was still dull, though the backyard grass seemed greener in the low light. For some reason all that color filling the living room windows was making my stomach contract.

I would just have to ignore myself. I had a list of questions ready. I would just get through them as fast as I could. But I prefaced these with a warning to the kind person on the other end of the line: "I'm pregnant and have a lot of morning sickness and I can't handle a lot of information . . . so maybe could you just tell me only what I need to know right now?" I was starting to get that uneasy feeling I have when people announce they're psychic. In some ways, this nice woman in Florida could tell me my future.

First question: "The woman at NORD said the baby I'm carrying has a chance of being born with this disorder and my other children could pass it on. Do you know the percentages of those chances?" I said it all as fast as I could, and closed my eyes to hear the answer.

The answer was my first surprise. "You can only pass on FOP if you actually have it yourself," was what I heard with my eyes closed. "If your son does, in fact, have FOP, then he has a fifty-fifty chance of passing it on." FOP, I learned, is an autosomal condition: it usually results from DNA altered at, or not long before, conception.

Suddenly there was no such thing as morning sickness, no such thing as a hard kitchen counter, no such thing as a cloudy winter day. "So, you're saying this baby—"

"Your baby has the same chance of being born with FOP as anyone in the general population," said the kind and matter-of-fact voice on the other end of the line. Oh! For the first time since I held up the white wand with the blue line, I felt the ground go back to its place under me.

"And my other kids?" I already knew the answer but needed to hear it.

"They have the same chance of passing it on as anyone else," said my new friend.

If the young woman on the other end of the line had told me her name, I hadn't heard it in all my nervousness. I found out she was Jeannie Peeper, and Jeannie Peeper—confident, professional, kind, happy Jeannie Peeper—explained, amazingly, that she herself had FOP. *Someone who had this was OK.*

But I wasn't done with my questions, and for the next one I had to hold my breath to listen again. "What are you able to do?"

"How much do you know about FOP?" Jeannie asked. I told her about the nightmares I had read in articles our pediatrician and a friend of mine had researched: living statues, deafness, mental retardation. I couldn't understand much and didn't want to know more. I was pregnant, for one thing, and didn't dare invite problems for this next child. I told her I had had one complicated pregnancy before and wanted to spare this baby from premature labor and toxemia.

"A lot of articles out there on FOP are outdated," said Jeannie matter-of-factly, miraculously. Practically everything I had just listed about FOP was false. "Living statues" was a brutal description, but catastrophic loss of mobility, I discovered, was the only accuracy in the list I had recited.

My blood started to move in the right direction again.

Still, I needed to know what only Jeannie could reveal. *What was she able to* do? "Could you just tell me what I need to know?" I asked in a small voice.

"I can walk," Jeannie said. "I can shower, put on my makeup, comb my hair. And I'm the head of an organization that brings in hundreds of thousands of dollars a year."

The sky lifted. I felt like my soul had been returned to my body.

"I tell parents it's not the end of the world," said Jeannie. *Thank you, thank you, thank you.*

And then Jeannie talked about a doctor named Fred Kaplan at the University of Pennsylvania. "All the kids call him Dr. Fred and they love him," she went on, telling me about this extraordinary man—as extraordinary as Jeannie—who had taken up easing the grief of FOP as a mission. I wrote the number she gave me for this doctor in blue ink on my palm—and the rest would be history.

My exchange with Jeannie Peeper changed me that day. It was one of the most important conversations of my life, and it was one of the first, and maybe the most significant, in a series of steps that would change the way I looked at things. Here was a woman who was my age, as it turned out, who was alive and well with a condition I could still not fathom or understand or accept. And she was helping others, running an international organization, making a lot of money for research. *Blessed Jeannie Peeper.*

It was my conversation with Jeannie one cold gray winter day that began to save me from FOP and taught me that *our worst worries and imaginings can bar us from the comfort of the truth.* I will forever bless and thank Jeannie Peeper—for that conversation, for everything she has done in the world, for the monument and example she has raised that is her life.

IN JANUARY 1996, not long after my conversation with Jeannie
Peeper, my father, Walt, Vincent, and I were in Manhattan for a trip
that was part vacation, part business, part medical pilgrimage. We
were there for a tour given for pistachio growers by a packing and
processing plant in New York, and our trip had been arranged by this
company because of the small farm Walt runs with my father. The
plant, with its moving bridges of nuts, mysterious silver machines,
churning chocolate, and shelves of every possible confection, was
like a Willy Wonka factory. Vincent was given metal scoopers to
take chocolate-coated nuts and all the bubble gum and jelly beans
he could eat or hold on his way out the door. He had made friends
with the only other child along, a little girl from Merced, and she,
like our son, alternated between awe and glee through the tour.

The FOP had not progressed, and I was starting to feel better into
my second trimester. Jeannie Peeper's facts about FOP had freed me
from undue worry and a nausea that had been like a prison cell. So
it was a happy visit to the East Coast. Vincent and his new friend
threw snowballs around the Rockefeller Center, two nine-year-olds
from the Far West exhilarated over snow in a place with skyscrapers
and an outdoor ice rink by a big gold statue. There was a moment,
though, on the sidewalk, when Vincent skidded over a slick of ice
and I threw out my arms and screeched out of all proportion to the
danger. At least that's what it would have seemed like to any casual
observer. A doctor along on the tour raised an eyebrow and joked
about my anxious mothering. He was right in a generic sense, but
completely wrong in that instance. We were still telling nearly no one
about the FOP, and my reaction to my son's slide on a slick sidewalk
must have made me look like a lunatic to that doctor.

The real reason for our trip east was for Walt and Vincent to
continue on to the University of Pennsylvania to see the specialist
whose number Jeannie Peeper had given me. In keeping with the
plan of safeguarding my pregnancy, I would not go along to Philadelphia. If the world's foremost FOP expert confirmed the diagnosis

once and for all—a fourth and final opinion—the anesthetic of denial would wear off for good.

Dr. Kaplan was (and is) Chief of Metabolic Bone Diseases and Molecular Orthopaedics at the University of Pennsylvania Hospital, an authority on bones on an invisible level if there ever was one. So when we were all back in California together and Walt handed me Dr. Kaplan's stationery confirming FOP, I knew that was it. There it was, a definitive FOP diagnosis, in black and white, with the seal of the University of Pennsylvania as official and binding and historic as anything ever signed in Philadelphia—and I knew it.

At the University of Pennsylvania, Dr. Kaplan showed Walt and Vincent the little labyrinth of the FOP Lab, with its labeled beakers and priceless DNA "Xerox" machines making copies of people's double helixes, and a small handful of devoted researchers, men and women in white coats with their names stitched over their breast pockets. And they talked in Dr. Kaplan's office, filled top to bottom with the photos and artwork of FOP children and their families. And Dr. Kaplan told Walt and Vincent about the mission to find a cure for FOP in this race against time.

"But he says Vincent seems to have a mild case," offered Walt, back home. He sounded hopeful. I saw this statement in the letter, the mildest manifestation Dr. Kaplan had seen in a child to date, a great range of motion in his limbs. "Even though they can't predict its course from that," added Walt. With FOP you can't predict anything at all.

"Kaplan's a great guy," Walt said, enthused. And for the first time since we had broached the subject of FOP, there was hope and levity around the topic—and there was a new direction to look to. "Vincent really liked him," Walt said. "He even took us to lunch." *A doctor who takes his patients out to lunch: wow.*

Then Walt handed me something: *What Is FOP? A Guidebook for Families.* Dr. Kaplan had given it to him for us. It was a spiral-bound booklet with a cover in blue and green watercolors. It was not an illustration of ocean life—my first impression—but the painting of a butterfly. Only I was not looking at a butterfly at that moment: all I saw were the blues and greens washing around it.

I held the manual feebly. How could I forget that plain manila envelope we opened so ingenuously, a lifetime ago?

It took me a few moments to say it, but finally I did. "I can't." Walt understood. He would be the one to study the FOP manual.

For some reason, I was still holding the *Guidebook for Families* after Walt had gone downstairs. So I shoved the guidebook to the bottom of a sock drawer. I wish I hadn't. But at the time I could not know the meaning of the butterfly, luminous and perfectly formed, and painted by a young man whose arms were crossed and locked.

WHEN YOU HAVE five children there are, of course, more battles than FOP to face. Sometimes I wonder if it is Vincent's require- ment for exceptional caution that has prompted our oldest to take adventurous leaps most people avoid; or maybe he is doing things as he was made to do them, starting with the crash C-section in which he was involved. I try to read events to answer these ques- tions, but sometimes I reach conclusions that have nothing to do with what I'm asking. Below is an example that involves two fights at Berkeley (make that four, if you count a lawyer and a professor) and a Disneyland parade:

It was a Friday afternoon in spring when Brian called from a pay phone on the Berkeley campus. "We've been arguing for two hours," he said, his voice tense. "The attorney's gotten pretty angry and he's yelling and he threw a book down on the student health advocate's table."

Near the end of his freshman year at Cal, Brian brought an appeal to the university over punishment for a fistfight. The fight happened the first week of September 2001, in the middle of a bas- ketball scrimmage at the university rec center. A student punched Brian and Brian punched back. The police were called in, and their report tagged our son as the assailant.

Our oldest—a high school valedictorian—had never been in a fistfight before, but his penalties—as we understood from the Cal lawyer—could be up to several hundred hours of community service and a black mark on academic records. The hours of service alone would be burdensome enough for a freshman at an elite institution like Berkeley, which is part bureaucratic jungle, part boot camp, part world-class think tank. (To illustrate, there's a posted spoof of a student, books in his lap, head in his hands, with the caption, "UC Berkeley: Where your best is never good enough.") Berkeley has always been famous for its challenges, so the community service hours that could be imposed seemed onerous enough, but concluding college with a black mark to follow Brian through law school applications was worse.

Worst of all, the police report was wrong.

Walt appealed to the university lawyer, who wouldn't budge from the sentence because no impartial witnesses stepped forth. We hired a Berkeley attorney who represented students in similar cases. The lawyer was able to reduce the number of service hours, but that was it. The black mark would stay. "That's how this attorney is," said our lawyer. "He's known for it."

We gathered character reference letters from teachers, family friends, and former employers. "If my little boy grows up half this amazing I'll be one proud father!" said our counsel when he read the letters.

The university attorney was not impressed.

We finally advised Brian to let it go. At the age of eighteen he didn't need a long battle against a major institution to disrupt his studies. But Brian prefers to do things *his* way, as a high school counselor once observed. So in spring of 2002, he scheduled an appeal, prepared arguments, gathered witnesses, and told anyone in class who asked why he was wearing his father's suit with running shoes, "I'm going to trial!"

That Friday afternoon before Easter when he called me from a pay phone, Brian had argued for hours with an angry attorney twice his age in front of a UC Berkeley panel of faculty and students, and he said to me, "I'm nervous." He had just finished telling me about the attorney raising his voice and throwing down a book. "Can you say a prayer, Mom?"

Brian may have been nervous, but it sounded to me like he was winning. I even began to feel some sympathy for the University of California lawyer: the poor man was probably at his wits' end, arguing helplessly in circles, yelling, pulling out his hair, ready to hit the ceiling or throw things. Brian had been engaging me in similar debates since age three, and because Berkeley's attorney lacked the authority to stamp a foot and say, *Because I'm your mother,* the University of California was sure to lose.

Brian called back a few hours later, exuberant. "I won! And the panel reprimanded the attorney . . ."

To his credit, the university lawyer handled the defeat with grace: "He looked over at me and winked," Brian said.

If I've learned anything from Brian's Cal experience, it is that I don't really want Vincent going to Berkeley. Nobody else in the family wants him there either. *You're not letting Vincent go to Berkeley,* says my mother-in-law, June, who took over the family farm and raised five children on her own after Walt's father passed away. June, as resolute as she is impassioned, has never shied away from a challenge in her life. *You're not going to have him at that place of locos!* says my mother, who does not back away from anything or anyone, herself.

They're both thinking about another fight, a more recent one, Brian's sophomore year, on Holy Saturday, when my cell rang at Target after I had filled up my cart with what was left of the plastic Easter grass. I never made it to the cash registers because when I answered my phone, I heard, "Mom?" from someone who sounded like he was speaking through a mouth packed with cotton. "They broke my jaw." It was Brian.

They? Who? Where? Ohmygod—ohmygod—ohmygod.

Telegraph Avenue flashed through my mind. That street has always looked like a place on the morning after a party—or a riot—and Brian played basketball with a student who had been shot in a bar there. I've never felt at ease on Telegraph, but Brian, on the other hand, at six foot two and over two hundred pounds, is my polar opposite. (When his newborn feet filled my palms, I said, *These feet seem large. Will he be a big man?* The pediatrician smiled. *Babies aren't like puppies,* he said.)

That Saturday, while Walt and I were on a date in the foothills,

holding hands and strolling though rivers of Monet wildflowers, Brian was in the university rec center in an argument over
basketball—again. This time around, he wasn't beating a lawyer or
defending himself against another student. He picked the wrong
people to rattle with his debating skills: two men—not students—
bigger than he was. One blocked Brian, while the other took a
running start from the side and slammed him in the jaw, breaking
it in two places. The men fled the scene, and Brian ended up in an
ambulance on morphine. (Walt made it to Berkeley in about two
hours that day.)

"He looks like a distinguished Englishman," said my mother, right
after Brian had his jaw set, too shocked to say much else at first.
Brian's lean, handsome face had swollen into another person's.

On our way out of the oral surgeon's office, Brian had mouthed
something to me that sounded like, "I have a midterm." A professor
he had e-mailed about a makeup exam had told him *no makeups*,
so Brian refused to come home to recuperate. I knew better than
to argue, so the day after the surgery, I dropped him off, groggy
with painkillers, at a review session he insisted on taking. I called
his professor—Professor X, I will call the man—to request an
alternate exam.

"We don't give makeups," said Professor X in a jolly tone that
would have been more suited to a yes. The final would be weighted
at 50 percent of the final grade, instead. That didn't sound like
a good deal to me, so I repeated that my son had been brutally
attacked on Saturday and—with no makeup—would force himself
to take a midterm on Wednesday. "Maybe you should just let him
take the exam," said the professor, still jovial. "It might get his mind
off things!"

The man did not seem impressed with a broken jaw excuse.

"If you expect him to take it, he will," I said, suppressing a rise
in my voice. "But he could incur complications." The oral surgeon
had told Brian to go home and rest, since infection would require
a hospital, surgery, and a metal plate.

"If he gets sicker," said Professor X reasonably, "he can take an
Incomplete." I was staring over at the gray curve of the university

stadium as he spoke. The stadium has that Roman Coliseum look to it.

"Then, in my heart, I'll hold *you* responsible!" I told Professor X—without stopping for air—that *I* had a PhD and *I* taught at a college and *I* had five kids, *one with a rare genetic disorder* and *I knew what was important and what wasn't.*

The professor's jovial manner was gone. "There's no need to threaten!" Was that what I was doing? *Oops. Uh-oh.* On the other hand, *Wow.* I threatened *him?* "Your son needs to talk to me himself!" he barked. "Can he talk?"

"He just had his mouth wired shut!" I could barely understand Brian myself. When I learned someone in the dorm washed and folded clothes for him after the attack, I asked whom we could thank. I thought he answered "Allah," but he was really saying "Oliver."

"This conversation has to end," said the professor. "Good-bye." And that was that. *Poof.*

From where I had parked on the Berkeley hills, I had a shiny postcard view of San Francisco, with its Transamerica skyline and the Golden Gate Bridge crossing the Bay. Somewhere in that glittering city was a prominent man who had just hung up on the mother of one of his students. Good going, *Mom.*

A little while later, a lieutenant called to ask if we still needed the police to contact Professor X about a makeup.

"Don't bother." I told him what happened.

"These professors, they don't live in the real world," said the lieutenant. "Some of them are legends in their own minds."

The man who hung up on me was actually well known outside of his own mind, but I was grateful for the sentiment. And it gave me a peek into the strange bedfellows Berkeley faculty must make with the police, who probably don't care for a circle etched in concrete in the Free Speech Plaza that says: THIS SOIL AND THE AIR SPACE EXTENDING ABOVE IT SHALL NOT BE A PART OF ANY NATION AND SHALL NOT BE SUBJECT TO ANY ENTITY'S JURISDICTION.

A week after I was in Berkeley, fighting with a Harvard-trained academic, I was at Disneyland, marching with Vincent and his high school band down Main Street, U.S.A. I wasn't there so much to march as I was to trail my son. I did that because during our last parade at the Happiest Place on Earth, Vincent got a side stitch and had to break formation by the Peter Pan warehouse. He was taken inside, where he tried to sit on a broken flying ship to rest, but was given a wheelchair instead. Meanwhile, Walt and I had waited in a panic by It's a Small World, not knowing why our son had not finished his route. Vincent was in better shape than his parents after it all, gleeful, in fact, because he had seen a familiar character in a green tutu turn around in the back lot. "Tinkerbell is a man!" he told us.

So for our last parade in the Magic Kingdom, I made sure to march with Vincent's band, and it was all good and exhilarating and without incident. And I asked myself: Why is it that I have to be in such opposite worlds in the space of one week: in Berkeley learning what to do about a broken jaw, and then in Disneyland trying to march in a parade?

But then it hit me: Berkeley and Disneyland are not opposite: they're parallel, parallel universes. Both are artificial utopias; both have unusual characters; and both have dangerous attractions.

Please let Vincent get into Stanford.

JANUARY 2004

IT IS JANUARY and it is summer. We are in Argentina. We have not been back to my family's homeland since before the FOP diagnosis, and something happens when we arrive in Mendoza, the province at the foot of the Andes. Here, as in California's Central Valley, vineyards are staked optimistically in dry lands, but here is as far south as the Incas forged their water canals and as far south as the Italian immigrants went to produce a new wine country.

"Welcome to Mendoza, my favorite city!" says Brian as our plane touches down at the little airport near the Andes. While he was studying in Chile, Brian made the trek over the mountain range, past the Aconcagua, to visit. It is weeks since he has been in Mendoza, but for me it has been ages, and this is my first time here with my grandparents gone. I lean toward a porthole in the plane and see the stark mountains, the ombú trees, and memories rushing to meet me: my grandmother, plump and girlish in her sober dresses, her hair still dusky, her joy so vivid, making plans, poking fun; and my grandfather, short and powerful, white-haired and grave, at his typewriter. I have felt them with me through the trials of FOP, through the births of our daughters, through my absence from Argentina. And I sense them more than ever in this province: in the green tunnels of sycamores, in the dry foothills of the Andes, in weeping willows, on the broken sidewalks, and in the Pampas smell of Argentine leather. It all filters in, settles in me, reaches something I cannot get to, gives me back what I don't remember. And I see my grandmother in her apron, leaning into a rolling pin, steam from apples dancing in a pot of water; I see my grandfather peering over his spectacles, indulgent, the books behind glass in his sacred library; there is the metallic smell of kerosene lamps, the paprika smoke of empanadas, the *asado* under the adobe dome, the patio tables, dark green, one long and one round, with more people to listen to you than you could count.

And all of those people to listen, they are all here now, ready to pick up where we left off. But something strange occurs the day we land: I lose my voice. This has never happened, and it happens exactly now, when I have the most to say and the greatest number of people who care to hear it. It is a severe viral laryngitis: all that comes out of my mouth is a rooster sound. I am told to drink red wine, keep quiet, write notes. I force out whispers, give up. All I can do is point, shrug, shake my head, and nod. This all happens, I know, because there is too much to say and too much I can't explain.

We go to my cousin Julieta's, to her house of thick white walls and black window grates. Coming in from the street you have to mind the *acequia*, the narrow canals I floated paper boats in long ago in runoff from the Andes. Julieta is a young version of my mother's mother, with the same exuberance, the same smile. In her garden of poplars and pines my uncles are tending the *asado*'s fire in the mild summer night, drinking Mendoza's *vino tinto*. The smoke and sizzle of sausages and ribs cut across the grain, dripping broth and basted with *chimichurri* reach me, and it is as if no time or distance has separated me from this place.

I've brought little trinkets marked in English for the children in the family. One of these gifts I will need to use myself tonight: a magnetic writing tablet with a tiny tape recorder along its side. Ten-year-old Facundo is busy testing it. "Facundo, *el Magna Doodle!*" I whisper, pointing at the toy. Facundo has olive skin and green eyes and looks back with a level gaze, as Argentine children are taught to do. He uncomplainingly hands me the gift and watches as I print a message to my uncle Jorge, my exuberant godfather with a full head of wavy white hair, who still rides into the Andes on horseback and outlasts newlyweds in conga lines. (Once, Jorge danced with Walt's mother, who can outdance anyone but Jorge, and he declared to her afterward, hand on his heart, "I marry with you.")

"Do you remember my daughter, Paula?" asks another uncle, Raúl, loudly. Raúl is still strikingly handsome into his sixties, a dark movie-star Latin. I've known Paula since before she was born.

"I've lost my voice, not my marbles," I write. The Magna Doodle tablet has little honeycombs for iron shavings, which follow a tethered magnet. I can't blame my uncle—no doubt I look daft, as all I do is smile, nod, and point.

"That's right!" says my aunt Margarita, taking Raúl's place. Margarita has exclaimed over Celine and Isabel, palms out, as if I had brought her the *Mona Lisa*, and they both glow back. How big is Walt's family in *Norteamérica*? she wants to know. "Are they used to seeing so many relatives in one place?" And I try to tell her, with no sound, that Walt's family is big and devoted, just like here, just like a Latin family, and they are always there for each other. Margarita smiles, looking exactly as she did the day she married my mother's brother, copper-skinned and daisylike. I should know, because someone tossed me, a child, on her lap as she and my uncle were readying to drive away from the Spanish church in the plaza, the three of us competing for room with her wedding gown. Margarita turns out to be good at asking questions I can answer on the Magna Doodle, and we get into a rhythm, with others checking in, inserting ideas. But then the wine begins to reverse our order, and Margarita begins writing instead of me.

"I've lost my voice, not my hearing," I print. And on it goes. The same party will be reconstituted at my mother's house, where conga lines will jump unbroken from the blasts of Brian and company launching fireworks that exist only in cartoons—rockets on poles, sending up streamers and stars of colored lights.

Through our visit, relatives comment, independently, on a light that comes from Vincent, and every aunt tells me she has been praying for him at a great gathering on my father's side, with more fireworks and guitars and another dancing Uncle Jorge. My godmother, my aunt Susana, wants us to make a pilgrimage to a saint in the province of Salta, to whom Vincent has been commended by my mother. The saint is too far, but we make a pilgrimage into the Andes to see the Aconcagua, the great sentinel.

THE RISE INTO the Andes from Mendoza is gradual, and we pass wide flat spaces of wild grass and little valleys. We stop on one level stretch to watch two long-necked guanacos hiding from traffic. We drive by a meadow of potato plants, flowering white, the striated rock rising as their backdrop. We pass *Penitentes*, a hill named for its great stones that are like stooping pilgrims making a climb on their knees.

We stop at a fabled church on Puente del Inca where thermal waters create mineral tunnels and eerie rock formations, tinted red with iron from the Andes. We watch a Chilean father strip off his shirt and lower himself into the earth and its warm pools. If only Vincent could bend that low—and if I weren't afraid of the mountain winds and bronchitis in his chest. The waters in the red rock are healing.

We enter the little church, a legendary chapel of gray stone spared decades ago by an avalanche that razed a famous hotel. The church has a great Gothic window behind the altar, filtering in light that polishes the wood pews and catches glints of dust in the air. I hear a bird fluttering somewhere inside and then see it batting at the window, which is open just wide enough for an exit. The five of us there, Walt, Vincent, Lucas, my godmother Susana, and I kneel on the hard pews to pray, and the bird stops to rest by the window. Señor, *let this bird, the color of smoke, take this prayer up to you, this prayer, as always, for my children, for a cure for FOP.* My second prayer is for Vincent to make it into the school of his dreams.

At a little market of souvenir vendors, tents and tables loaded with trinkets, across the street from the stone church and mineral baths, Vincent buys a bird carved out of the Andes. It is rock-shaped into a small owl, a striated brown stone polished by the dark hands that sell alpaca jackets. There are other souvenirs: baby sandals, vases, frames, all ossified as curiosities in a rust-colored coat of minerals from the thermal waters. I find Brian a black-and-white alpaca jacket for his UC semester in the Italian winter, coming up this month. I buy a chunky white rosary as wide as a belt, made from pieces of the mountain.

And finally we come to a stretch where we find the Aconcagua, whose name is "stone sentinel" in the Inca tongue. The mountain rises, guardian of a continent, its summit brilliant with snow. Here is the western world's highest reach. The summer air is cold around us and the wind is hard and you can hear it. I feel stronger, somehow, this close to the Aconcagua.

In between the Aconcagua and Mendoza is Portillo's ski resort, now idle, ski lifts swinging empty in the air. We stop to walk around, and Walt spots a condor. I peer up into the clean blue of a sky that seems infinitely higher and farther in the Andes. Walt is pointing. My aunt Sussy has her head back, her brown bob ruffling in the stiff wind. Vincent and Lucas see. It takes me a while of blind searching through the blue, and then I discover two apparitions, wings unmoving, crisscrossing space. There is a soaring feeling you get when you find creatures that can sail so casually over something like a mountain.

8

SADIE HAWKINS DAY

FEBRUARY 2004

*One doctor suggested we roll Daniel's hand over a ball to
make the vein stand out, and it really works. And then I am
the tourniquet, holding just the vein, since I don't trust that
the rubber hose tied on the upper arm won't traumatize the
underlying muscle. We then have another person holding
Daniel's arm still, after careful coaching on what they can
and cannot do.*

*That makes four people involved in the process: the
phlebotomist, the tourniquet (me), the holder, and Daniel.
It's quite a sight, I'm sure, but it gets the job done, and
safely. By the way, I tell Daniel that he can scream his head
off, if he likes (and he does!). It doesn't mean he isn't brave.
I once read that courage is not being unafraid, but being
afraid and doing what needs to be done anyway.*

—JERI LICHT, mother of Daniel, ten, diagnosed at age three, New Rochelle, New York

THE FOP GUIDEBOOK I pushed into a sock drawer didn't actually stay there until our fifth baby was born. I fished it out now
and then and stared at its cover, but always shoved it back unopened.
Once, to keep myself from reading the manual against my will, I
flung it at the top shelf of our closet, where it lodged behind boxes
of keepsakes and stacks of old lesson plans. I knew there was no
way for me to get to it there in my pregnant state.

Not long after Isabel had been safely born, I climbed on a bar
stool and pulled out the guidebook from its dusty spot. For the last

time, I studied that butterfly cover with its sea colors. My mouth was dry, and my heart was galloping, but there was no longer any good excuse to protect myself from FOP.

I remember that summer as one of unrelenting heat, heat like a glove, heat that punched the power out of two towns in one weekend. But I don't remember feeling hot the day I sat cross-legged on the carpet in the master bedroom and opened that guidebook, flipping through pages and pictures, ready for blood, sweat, and tears. What I found instead, strangely enough, was *reassurance*. And when I was finished reading and the earth was still on its axis, I realized: *As bad as it is, FOP is less bad than I have been capable of imagining it.* I learned, among other things, that the facial muscles were spared, the eye muscles were spared, the heart muscle was spared, the fingers were spared. And it could spare all of you entirely—for years.

I had held on to my fears about FOP for nine months, like secrets. And in "relegating" the truth to my husband, I had deprived myself of the truth's relief. I thought I had learned a lesson on all that after my conversation with Jeannie Peeper. But I had really just started to understand what would take years to learn, what I am still learning.

AS I SAID before, in 1997, Vincent's second major FOP flare-up arrived symmetrically. It arrived on his left side instead of his right, and it arrived almost exactly a year to the day that his first flare-up appeared. As it had the year before, the FOP started with a little lump that grew and shifted. He developed the contours of a bodybuilder on one side, with a swelling that made it hard for him to keep his arm down. The pain kept him from falling asleep and it woke him in the middle of the night. It was a pain that kept Walt and me up even when Vincent was already breathing evenly in the dark.

The second flare-up was exactly like the first, but exactly unlike the first in that the future was already mapped out for us on Vincent's right side: the network of FOP bone on his rib cage and back, the lost arm motion.

Impossible to watch helplessly again as our son would surely and painfully lose what he had lost a year ago—all over again, as in a mirror image. We knew exactly what FOP was. We knew it from the studies I had ripped up. We knew it from the guidebook I had shoved in a drawer. We knew it in the flesh.

The time after Isabel's birth when I finally read the FOP *Guidebook for Families*, I absorbed all the *real* features of the disease, and the warnings were seared in my brain. But I had only skimmed the table of medications. As we knew—since FOP was incurable and untreatable—the medications hadn't worked. They had all failed. So what was the point in reading about them? As far as I was concerned, the list's value was, if anything, historical, not medical, like a packaged Victorian remedy a docent once let me hold on a school field trip to the Meux Home Museum in Fresno.

But in the summer of 1997, during that symmetrical flare-up, I flipped over to the medications page again: there it was, the grid of failed drugs, all useless: Accutane, the acne medicine, with its side effects of dry eyes, dry mouth, mood swings; indomethacin, the anti-inflammatory, with its risks for the digestive tract. And there were other hopeless drugs with names like mythical deities that meant nothing to me.

After a week of watching FOP start its work all over again, in desperation, in a rage at the disease, we knew we would have to try something—anything—even if nothing worked, even if it was just a placebo. *Anything*, even if it postponed the inevitable for just a few days, would be better than standing by helplessly before the enemy.

I called Philadelphia to ask about the failed medicines in the guidebook. Dr. Kaplan was away, but I reached his partner, Dr. Glaser, who sounded kind, conscientious, and—to my worried-mother's ears—maybe a little too *young*.

"What can we *try*?" I asked Dr. Glaser, after describing the symmetry of a disaster that was replicating itself exactly a year later. I sat cross-legged again, on the blue carpet of the master bedroom, holding the opened guidebook so hard against me it was leaving a spiral imprint on one of my calves. I had a finger on the grid of drugs, straining to understand Dr. Glaser's answers.

The names of the medications felt uncomfortable in my mouth, and I wanted to sound sure of what I was asking, but I had no sense of where to stress syllables. "In-do-me-thacin?" I said carefully, and Dr. Glaser tossed the word back easily in a sentence; but then he said, "Indocin." Indocin: I liked his version. Yes, we would try Indocin. It sounded right. Indocin, the word turned into a wise old man with dark skin and magical herbs. But Dr. Glaser was saying no, maybe not Indocin. We discarded the word, just like that, *poof.*

But the list went on, so I would just go ahead and choose a word that looked better, maybe a more familiar one: "prednisone?" I knew how to say it, at least. We had used prednisone before, when Brian was three and his joints and hands and feet swelled with an allergic reaction. Of course, I knew allergic swelling had nothing to do with FOP swelling, but maybe swelling was just—swelling? And I liked the sound of the word *prednisone,* solid and full, like *pregnancy.*

"At his age we don't know—" Vincent was ten years old, and I remember, just from using the drug with Brian, how desperate the situation got before any of the three doctors he had seen at the time would prescribe steroids for a child.

But we had to try something, *anything.* So I said to the young and kind Dr. Glaser: "We already know what FOP can do. Can prednisone be worse?"

Dr. Glaser asked for Vincent's weight and calculated his dose.

Almost as soon as Vincent started taking the prednisone tablets, pink for twenty milligrams and white for ten, his pain disappeared and so did the visible signs of FOP. The swelling on his back went down, the bodybuilding contours vanished, and he was able to walk without holding his arm out. He could, once again, reach for glasses in the kitchen cupboard, and he was able to sleep at night.

It was a miracle.

A few days into our jubilation over prednisone's effects, a fellow FOP mother, Jennifer Snow, called. We had met Jennifer, her family, and her exuberant blond kindergartner, Stephanie, the year before at the annual FOP fund-raiser dinner the Snow family held with the support of the entire town of Santa Maria. Stephanie had been diagnosed with FOP at the age of two, and seemed to pay no mind to her stiff little shoulders and neck, bouncing on a trampoline, riding a bike with training wheels, and charming a whole town, its city officials, and television camera crews. Stephanie herself had already envisioned a cure for FOP. "Make it cherry flavored," she told Dr. Kaplan.

"I'm taking Stephanie to the pediatrician," said Jennifer over the phone that summer of 1997, her voice tense. "I'm worried about her jaw." Stephanie had fallen, and seemed fine—but then her jaw began to bother her.

My blood froze. A percentage of FOP patients lose jaw mobility— one of the disease's most chilling features. It was for submandibular flare-ups that prednisone was listed in the guidebook, recommended to ease breathing and swallowing. But it was not listed as anything that could keep a jaw from clamping shut.

I knew our one-subject experiment with prednisone didn't translate to any manner of scientific proof. There was no real way to know if FOP had just decided to do an about-face (a trait of the disease), or if the prednisone was actually attacking the disease process.

I was no scientist. But I *was* a desperate mother on the phone with another desperate mother, and so I gave my recommendation: "Try prednisone." I described our success. "Tell your doctor. It works like a miracle!"

If only I had studied the medication tables in the guidebook during Vincent's first flare-up in 1996, I was to think at the time. *I might have saved his right side.* But I was wrong to think that way, because the timing would have been wrong—and this fact would not be made apparent to me until later.

Vincent stayed for months on the miracle drug and he developed the swellings of Cushing's syndrome, a side effect of long-term prednisone use.

My child's normally slender frame had gradually swollen, and so had his beautiful freckled face. "What happened here?" asked the principal of our school, taking me aside in alarm when school started in August 1997. It was not the FOP that was showing, it was the steroid's side effects. It is still a surprise, today, to look back at photographs of Vincent during that time and see a completely different boy. The prednisone told the world that something had changed. Up until then, FOP had been hidden well enough. Cushing's syndrome, producing the full, round face characteristic of prolonged prednisone use, made it obvious that something was not right.

Meanwhile, Stephanie Snow had been prescribed the same drug with uniformly miraculous results. The pain in her jaw disappeared, the FOP retreated, and she wrapped up her treatment in a matter of days, with no side effects.

Vincent did not have the same luck. Every time we began to wean him off the drug, the pain in his arm would reassert itself, the FOP inflammation would start in again, and his mobility would suffer. So for as long as we could, we traded FOP swelling for facial swelling and weight gain.

Another one of the prices of this treatment was mood swings. The last thing a child battling a nightmare disease needs is a depressant, and that is what prednisone was for Vincent. All things considered, when I look back and see his smiling face in photos, the full cheeks so unfamiliar to me then and now, I see how bravely he held up under the assault of both the disease and our failed experimental course.

)

"WE'RE GOING TO have to discontinue the prednisone," said Dr. Henrickson, when we took Vincent in to see him in October 1997. Dr. Henrickson agreed that since inflammation itself triggered a chain reaction of trauma to muscle tissues, if we could short-circuit the inflammatory response, we could spare muscle and connective tissues injury caused, not by falls and bumps, but by the immune system, which has, of late, been identified by Dr. Kaplan and his colleagues as a player in the FOP process. The prednisone was working well under that theory, but we could no longer afford to pay its price. Impossible to sustain the side effects, but more important, the long-term use of a steroid would begin to threaten internal organs. Prednisone's risk factor finally outweighed the risk of doing nothing at all.

After three months of prednisone maintaining mobility in Vincent's arm, after three months of trying to taper down the drug and still keep arm motion intact, we conceded defeat. And FOP retaliated: it rebounded with a fury and a vengeance the likes of which we had not seen a year before. It was as if the disease were a mythic creature taking revenge for the few months of time and mobility we had purchased for our child.

Children in Vincent's class sent cards; friends set up prayer groups; entire churches prayed—and continue to do so; friends brought over food. But nothing kept the FOP at bay that fall. After he turned eleven, Vincent lost the ability to reach high enough to comb his hair, bend low enough to tie his shoes, and extend his arms to pull a shirt over his head.

Why did the prednisone work for Vincent only during the months that he was on it? How was it that the drug had defeated Stephanie's jaw flare-up in just a few days? Was it that her FOP had retreated on its own? Did individual reactions to medication make that kind of difference? The answers would come in time, and they would be surprising. They would imply, once again, that there is a mysterious "schedule" in things. But at that point, all we understood was that our one-subject experiment had failed.

When you figure that the most likely way to get what you need for your child is through persistence, it can get confusing when you have to know when to hold off or stand back. I like to think I've been training myself all along to push through one challenge at a time, but then something happens that shows me that worry coils up somewhere in my psyche, popping out crazily like a broken jack-in-the-box. I keep learning what "trying too hard" means.

One February, when the rains had cleared the horizon, we made our way over the foothills, up to the giant pines and redwoods, the forests still elegant with snow. We've taken at least one ritual trip up and down the mountains every winter to sled, make angel wings, and roll snow into giant balls to stack and decorate. For the first nine years of Vincent's life the trip was as it was for any family, but after we learned what FOP really was, every glassy puddle or slick stretch meant panic for me.

It was two winters ago that we parked at a little inlet full of SUVs and minivans, joining parents with toddlers handling snow for the first time, teenagers recklessly sledding down a rise, little kids finding out how far their feet could sink. We all got out of the van near a small hill with frozen patches along its base. Then it happened.

Vincent tensed as he slid—it seemed an instant of eternity, longer than it actually lasted—and I shrieked as if my shrieking could somehow protect my son, his balance, the grip of the ice, the rotation of the earth.

But—Vincent did *not* fall. And before turning away, he looked pointedly at me, his dark eyes furious. "I'll wait in the car," he said. No argument would persuade him to join us.

And in the cold mountain air was that little sting of grief that Vincent would miss more than he had to because of my overreaction, which had caused mothers, fathers, and children to turn their heads and look.

Walt and I watched Isabel and Celine take turns riding a sled down a little slope. I slid along the snow with both girls in my lap in waterproof coats. We forgot everything in the novelty of the mountains.

Our spot on the hill was too crowded with families to make angels or snowmen, so we finished sledding and made it back to the minivan, passing lines of parked cars and mothers unscrewing thermoses of hot chocolate. Vincent sat in the front seat, looking unhappy, but not for the reason I thought.

"I hurt my leg a little," he said. "I tried that over there and landed wrong." He pointed at a small rise by the van, where he had gone off on his own. Something in me sank. What could we say? As it turned out, my anxiety had provoked exactly what it meant to prevent in my sixteen-year-old.

There was another time when my fears invited what they promised—falsely—to ward off. It happened when Vincent needed a routine blood test, and I had called the hospital for the name of the most skilled phlebotomist there was. I wanted the best phlebotomist in the world, one of those people who can find veins and draw blood like a magician. Blood drawing requires careful precautions for FOP patients and is best carried out by practiced souls with a butterfly needle, the tiniest kind, the ones they use for anyone with hemophilia. So I made sure to get the name I needed, made sure we arrived at the lab when the best phlebotomist was there, and called ahead to double-check.

The best phlebotomist in the world was a friendly young man with a mustache, and he seemed happy to help. "It's *really* important that he have no trauma," I said to him and his assistant, a young Latina who was lining up glass tubes. I glanced at the hinged desk where the blood was drawn. "And you need to get the vein *the first time*."

While Vincent was out of the room, I went on with so many anxious explanations and warnings that the confident, jolly look staff people have in a children's hospital was gone by the time I finished. So when the moment to draw blood came, the top phlebotomist in the world had to take a stab at it more times than I've ever seen anyone take a stab at it. "Nobody's ever had that much trouble," commented Vincent as we left the lab with cotton taped to the inside of his elbow. No damage was done, thank God, but I learned exactly how contagious fear can be.

Besides learning how we can be catalysts and accomplices when things go wrong, I have also discovered that even if you *are* trying too hard, the universe will try to even things out now and then and—every once in a while—do you a little favor.

It was a rainy weekday three winters ago, a day Vincent's high school had off, and he was in his room hooking up a Nintendo game box. I was watching my printer make a Rubén Darío handout for a class at the university when the doorbell rang.

I opened our front door to a man I had never seen before. He was in a gray uniform, his face was sober, and standing next to him, of all people, was my son—Vincent. Over the man's shoulder I saw a golf cart with another man in uniform at the wheel. The day was the same color as our one-story stucco house, the sidewalk, the uniforms, and the rain, which had turned to a drizzle on wet asphalt.

"Is this your son?" said the man at the door, nodding to Vincent. I nodded back.

The whole gray day was like a black-and-white film, an episode of "The Twilight Zone." There was my son, but my son was also on the bottom bunk in his room, connecting a black box with cables to little ports under a television screen. Vincent, who has never gotten in trouble for anything in his life, was in two places at once, and in the place right in front of me, he looked guilty.

"We saw him riding around the basketball courts at the school on his scooter."

Vincent doesn't have a scooter. I looked at Vincent and there it was, bright and silvery at his side: Celine's new Razor. "We thought he was a truant," said the man. Truant? The charge was as fantastic as the idea of Vincent riding a Razor around a school in the rain, as impossible as the idea of another Vincent in his room playing Nintendo at that moment. "We asked him why he wasn't in class, and he told us he goes to another school," said the man.

"Right," was all I could say, still as distracted by the sudden appearance of my son on the doorstep as I was by the idea of Vincent riding a scooter alone on a slippery blacktop. "We're at the Catholic school. It's not in session."

"That's what he said." The man looked over at his coworker at the wheel in the golf cart. His friend raised a hand pleasantly. The rain was picking up its tempo. "So we brought him home."

Vincent came in the house a bit sheepishly, but I was too surprised—and glad—to scold with any conviction. I was secretly thrilled he had had this adventure—one I never in a million years would have authorized—and that it had turned out fine, brilliantly, in fact. Vincent had gone out, fourteen-year-old that he was, and zoomed around a school in session in the rain. And he had been brought back safely. It was a little miracle.

And last year I witnessed a full-fledged miracle. It happened when we were visiting Brian's school during the famous Cal–Stanford football game at a stadium packed with seventy thousand fans: drunk fraternity boys, milling students, kids in blue and gold "F—Stanford" T-shirts. There was rivalry, friendly and unfriendly; crowd surfing, loudness, chaos, laughter, and rivers of people. Crowds are especially worrisome when you can't have bumps or sudden wrenching, and we try to avoid them. But this was the Big Game.

I was following Vincent, who was behind Walt weaving efficiently through the throngs. When he made a move to avoid bumping into a group of girls, Vincent stepped up onto a low curb of concrete, and I saw him lose his footing. He started to fall backward over the bleachers, and once again, everything took on a slow-motion quality, lasting forever, like a scene in a film. My son was at the top of the pyramid made of concrete and steel and wood. I screamed, and used words that caused even the "F—Stanfurd" T-shirts to turn around. Whatever unseen force or descending angel reached my son, it overlooked my language. At the last split second, Vincent was righted. The fall would have been catastrophic. It took me a good hour of staring at red-and-white figurines versus blue-and-gold figurines on a green backdrop, a hand at my throat, to come down from the near-miss feeling.

Not long after the episode at the Cal stadium, we were at a Taco Bell in between rushed pickups and drop-offs, and I was telling my kids about a scene in a memoir that seemed unbelievable. The narrator described falling against an unseen rescuer after escaping a fire; the person behind her failed to appear in a newspaper photo taken at a key moment, making the rescuer seem supernatural. "The person could've just slipped out of the camera lens," I said. "Ridiculous." Even I can only suspend disbelief so far.

Vincent unwrapped his taco and then said, in the understated way he has, "That happened to me, though."

I looked over at my son calmly taking a bite of tortilla. *I knew it.* I knew I had to have witnessed something out of the ordinary at the Berkeley stadium, that split-second defiance of gravity. "It was at the Stanford–Cal game, right?" Vincent shook his head no.

I wracked my memory for anything even remotely similar.

"At the Supreme Court," said Vincent.

A few years back, when Vincent was twelve, we made a trip to Washington, D.C., and to the FOP lab at the University of Pennsylvania, eighteen of us, with cousins and aunts and uncles. In Walt's office there is a photograph of all the children, oldest to youngest, positioned at the bottom of the steps of the Supreme Court, with Lucas breaking the line in a can-can kick.

"On our way up," said Vincent. I remember the ascent on the marble steps, thinking about plaintiffs and defendants who had trekked through history to the highest tribunal in the land for a last shot at justice. Walt and his sister Joan's husband, Robert, another lawyer, struck a boxing pose at the top, flanked by the Greek columns, the golden doors of the Court behind them.

"I started to fall backward," said Vincent. He took a sip of Sprite.

Vincent has a tendency to talk as Walt does sometimes, with pauses before key statements, without too many changes in tone. You never know if they're about to tell you we won the lottery or the car broke down.

"And?" We waited. Isabel was holding a little bag of unassembled plastic that came with her Kid's Meal.

"Someone pushed at my back. So I didn't fall." *Lucky I missed that particular miracle.* "When I turned to look, there was nobody there." Vincent told it all matter-of-factly, in that math-and-science way he has, his dark eyes steady.

"It wasn't one of the cousins?" I asked.

"Nobody else was near me. I looked around." Vincent is nothing if not accurate. *Sharp Eyes,* someone called him once. He crumpled up his taco wrapper.

"And you felt—what?—on your back."

"I don't know. Like a hand, maybe."

"Why didn't you tell us then?" Not that the event would have been either more or less believable at the time. The other kids sat chewing in silence.

Vincent shrugged, that shrugging gesture he has where his shoulders rise a little stiffly. "I guess it sounded funny." He still didn't seem to give what he had just said any dramatic significance, even in the telling, even as the rest of us sat searching back with our eyes for that memory.

I know of another little gesture of unseen orders, one made

when Vincent was to go to his first dance, Sadie Hawkins, where the girls invite the boys.

Vincent was asked to Sadie's by a lovely girl with shy brown eyes in the marching band, Clemencia. One cold clear February night before the dance, Clemencia's family came by to take Vincent on a Sadie Hawkins shopping trip. Clemencia's parents, I discovered, were from Mexico, so we spent a good while rattling off in Spanish, and by the time I had to list FOP precautions, the teenagers had tuned us out, sparing Vincent the embarrassment of my recitations. A few hours later, he and Clemencia returned from a trip to Old Navy, happily holding up matching khaki camouflage gear.

The Saturday morning of Sadie Hawkins the phone rang. It was Leonor, Clemencia's mother, distress in her voice: "My daughter wants to apologize," she said. Clemencia had the flu.

Vincent retreated to the family room computer. Brian was on his way to a friend's to have cornrows done in his hair for the dance, and Lucas was at a basketball game. While I was glad for the other boys, my throat tightened for Vincent.

But it was a sunny day, at least—a clear blue one—the Sierra Nevada appearing like a good omen. The day was so pretty Walt decided to cheer up Vincent with an outing. "Come on," he said. "We're going to the park to feed the ducks."

"No, thanks," said Vincent, expressionless, at the computer screen. *What fourteen-year-old boy wants to go to a park to feed ducks?*

"Let's go!" called Walt, following Celine and Isabel to the garage with baggies of bread. He extended the invitation again. Vincent refused again. Walt tried again. No answer. Almost out the door, his father asked one last time.

"OK," said Vincent abruptly. "But I'm staying in the car."

Walt found a spot for the van on the park perimeter and took the girls down a grassy rise to the oily lake patrolled by ducks and geese. Vincent stayed put in the car. The girls had just started flinging bread chunks at the birds when a swarm of seagulls started to loop and dive-bomb for crusts, making everyone laugh. "Vincent should see this," Walt said, and he ran back to the car.

The moment Vincent was swinging his legs out stiffly from the passenger side, a pretty young Latina in sweats, with long dark hair, was running past. She stopped.

I could tell by his stance that Vincent knew the girl, and Walt left them discreetly.

After a while the girl jogged off and Vincent appeared at the lakeside. His face was transformed, radiant: "I'm going to Sadie Hawkins!" he announced.

The young runner Vincent had just seen by chance was a friend from school. She had asked if he would be at the dance, and when he explained his date was sick, she invited him to join a big group of friends that was meeting at a grand new arcade restaurant, John's Incredible Pizza, for a preparty.

Vincent wore his khaki camouflage pants to Sadie Hawkins, and that night, instead of a first awkward couple's pose, he brought home a professional photo of himself in the center of a crowd of friends.

OF COURSE, VINCENT never goes to the park, which happens to be on the other end of the city from the Catholic high school, a freeway drive from the house where we lived his freshman year. The friend who jogged by lived in another town. So, up until that Sadie Hawkins Dance day, Vincent had never coincidentally run into any classmates—many of whom live in distant San Joaquin Valley towns.

I said to Walt on that afternoon at the park that I knew Vincent was surrounded by angels. Then Walt told me the name of the girl who jogged by at just the right moment: *Angélica*.

FEBRUARY 2004

AT THE CT scan, a grandmotherly woman wearing cartoons on her medical togs is gentle as she guides Vincent into the white hoop contraption. She brings him a triangular foam pillow to install under the leg he can't fully straighten. Of course, she has no clue why she's putting the pillow under his leg, and I hover and help her adjust it.

She seems to understand on her own, however, that his leg mustn't be moved. "Does it hurt?" she asks.

To save us all time—even though his leg is fine now—I answer in the affirmative. "And his arm . . . so you mustn't—please don't, don't move *anything*," I just tell her. She nods, as if to indicate, *Say no more.* I learned this shorthand for low-risk procedures and even for markets; when a clerk tries to hand my son a king-size box of Tide to lug I'll say, "He hurt his arm." It's true in its own way.

We are here today in Medical Imaging to check for fluid in Vincent's lungs. He has had a cough for months, and antibiotics, syrups, and inhalers have been useless. FOP puts the lungs at risk for pneumonia during minor respiratory illnesses because its corset of bone limits rib cage expansion.

At seventeen Vincent is certainly old enough to fend off any well-intentioned technician pulling on an arm. So I don't need to stay in the room. But of course I do, and wear not one, but two of the blue lead aprons hanging from hooks. I take a chair in the corner and just sit, while an automated voice drones pleasantly: "Take a deep breath—hold it—breathe." There are sparks in a little porthole of imaging equipment, and I wonder how much gratuitous radiation is whooshing around me with its washing-machine sounds. I'm close enough to see Spiderman stickers and the side of the slide moving my son back and forth through the big white ring.

"Take a deep breath! Hold it! Breathe!" I say as we walk down a hospital hall lined with photos of children. The machine's mantra is still in my head. Six years back, after his concussion, Vincent had a CT scan. "Did the voice say, 'Think. Hold that thought. Release'?" I ask. We laugh.

We pass the lobby's rotunda, light streaming from high windows, onto the blue-and-green carpet, the round map of the world. In another lifetime, it seems, my son and I waited in this rotunda while a *Newsweek* photographer set up silver umbrellas. We stood on India and the photographer found us a papier-mâché giraffe and a bouquet of confiscated yellow, purple, and green balloons for the shot. It is a happy memory, but it makes me ask, "Do you feel funny here, as an older kid?" He is now over six feet tall.

"I hadn't really thought about it," says Vincent, and I'm glad. We are outside the castle, and Vincent notes that the animal topiaries have finally filled in on their wire skeletons. It is a clear, blue February morning, and we can see the Sierra Nevada, its rugged expanse of dark rock brushed here and there in metallic white. The horizon seldom reveals these fabled mountains, but today there is a sky washed in Monet hues, and the distant peaks look like they have appeared as proof of something.

Twenty minutes later, after we park in front of the high school, under the Spanish mission bell tower, we have our chronic discussion over Vincent's backpack, which should be featherweight—but isn't. He must protect the flare-up in his left arm.

"Why can't you have Peter carry it?" I ask. Peter is Vincent's best friend since first grade, and I have a picture of him with Vincent at age seven, little boys flying like planes over the yellow half-moons of the playground blacktop, their arms stretched wide, wide, wide, both of them laughing. Peter is blond and wiry and enthusiastic, as thoughtful and brilliant as he is absentminded, and he has relied on Vincent's eye for detail through the years. *He'll always know if something's missing or out of place,* says Peter, with his open hands: *He's nitty-gritty.* And for Vincent, Peter is the most authentic, steadfast friend anyone could ever wish for—and he is well named: Peter, the rock.

I take the green backpack from my son, unzipped. It yawns open and the contents spill and scatter—math papers, pencils, colored folders. I gather them all up and offer to put things back, but he refuses my help angrily, stuffing it all in himself.

"You never leave me alone! You never leave me alone!" says my son, pushing into the breezeway's double glass doors.

For eight years I have been hovering, hovering, willing the world safe around my child. But my high school senior is not a child. Next year he will be away, on his own. I won't be there to wrest a backpack from his hands or stop and listen to his breathing at night.

I watch my son move off with his dignified gait, past the high school's gelid blue pool and its floating lanes. And I'm glad he's angry.

)

DR. KAPLAN WRITES a letter of recommendation for Vincent
to Stanford. His recommendation for a boy whose triumphs and
disasters he has followed from age nine is an entry in a future volume of the Encyclopedia Britannica. "If that doesn't get him in,"
says my friend Cherie, Peter's mother, "nothing will." Cherie's eyes
are teary. In Vincent's file is another, equally powerful, letter by Dr.
Henrickson, who is also a UCSF clinical professor. Dr. Henrickson
compares Vincent to the scientist Stephen Hawking, and he tells
movingly of the privilege of knowing this young man. There is no
way Vincent *cannot* get in with these letters, with a 4.67 GPA, an
internship with a doctor, a school ambassadorship, his resolve in
marching band, his school newspaper articles, his volunteer work
in the California Scholarship Federation, and on and on.

Vincent himself writes a letter, one to a little boy in Texas
diagnosed with FOP this month, near the same age Vincent was at
the time of his own diagnosis. "I'm going to be a doctor," he writes.
"And hopefully next year at this time, you'll be hearing from me
from a dorm at Stanford."

)

FEBRUARY 2004 TURNS into what I can only call "Hell Month."
This month we take Celine to the ER down the street, to the hospital behind the orange groves, after she slips in the kitchen and
fractures her arm; Brian calls from Italy after having to negotiate
emergency—albeit minor—surgery in rudimentary Italian his first
week of UC study in Europe. Walt's mother, the indomitable olive
farmer June, is in a hospital in Los Angeles. Vincent has a chain of
flare-ups, and the CT scan of his lungs reveals some fluid. I cannot
remember a stretch this difficult in years.

Vincent's pulmonologist wants to schedule a bronchoscope to
track down pathogens behind the relentless cough. This involves
sedation and a trip to the OR, a slightly risky medical procedure for
someone with FOP, and I need just one more opinion again. A bleak
rainy Saturday after this news, our good friends Plamen and Kathy

Yosifov show up at our door. Plamen is the premier adult pulmonologist in the Valley. He examines Vincent, thinks one more antibiotic is worth a try, but says it would be good to know which pathogen is causing the cough. I beg our pulmonologist's office for one more antibiotic trial. The doctor's nurse calls back on an afternoon I am hunched over at my desk, crying because we may have no choice but to go with the OR procedure. "What's your pharmacy number?" the nurse is asking kindly. They will order one last antibiotic, one we have never heard of, Omnicef.

The Omnicef works.

After months and months, the coughing sound is gone. It is gone, *thank* God.

And then, one by one, three of us: Mom, Isabel, Celine, start scratching our heads. I begin to brace myself every time I see anyone's hand go to her neck, her hairline, behind her ears. And it is all I can do to keep from imploding one day as I comb something out of my bangs at the bathroom sink.

I stand against cold tile, leaning toward the mirror, my hair dulled by pesticides, and calculate incubation periods. We either picked them up at the girls' school or somewhere between the airports of Ezeiza in Buenos Aires and LAX. This has never happened before. In my whole life.

So today I am at a specialty market on the other side of town from our house because our pediatrician's nurse—my lifeline, Laura Lee—recommended a natural remedy that works better than pesticides. This market is in a fancy part of Fresno, with mansions and expensive cars. And while there is no place where I feel OK asking, "Which aisle has the lice shampoo?" I'm especially queasy over having to get something called Zero Lice in a place like this. I call from my car to avoid asking in person.

Inside the upscale market, I see well-dressed, well-toned women moving languidly around the specialty breads and salad bar. I can't just walk in and walk out of here with nothing but a head-lice potion, so I get camouflage ingredients: baguettes, a vat of organic apple juice, broccoli. And after a few trips in and out of the natural supplements aisles, I know I'm lost.

I have to ask out loud.

A young woman wearing a batik wraparound skirt leads me to a top shelf across from the vitamins, relating a niece's recent trial. "It's going around," she says, and pulls down a little teal box. She recommends a preventative shampoo from Australia with tea-tree oil. I let her hand me four samples of the natural remedy and three bottles of honey-colored shampoo.

I feel less uneasy now, but I still have to make it past the checkout counter. There is no line, at least, so I heave my apple-juice vat onto the moving belt and bunch bottles and boxes together in between the baguettes and broccoli. Better to take the bull by the horns and state the obvious? That I'm buying a lot of lice killer? Or just pretend I'm any other shopper?

"There's been a lice scare at my kids' school," I hear myself say. *A lice scare that we maybe caused,* I don't say.

"Yeah, they're all over the place." The young cashier is nonchalant as she swipes the little boxes and shampoo over the scanner. I'm not nonchalant.

"I hate it when you get lice," says a voice next to me in line. I look over and up at a very tall, very distinguished man with long gray hair in a ponytail. He has the worn good looks of an old rock star.

"It was murder in the commune when someone brought lice home," he says fondly. "Especially if you were a hippie with lots of hair." I glance involuntarily at the ponytail reaching past his shoulder blades.

"Really?" I say. I'm not sure how else to respond, but I'm suddenly feeling oddly lighthearted. *Solidarity, in the poshest market in town—of all places.*

The man smiles broadly at the girl at the register and me. "And it was really bad if you were the one who brought it home. Everybody hated you."

The young cashier listens agreeably, hands me my bag of bottles, and lowers my vat of apple juice into the cart.

I smile and say good-bye to the man. He nods as he reaches for his wallet.

"And don't forget to put all the bedding through your dryer!" he calls back to me over his shoulder.

And as I get in the car, that unwashed feeling of loneliness and woe lifts; it is gone completely. I will never see the tall thin man with the gray ponytail again, but for today, he has made all the difference.

I am in the February twilight, and the clouds are gray and magenta fish rising in the watery blue.

9

SKELETON KEY

MARCH 2004

*I usually discussed with Ashley possible recourses that we
could take: "If such and such happens, we could do this."
But there is always "if" it happens, we can do this or that.
She would respond, "Do you think I'll be that way, or do
you think that will happen to me that way?" I could only
answer with, "It might, but let's say it might not." With the
progress in research, the idea of hope is and will always be
there in her mind.*

— CAROL KURPIEL, mother of Ashley, twenty-
three, diagnosed at age three, Atlanta, Georgia

ONE MILD SPRING day I took a stroll with four-year-old Celine
to a neighborhood mini-mart. She rode her bike with training wheels and pink handlebar streamers and I walked alongside.
On our way, I spotted a lifeless tabby cat in the bike lane, its eyes
open and glassy. To shield her from the sight, I positioned myself
between Celine and the animal, distracting her with stories and
questions as we went.

On the way back, Celine spotted the lifeless figure before I had
a chance to shield her again. "Look!" she said, stopping her bike.

"Yes, the poor cat's dead," I explained.

"But its eyes are open," said Celine.

"It's still dead." The animal looked intact, probably sideswiped
by a car.

Celine studied the tabby for a while. "Why can't we have a cat?"
she asked, finally conceding to move on.

"I'm allergic to cats."

"How about if we just get a dead cat?" Celine's blue green eyes in her apple-cheeked little face were looking up at me earnestly as she pedaled. She made it sound like a perfectly reasonable request.

"What would we do with a dead cat?"

"We could look at it," said Celine. "And then we could bury it. We buried Teacher Blanche's cat in her garden one day." Blanche Nosworthy had not shielded the preschoolers from this loss.

I realized that though Celine might be too young to fathom the reality of death, she was not too young to start to accept that life held loss in different forms.

In some ways, I considered, meeting loss in FOP and accepting the possibility of unreal future loss might not be so different. I had tried to shield Celine from a dead cat that she ended up accepting so naturally, she even suggested we get one for ourselves. Even if she was thinking as a four-year-old thinks, Celine seemed able to process the understanding of loss, and life had already exposed her to it in the garden burial at Blanche's—before I even knew.

How much emotional protection did Vincent need, then, between FOP and himself? In March 1997, he had already suffered FOP's first real visitation, so he knew too well what FOP and loss meant, knew it much better than his parents. But Vincent had not met any adults with FOP.

The question was: could Vincent accept FOP in others with advanced cases? Was it right to shield him from it? Wrong? As a child, might he accept everything more naturally than his parents? Or not?

In March 1997 the Make-A-Wish Foundation funded a trip for us to Disney World in Florida for the second international FOP family gathering. Jeannie Peeper, as the head of the IFOPA, and her crew made it possible for patients from around the world to fly to Orlando for the event. So at the Caribe Royale Hotel, a tropical resort, there would be medical and dental exams, lectures, workshops, and dinners.

We were unsure how to proceed with Vincent meeting older patients with the same progressive disorder. *Would it hurt or help?*

"Just ask him," said a child psychologist. She could no more make predictions than we could. FOP was still relatively new, and in many ways, we were, all of us, still in and out of denial zones. FOP would become more real the moment we met it in others. (Years later, a wise Armenian counselor would say: *Parents cannot always take their children's pain away. Their job is to teach them to bear it skillfully. Pain deepens us.* Thank you, Signe.)

"Vincent, do you want to go to the FOP reunion in Disney World?" Walt and I asked. *What a question.* Our son's face lit up. *Disney World!*

I made sure to rephrase the plan: "When we're there we'll meet other people, grown-ups who have FOP. Some have much milder cases, like you." Vincent did not answer right away.

Had Vincent been younger—four, like Celine—or older, his response might have been a different one. While age ten can still be young enough to enter into the fantasy of Disney, it is also pragmatic enough to know that something like FOP, no matter how unreal, is no fiction. Ten—ten and a half, to be exact—halfway between birth and adulthood, would be precisely the age that would make such a decision most difficult.

"What do you think?" I asked again. We were in the blue two-story, in the big room Vincent and Lucas shared, a bedroom with a built-in desk of oak and a picture window facing west, where the sun dissolved into streaks of neon behind the eucalyptus. "If you'd like to meet other families, that's fine. And if you don't, that's OK, too."

The light in Vincent's bedroom window was turning coppery and it would soon be gone. I could not read my son's expression. I did not know whether he would answer my question in the affirmative or not, if he had come to terms with FOP in ways I could not anticipate—or hadn't. "I want to go," he finally said. "But I'll meet everyone at another reunion."

One child at a time. One day at a time. One generation at a time. It would be good for Walt and me to meet other FOP families. So we made our plan: my friend Candy, Isabel's godmother, would fly from L.A. to Orlando, and she would take the children on rides and stay with them while Walt and I went to medical exams and meetings.

The flight to Florida was a good one. We were with five kids, ages eight months to thirteen years, who were more than happy to board a plane to Disney paradise. Once we landed in Orlando, however, and passed into the bright airport terminal, things changed. Our littlest was hungry, and four-year-old Celine started to question things. "Is *this* Disney World? Is *this* Disney World?" she asked unhappily as we passed airport gift kiosks with hanging Mickey Mouse dolls. "*Is this Disney World?*" she wailed as we trudged over linoleum, onto people movers, and past jets framed in glass walls. "I want to go to *Disney World*," she explained, as if she had been a victim of fraud.

Pushing a stroller ready to tip backward with bags of every size on it and hunting for airport vans, we were too harried to sound convincing to a preschooler. It was Vincent who patiently explained that Disney World didn't have jet runways, mollifying Celine, but her mood, I thought, was rooted in my own buried worries, worries that I, too, might be in the wrong place.

The airport proved not only to not be Disney World, it also turned out to be much more distant from the park than we knew, adding a fourth leg to a trip with five kids that included an indignant baby, a self-righteous preschooler, and an apprehensive mother. At the wheel of our airport van was a young man from Haiti. I will not forget this Haitian driver, because I think he was sent, like others whose paths I've crossed and have never seen again, as someone to look to. During the long ride to our hotel over freeways bisecting the tropics, we learned he was an exile, far from his family and home. But there was gladness in his eyes and in his wide vowels and sudden laugh.

"How do you like Disney World?" I asked, as we passed the arches of the park.

"I've never been there!" he said, and his answer was not a lament, it was more of a punch line. And I saw that he had turned whatever his loss might be into spirit, unaware that he imparted this spirit to us, not knowing he had left a lasting impression on a boy whose trip was funded by Make-A-Wish.

THE AIR WAS warm and humid outside our Orlando hotel, a palace in Mediterranean rose, surrounded by flashy palms. We spied
a game room on our way to the elevators, where we saw two boys
near Vincent's age, their backs to us as they played Nintendo. Even
from behind, one of the boys looked familiar, *familiar* in the literal
sense, as when you meet someone with your own smile or shape
of nose at a relative's. In this boy the resemblance was in his back.
When he turned, stiff shouldered, not looking in our direction, I
saw it. When he moved off with his friend in the conspiring way
boys have, *I knew.* He was the first boy besides Vincent I had seen
with FOP. I'm not sure Vincent recognized himself in him—he was
taken with the rambling blue pool framed in the windows of the
hotel. Walt saw it, though. And I think he also noticed what I had,
that this young boy looked fine, thrilled, like any other happy kid
playing Nintendo, ready for Disney World.

It was at the hotel's tropical pool flanked by palms that Walt
and I met Jeannie Peeper in person, a year and a half since that
cold January she restored life to my soul. Since that time, I had
spoken to Jeannie on the phone often, learning how to apply frozen
compresses, hot compresses, how to weather flare-ups. What Jeannie was telling me in those conversations, though she didn't put it
into words, was that *everything would be OK*; it would pass, the pain
would pass, life would return to normal, maybe a "new normal,"
as an extraordinary FOP mother I know, Marilyn Hair, calls it,
but *normal nonetheless.* I heard that message in her voice, in her
calm, steady tone, a voice with midwestern vowels and hard *r*'s and
optimism.

From our phone conversations I had conjured a portrait of
Jeannie in my mind the way you imagine characters in a book. She
would be fair and sturdy, with short brown hair and even, pleasant
features. I did not see a woman compromised in any way: there was
none of that in her voice. Hadn't Jeannie told me she could shower,
put on makeup, run an international organization? The Jeannie I
knew, the woman who had saved me from the nightmares of my

imagination, was a midwestern girl who moved with a little stiffness, maybe a bad back, and that was all.

There is a reverse kind of Doppler effect when a voice you've heard across a distance belongs, suddenly, to someone in person, right there before you. Everything except the sound you know changes pitch. I felt this dissonance on recognizing Jeannie's voice in a beautiful woman by the hotel pool. She was nothing like the plain and sturdy midwestern girl I had "heard" from far away. Jeannie was immaculately made up, with light blue eyes, a perfect nose, and a heart-shaped face. She was as slender as a dancer, elegant, in a suit that hid her delicate bones. The color of her shoulder-length hair—brown—was the only feature I had "heard" right.

There was Jeannie—flesh-and-blood Jeannie—who had rescued me that morning I had picked up the phone to call a worrisome number. She had reached out to me with arms that were permanently crossed. And her steady, reassuring voice had carried across the country from a locked jaw. There was Jeannie Peeper in her wheelchair: regal and perfect.

It was right there, by a hotel pool, standing before an old friend I had never met, that I understood that whatever FOP had done to Jeannie Peeper, it had not hurt *her*. Like the young Haitian who had driven our family to our meeting place, Jeannie had turned her loss into a monument of spirit.

"It's nice to meet you," was all I could say by that rambling blue water.

I put my arms around Jeannie Peeper at our first FOP gathering and was hugged back. And as someone who knows better than anybody what it feels like to get lost and make it at the wrong time for things, I knew I had arrived to find Jeannie Peeper at exactly the right moment and place in my own winding path.

)

DR. KAPLAN'S "examining rooms" were in a hotel suite with doctors and medical residents from the University of Pennsylvania in white coats or lay dress drawing blood from their patients seated on sofas or ballroom chairs, carefully inserting butterfly needles to find veins on the insides of elbows. The blood tests were to check for levels of a bone-building protein present when FOP is active. Because the protein appears in urine as well, little plastic containers were handed out. All of this gathered data could help, someday, lead research to the skeleton key to unlock FOP's secrets, the mysteries of bone formation.

Dr. Kaplan was joined by Dr. Eileen Shore, petite and blond, who codirects the FOP lab with him, and the famous, bearded Dr. Michael Zasloff, a pioneering FOP physician at the University of Pennsylvania. If Fred Kaplan is the father of this orphan disease, then Dr. Zasloff is FOP's grandfather (since I am not a scientist, I can create these metaphors that defy scientific explanation). Vincent sat on the edge of the FOP clinic-suite examining bed. "Simon says, touch your shoulders," instructed Dr. Kaplan—Vincent could not; *raise your left arm*: Vincent could; *raise your right arm*: Vincent could not—fully; *bend at the waist*: Vincent could, though not very low; *Simon says, turn your neck*: Vincent could, with some stiffness. "Vincent, great!" said Dr. Kaplan, pleased at Vincent's range of mobility. We were all pleased—enough. Though he had lost precious movement in his right arm the summer before, his other side was still intact. I suppose we had all come to accept, in some fashion, that FOP had done what it had done.

In another suite we waited with another family and their daughter for the FOP dentist, Dr. Burt Nussbaum. The other family's little girl, a bright five-year-old, seemed to show few signs of FOP other than some stiffness in her neck. The wait for Dr. Nussbaum was especially important because there were stories of people who had not known what FOP could do until a Novocain injection for a routine filling had left them with their jaw clamped shut. Dr. Nussbaum had written in 1994 about his first FOP dental extraction, a successful one, and thus became, as he told me later, the leading FOP dental expert under the medical maxim "Do one, write one, teach one."

"You have to be scrupulous in the care of your teeth," stressed Dr. Nussbaum, who examined Vincent. I remember the dentist as no-nonsense and droll, with auburn hair, a beard, and glasses. To convince insurance companies of FOP's rarity and attendant need for rare precautions, he would illustrate: "Take all the people in Times Square on New Year's Eve with Dick Clark. OK? Double it. And then you would find *one* person with FOP."

Dr. Nussbaum looked more like an old college friend than a dentist. Maybe that was because we were in a hotel suite where there was no tiny sink or scent of fluoride pastes, no looming equipment with insect elbows and drills.

"You can fix it with braces," said Dr. Nussbaum, referring to gaps on either side of our son's front teeth. After the FOP diagnosis, we feared such anomalies might not be correctable—considering the risks of dental procedures.

"He can wear braces?" we said. *He can wear braces.*

"Make sure the orthodontist never has him stretch his jaw for longer than a few minutes at a time," said Dr. Nussbaum.

Two years of silver tracks and two retainers that would get lost and fished out of restaurant trash cans resulted in Vincent's straight, white, perfect teeth.

After visiting Dr. Nussbaum, I saw a tiny blond girl in a wheelchair, one leg elevated in a big white cast; she had fallen at the hotel, and she was there, as pale and determined as her parents, accepting condolences, her father a powerfully built man with filigrees and curls of blue ink running up and down his arms. I remember, also, translating for Alicia, a mother with long dark hair from the province of San Juan, wife of a trucker in Argentina, who cried with me when we said good-bye; and I remember a fourteen-year-old in a checkered suit, Carla, from Buenos Aires, whose mother rides several buses a day to clean houses; and Ricardo, the father from the Argentine ski resort of Bariloche, who invited us to bring Vincent to the thermal waters in his town, where he could stay as mobile as Ricardo's eight-year-old son, Jorgito.

I can still hear Dr. Kaplan saying, in one of the banquet rooms divided by a hard corrugated curtain, "FOP is a hell of a way to make friends."

I don't regret letting Vincent keep away from the realities of FOP on our trip to Orlando. Vincent's choice was set by his own timetable on his own winding path to acceptance. And at Disney

World he took as many rides as he could on those days of humid heat and drizzles and tropical clouds. He rode attractions he might have trouble getting into today; he rode fast and slow, high, low, around, sideways, backward, and upside down, stopping to chart a course with his father and brothers and Celine on maps with cartoon icons and bright legends. I was happy to push a stroller through Cinderella's Castle and Main Street U.S.A. with Candy, feeding Isabel pineapple ices, stopping for Snow White, trolleys, and barbershop quartets. The one time I tried to escape on a flying elephant, my friend held on to my angry infant flopping like a fish. In compensation, we—all of us—rode the carousel, with its Disney tunes and candy colors, finding ourselves in an axis of mirrors, catching the glorious consolations of Fantasyland.

IN OUR EARLY experience fighting FOP we not only followed the counsel of Western physicians, we also tried out "alternative" or "complementary" medicine, which has a mixed reputation and a wide range of practitioners. I will not talk about the women with incandescent eyes and a car plastered with bumper stickers who promised to change my child's DNA with essential oils. And I will not talk about the hotel healer who had people fainting and crying in a ballroom my mother snuck her grandson into. And I will not say anything about the Reiki practitioner who haggled over fees while transferring energy from her palms to my child's chest. I will not go into the session at the chiropractor who had me pluck a strand of my son's hair for lab analysis, or the homeopath who tested Vincent's electrical charges with something like a seismograph. When a friend suggested an irisologist, someone who reads the eyes, I drew the line.

I will talk about only two healers. The first was Harvard-educated Andrew Weil, MD, at the University of Arizona, and the second was a Tibetan monk, Yeshi Dhonden, who was a personal physician to the Dalai Lama for twenty years.

When Vincent saw Andrew Weil, American icon for complementary medicine, he was still suffering from the side effects of our first prednisone trial in 1997. Dr. Weil, tall, with his trademark salt-and-pepper beard and full-faced smile, appeared in the examining room to shake our hands, and listened soberly to our FOP story. He then conferred with a staff that included practitioners of Chinese-medicine and other non-Western health professionals. For a different patient he might have tried acupuncture for pain, but because of the risk of needles, that avenue was closed.

With Dr. Weil that day was one of his medical residents, Russell Greenfield, a kind young redhead who took a keen interest in Vincent. It was Dr. Greenfield who followed up later by phone and fax. "When you're here next time," he said to our son that day in Tucson, "we could go to a baseball game." Though we did not return to Arizona, Dr. Greenfield never forgot Vincent. Over the years, he and his wife have contributed regularly to FOP research at the University of Pennsylvania in Vincent's name.

Our visit to Dr. Weil was informative and out of it came a special connection to a dedicated resident. But the natural supplements of ginger, black-currant oil, and other herbs for inflammation, like everything else we were trying, seemed no match for FOP.

Not long after our visit to Arizona, another FOP family referred us to a Tibetan doctor working with an American physician for non-Western treatments. I had met the other FOP family's child, a cherubic, glowing eight-year-old, at a Snow fund-raiser in Santa Maria. The little girl's head was inclined forward from an old neck flare-up. Her parents found Yeshi Dhonden and his associate, Marsha Woolf, who fly several times a year from Boston to see patients, their fee, a voluntary donation.

While our meeting with Andrew Weil was very much like a visit to any modern Western medical complex, the visit to Dr. Dhonden was very different. To see the Tibetan monk, we traveled from Fresno to an apartment in Santa Monica near the ocean.

Our appointment was in a tiny parlor with a scent of beeswax, where we left our shoes at the door. There were Eastern rugs spread across the floor, and a cluttered little altar with Buddha statues and candles. The spice colors of the room seemed to absorb an angst no doctor's office could; there were no fidgeting children or bored mothers flipping through magazines. There were, instead, people seated on floor pillows waiting in various postures of pain.

In the next room, a Tibetan man in Western dress was at a desk heaped with little plastic bags of what looked like brown beads, and a young blond woman handed out forms and instructions from her card table. Then I saw the monk, in dark orange vestments, a translator at his side. I could barely hear the unfamiliar syllables they traded over each patient, but I still found myself talking in a whisper to the girl taking donations at her makeshift desk.

When our turn came, the translator, a young American with fair hair and Western clothes of an Eastern make, took us to Dr. Dhonden, who sat on a chair for each exam. I remember the monk as one of those people who could be any age, spare and compact, his brown hands elemental, like tree roots. His smile at Vincent was luminous, but it faded quickly into an expression of calm I've seen only in contemplatives. The monk held Vincent's hand and wrist, feeling his pulse, probing his palm with a thumb, kneading each finger; he then pantomimed for Vincent to remove his shirt and palpated the knots and ridges of extra bone growth along his neck and back.

Dr. Dhonden addressed us in Tibetan and the translator explained: "In him, the disease is new and it should not take long to cure." I could barely half-believe these words, but still, they made me almost giddy. In any event, "cure" had to mean "treat," in translation, I decided. Vincent had, indeed, experienced a late onset of the FOP, with no incapacitating symptoms until relatively recently. He was told to avoid pork, because of nitrates, and—for some reason—maple syrup.

Marsha Woolf, the American MD, sat down beside me. She was a sturdy, matter-of-fact clinician who seemed of a different time altogether than the monk. She was dressed informally, in Western clothes, but I could imagine her in a lab coat scolding residents. She told us that individuals suffering from the same condition could have different imbalances causing the illness; that not every child with FOP, for example, would require the same treatment. "In Tibetan medicine there are three humors that need to be balanced: blood,

bile, and phlegm," said Dr. Woolf. Her list of vital fluids had the
familiar ring of antique fictions. Don Quixote would have been fed
lettuce to cool a bilious brain. Could modern medicine offer better
explanations for why people could be turned into bone?

"Which humor is out of balance in our son?" I asked.

"All three."

The young woman at the desk gave us three bags full of what
looked to be wooden beads of varying sizes. These were the herbs
that would begin the regimen, with specific instructions: no food or
other medicines within an hour of a dose; Vincent would have to
bite down on a pill before swallowing it with warm water. Attached
was a prescription in the loops and swirls of an ancient alphabet
that would go to India for more herbs, and a *precious pill* individually
wrapped in pink silk with a tiny thread tying it shut.

As we said good-bye, Dr. Woolf noticed a silver pendant I was wearing, a gift a friend had brought me after a trip to India. I had received
that necklace the week Vincent was diagnosed with FOP.

The pendant, which I still wear, is turquoise, with the dark cracks
that give the stone its character, and it is fashioned as a little box.
Everyone who touches the box tries to force it open. But the piece
is soldered shut with silver. It looks like an ancient amulet.

I handed my pendant to Dr. Woolf for a better look. She ran
a finger along the fissures in the aqua. "In Indian tradition these
marks are the blows meant for you that the stone absorbs on your
behalf," she told me. I studied the turquoise as if I could trace the
tracks of FOP there.

"Would you like him to bless it?" she asked, looking back toward
Dr. Dhonden. *Yes, please,* I said, and she motioned him over as he
prepared to leave their last patient. The monk accepted my aqua
stone in the cluttered anteroom, handling it familiarly, and for a
moment he reminded me—oddly—of a mechanic feeling for a
broken part. He stood there, eyes cast down, hands closed over the
turquoise on its silver rope, lips moving over secrets that only God
could hear.

WITH ALL MY heart, I wish I could say the Tibetan herbs worked. We did our best with the beads, cracked and consumed with warm water, balanced carefully in a chaotic schedule with other medicines and foods. I became alarmed at the hardness of the beads and the noise Vincent's molars made on them. Someone had suggested a mortar and pestle, but I devised my own method for cracking the pills, unaware of its oddity until one day when a friend saw me scurrying around the kitchen, reaching in cupboards, pulling out *precious pills*, warming water, checking the clock, counting out brown beads, grabbing a hammer, and then *thwack—thwack—thwack—*

"You're hammering things?" exclaimed my friend as I gave a last *thwack*.

I had gotten so used to smacking the beads with the edge of a big pickle jar, a can of tuna, and finally a hammer I kept by the breakfast bowls, that it didn't occur to me to explain what I was doing.

Maybe it was the schedule, the hammering, the heartburn from the herbs, or our impression that the beads didn't seem to help. I don't know. The fact is, we left off going to the Dalai Lama's doctor. But I will never forget something the father of the little girl whose head was bent forward mentioned to me a year later.

At one point this father, desperate at the beginnings of the disease process, took his daughter to Tibetan monks, who chanted and prayed for his little girl. And the monks said something similar to what the Filipina healer I wrote to had pronounced: "They told me she is paying for a sin in a past life," said the father, untroubled by this view so foreign to his own beliefs.

The night the monks prayed for his little girl, the father told me, his daughter dreamed of a creature made of flames chasing her in a forest. Out of curiosity, the father relayed this dream to the monks and learned that in Buddhist mythology such a creature had a name. And it signified purification.

While fire has long symbolized transforming energy (in Catholicism, the Holy Spirit, who forgives and heals in the Sacrament of the Sick, has been represented by a flame), the father's account gave me chills: I remembered the Filipina healer's dream about a soul passing through a flame. This healer and the monks, it seems, believed in suffering as an inherited penance. But I will not give my response to these different beliefs until the end of my story, when I can better illustrate what I have found.

MARCH 2004

THE FIRST LEAVES on the fig tree outside my window are here. The foothills are green, the mountains are navy blue, and the wildflowers are splashes of mustard and goldenrod over fields. Most of the Valley's tree blossoms have scattered, bridesmaid pink in plum and peach orchards, white stars from the almonds. And our daughter Celine also starts to bloom: she is turning twelve, her arm cast is off, and people have noticed the changes: *How beautiful you are*, they say, aware that she is different.

Today is Celine's birthday, and she has gotten up early to bake chocolate-chip cookies for her classmates. At Friday Mass, she stands in the front of the church in her blue plaid jumper, alongside everyone born in March, and the whole school sings "Happy Birthday." The younger children are shyly pleased by the attention, but the older students, those Celine's age, look like they're facing a firing squad.

I am picking up the daughter of a fellow Late Club mom (usually it is my friends Mira, Kathy, and Corey who help *me*). As we drive past orchards with scattered blossoms, Isabel's friend Rachel expounds: "And then if you get in trouble, it's '*no recess for you!*'" Rachel rolls her r's in imitation of the Spanish nuns, sounding like a character who sells soup on *Seinfeld*. "And then she says, 'I'm sorry'! And she's not one bit sorry. Not even 1 percent sorry!"

I, on the other hand, *am* 1 percent sorry to have my mind half on everything I am doing these days and half on what will happen with Vincent's Stanford application. It is for this reason that we have sent the invitations for Celine's birthday party too late. And it is around this time that I begin to hear, "Have you heard from Stanford?" The answer is supposed to arrive in March. If the news is what we have been praying for—and why shouldn't it be—I will

get a little plane to fly over the Valley with a banner announcing:
VINCENT GOT INTO STANFORD.

It is still too early to hear from Stanford, but too late to get
everyone to Celine's party, and the latter is a defeat I take personally, considering my Late Club reputation. But as it turns out,
Father Sal's brother, Edgar, is eager to come over, and so is Celine's
good friend Vera; and other classmates can make it, and the party
swells. Celine and her guests fill water balloons, bat a piñata, eat a
sheet cake decorated with pink balloons and streamers, and have
a glorious spring afternoon.

IT IS A cloudless day, one that invites good news.

Vincent and I both approach the green mailbox as the girls slam
car doors and skip into the house. Vincent spies the envelope as I
fish it out from a stack of junk mail.

We stand in the dining room, blinds half drawn, light absorbed
by the long mission table, so we are washed in sepia, like an old
photo. The table holds neat stacks of textbooks, a second set we buy
every year to spare Vincent's joints the trauma of a heavy backpack.
Alongside the books are ruled sheets with the tight, microscopic
notes he makes into the night. But none of that matters now. The
clock has stopped.

I am at Vincent's elbow, not breathing as he unfolds a piece of
paper. At the top is the school seal with the California redwood in
silhouette, and under it the distinctive cardinal letters: STANFORD.
And it says:

March 2004

Dear Vincent,

*I write to tell you that we are unable to offer you admission
to Stanford University for the fall of 2004. I appreciate the
thought you put into your application and into selecting
Stanford as the place to which you applied early.*

Silence.

In the enclosure I read the last paragraph:

> *Sometimes a candidate is denied admission, while some-*
> *one he or she knows, whose rank in class or test scores*
> *are lower, is admitted. This occurs both because we value*
> *hard-to-quantify personal qualities or achievements,*
> *and because schools, programs and individuals vary so*
> *widely. While you might know another applicant's rank*
> *in class, GPA and test scores, only admissions officers*
> *see the entire applications, including the student's writ-*
> *ing and teacher and counselor recommendations. Each*
> *applicant presents a unique combination of achievement,*
> *potential and intellectual vitality, blended with personal*
> *qualities. It is the composite of these factors that influ-*
> *ences our decisions.*

Vincent is very quiet; he has receded from me, and I am the one holding the paper now. I cannot reach him, no words to help it. But for the earnest expressions *unique combination, hard-to-quantify personal qualities, composite of factors*, there is only one word, one compound word, and I will not say it out loud.

RAGE, RAGE

APRIL 2004

I worry every day about Whitney's emotional insides: we are only eighteen months since diagnosis and she really won't talk about "it." She sees a school social worker two times a week after school, which has been a blessing. She had become very angry with me . . . and when she had the biggest flare-up, she had a total meltdown. The first time since her diagnosis, she was screaming that this was all my fault. I was at first in shock, but then I felt a relief that she yelled, screamed, and cried, and I stayed quiet during the episode. I was so afraid of doing or saying something that would be a huge mistake. I just wanted her to know it was all right to be angry and I wanted to give her a safe place to have her meltdown.

—HILLARY WELDON, mother of Whitney, thirteen, diagnosed at age nine, New Vernon, New Jersey.

ONE AFTERNOON IN July 1997, around the time of Vincent's second major flare-up, in a mood of despair, I took a walk. It was a hot Saturday, and I had given our littlest a bath in the laundry room, where a long sink shared counter space with salads of clothes. Walt had been at his office, and the moment he walked in the door, I took off. There were no clouds that day, but the mountains hid in the Valley's perennial haze.

I took my usual route of sidewalks flanking the edge of our new neighborhood, along a gray concrete fence and houses in gray drywall stage crowding into tiny lots. I walked past saplings tied to stakes where there had once been orchards. Everything around me was in a state of transition, and it all looked like a change for the worse.

The rhythm of walking didn't bring its usual relief, but the grayness began to turn into something else, a vague anger. And it was after I rounded the corner of gray concrete fence and crossed a street gray with construction dust that a line of verse popped into my head: *Rage, rage against the dying of the light.*

Who wrote that? I was supposed to know, but life was making me lose my literary edge. For the rest of my walk the line nagged me. Was it from *King Lear?* Something else by Shakespeare? *Who wrote that?* I kept reaching for the answer as I walked, and then forgot all about it when I got back to the buzz and din of home.

But that night took place one of the strangest coincidences ever, the closest thing to a bona fide psychic experience I have had in my life.

The answer to who wrote the line of poetry that had popped into my head on a desperate walk could have come to me a day later, a week from then, maybe in conversation with a friend or colleague years later, long after the words had stopped irritating me. But it arrived that night, in the *Fresno Bee.*

I had not opened the *Bee* all day, so unaccustomed was I to picking up the newspaper until evening, or not at all, with the demands of a one-year-old—of five kids. So that Saturday night I was standing at the kitchen counter by the phone—the same spot where I had talked to NORD and Jeannie Peeper—paging through an inside section of the paper. A headline caught my eye: "A Lesson in Courage." This title was at the very top of the right-hand page, and the first words of the article beneath it were: "In 'Do Not Go Gentle Into That Good Night,' Dylan Thomas begged his dying father, 'Rage, rage against the dying of the light.'"

I felt a faint charge of electricity: Dylan Thomas, the Welsh poet. There it was, my answer. *What are the odds?* But as I went on to read the article I realized this "answer" included more than just an author's name. "A Lesson in Courage" was about a child with a serious, chronic disease, and it was about the courage of the parents. Where I had fallen into despair, this child's mother had picked herself up and fought. The charge I felt that night became something larger, and it suffused me with a profound sense of peace (paradoxical, considering the words that had started it all).

I had been given my own lesson in courage: *Rage, rage against the dying of the light*, fire to dispel the gloom. It was as if I had been sent a personal message—in the newspaper. It was as if I had been told: *Courage: Fight the good fight.*

After that day, though not immediately after, I raged against FOP in print, and against any editor who didn't see how important my child's story was, and why I was the only one allowed to write it (I couldn't trust anyone else to know what to say and what not to say). What I wrote was an essay rejected everywhere, even by the *Fresno Bee.* And its title, when it was ultimately run by a publication, was about fighting the good fight, and it was titled—by editors, *not by me*—"My Son's *Fight* with a Mysterious Disease." The essay nobody wanted to print appeared in *Newsweek*, dated July 12, 1999. My own lesson in courage, the article I found in the *Fresno Bee*, came out on July 12, 1997. The chaos of life—even for someone like me, with no sense of time—seemed to have a calendar.

And there is more to the aftermath of that line of poetry that came to me on July 12, 1997. And I did not piece it all together until many years later.

The summer of 1997 was, of course, the summer Vincent began his second raging flare-up, the summer his left side swelled with a massive hump that revisited him. And with all that I knew that season, I could not stand by helpless as before, watching in despair. I "raged" for anything. That was the summer Dr. Glaser prescribed the prednisone, the only medicine in the list of pharmaceutical syllables whose name I could pronounce.

Of course, the prednisone didn't ultimately work for Vincent in 1997, but it helped Stephanie Snow, and over time, through trial and error, physicians discovered the drug did, indeed, have a window period of some efficacy, when it could—*though not consistently*—short-circuit the inflammatory bone-making process.

"We learned this from a little girl called Stephanie Snow," said Dr. Kaplan the morning I was in a hotel-suite-turned-medical-office, translating for him and Dr. Michael Zasloff at the 2000 symposium. Before I could turn to my Peruvian friends Teresa and Reynaldo, to repeat Dr. Kaplan's words in Spanish, I had to stop and stare at him. There was our beloved Dr. Kaplan, in his dress shirt and tie, the soul of clinical precision and scientific research. And I—late and lost as I usually am—felt compelled to correct him, precisely then, precisely there.

"You found this out from a boy called Vincent!" I said, thinking back to the summer of 1997, back to my afternoon on the phone with Jennifer Snow. *Prednisone works like a miracle.* And then, of course, the miracle backfired.

But as it turned out—and this fact was only evident in retrospect—Jennifer Snow had called us *the first day* her five-year-old had begun having trouble in her jaw. Because of Vincent's apparent success with the drug at the time, Stephanie was also prescribed prednisone, and her pediatrician decided to double its usual dose. Stephanie started this treatment *at the start* of her flare-up. But by the time Vincent had gone on the drug, his FOP flare-up had already begun its work.

In 1997 our doctors couldn't know that prednisone had any real chance of retarding FOP's advance if it was given in large bursts *immediately* at the onset of symptoms. By 2000, they had learned how to employ prednisone, with varying results, but it wasn't until that afternoon I was translating for a family from Peru at the Third International Symposium on FOP in Philadelphia that I discovered my own son's contribution.

"The inflammation is like a fire," Dr. Kaplan explained at the symposium as I translated for Teresa and Reynaldo, parents of tiny, angelic Maria Claudia. "We learned you have to try to put it out with the prednisone *right away* before it does its damage, before you can't stop the flames and they destroy your house."

Vincent's FOP had inflamed too much muscle tissue by the time we started the prednisone in the summer of 1997, too late—and the FOP raged out of control. But because of Stephanie Snow's success dating back to those days, prednisone dosing evolved into a standard first line of defense against FOP flare-ups.

Vincent's miracle with prednisone was not failed—it was imperfect. But it was a perfect lesson in courage, and in how to fight fire with fire.

APRIL 2004

IT IS THE morning after, the hangover from Stanford's rejection letter, and it is also April Fool's Day. Today feels like a prank. In protest—and because it is the only clean one—I pull on Walt's Stanford sweatshirt, inside out, the tag sticking out like a tongue, for my morning run.

I jog past the California redwoods and weeping willows, across a field of weeds and wildflowers, past a corral with horses, one of them old and worn and watching me. The animal's dark mane is sparse, his ribs show under an auburn coat, and he looks resigned. Past him is a wooden fence draped in wisteria, its lilac clusters mixed in with dead shoots.

Walt and I lay awake last night, too angry to sleep. I told Walt about my earlier plan for a plane with a banner announcing Vincent's acceptance. "Instead, how about we fly a little plane around Palo Alto with that expression they have on the Cal T-shirts?" I say. Last year in the laundry room, I found one of the blue-and-gold T-shirts with the unsettling wording popular at the Stanford–Cal games and threw it out. "Thirty thousand students would pitch in for that plane."

"Or we could put up a blue-and-gold fence around the school . . ." says Walt, remembering Christo, the artist who swathed an island in colored plastic and planted yellow umbrellas on the Grapevine's mountain pass.

Never mind that Vincent has been accepted to Claremont McKenna, an elite college that took 265 out of 3,528 applicants. Never mind that our son has had congratulations from UCLA, the school with the highest number of applicants in the country, and heard a yes from places like UC San Diego, with Sally Ride, the astronaut; and from Davis, with its agricultural prestige. And he has been accepted to Berkeley, top-ranked public university in the world.

But we would have to take one feature from all of the above to create the ideal college for a gifted intellect to transcend FOP. Vincent would need a small school that could shelter him, like Claremont; that could give him the world, like Berkeley; with no hills, close to family, like UC Davis; with a famous medical center, like UCLA; with temperate weather, like UC San Diego. All of that intersects at just one school. And today, this school's name is best introduced by a word on a T-shirt I threw away.

I find Vincent working on the computer when I get home in the afternoon. He has not spoken about the decision since its arrival. With a half turn, he says, "Cristina got into Stanford."

"Is Cristina going to go?" I have known Vincent's friend since grade-school days.

"She's not sure." Vincent goes back to the keyboard.

What do you say when your child strives, body and soul, for a prize handed to a friend who may not want it? Do you say: *Life isn't fair?* Do you say: *Everything happens for a reason?* I might as well be chirping *Have a nice day.*

"Think about all the amazing schools that want you, Vincent: UCLA, Berkeley, Claremont." But right now the finest colleges in the world are nothing more than fancy consolation prizes.

So we are just silent. I see my son's stoical gaze. I am not feeling like such a stoic. I hug him from behind, my hands over his heart, which beats hard against the bone corseting his chest.

People who love Vincent are not at all stoical about the Stanford decision: a high school teacher lets loose an expletive and compares Stanford to the DMV. A doctor says "absolutely appropriate" to the idea of flying a little plane around Palo Alto with a four-letter word. Friends' eyes fill with tears. *That place is a sham,* says my mother. *Stanford's not what it was when Walt was there,* says my mother-in-law. "It's their loss," says Brian from Italy. "He should go to Berkeley; he'll like it there better, and I'll be there, but if he still really wants to go to Stanford, I know a friend who appealed."

Meanwhile, in Italy, Brian is helping with letters and translations for the FOP battle.

One of the projects to track down the FOP gene involves gathering DNA data from multigenerational FOP families, parents and children who have the disease. DNA studies at the FOP lab have narrowed down the gene's location in much the same way a missing person might be found. From looking for this "person" anywhere in the world a decade ago, to knowing this individual was somewhere in the populous stretch between New York and Philadelphia a few years ago, to currently finding the college dorm where this (anonymous) person resides, great progress has been made. To date there have been seven such families located in the world. If ten families can be found, the search for the gene can be exponentially accelerated, and the information gleaned could make it easier to target the disease process with tailor-made medications. Unlike investigations into most other genetic disorders, FOP research is radically hampered by the features of the disease itself. Because trauma accelerates FOP's advance, the only tissue samples from living subjects available are those from biopsies ordered before an FOP diagnosis was made. It is for this reason that the DNA in the multigenerational families is especially precious, yielding common denominators, signposts in the gene hunt.

Because Brian lives in an international student community, his time studying in Trento offers a unique opportunity to translate a message to boost the effort to identify FOP patients and the hunt for multigenerational FOP families. Brian will try to have the passage translated into the native languages of friends he sees on a daily basis: Punjabi, Cambodian, Albanian, Serbo-Croatian, Polish, Hindi, Hebrew. In addition to these students, my best friend from childhood, Viviana Schwarzbein Ortolani, who lives in Padua, will help, as usual, with the translations. Since she first heard about FOP, Viviana began interpreting medical messages, and she recruited friends to translate FOP materials throughout Europe, getting the word spread on television, and other media, giving a great boost to the desperate quest.

This is the paragraph Brian and Viviana will try to have translated and spread around the world:

Urgent Attention Is Needed for Rare Disease

Fibrodysplasia Ossificans Progressiva (FOP) is a rare genetic disorder that turns muscle and connective tissues into bone and can appear in the first or second decade of life. FOP children appear normal at birth except for a congenital malformation of the great toes (usually a missing joint). Children with FOP develop painful tumorlike swellings that can rise, shift positions, and disappear, and which progressively immobilize the body within a "second skeleton." FOP's progress can be spontaneous, or it can accelerate with trauma. Currently, there are about 400 identified cases of FOP in the world. At present, there is no proven effective treatment for FOP. However, scientists at the University of Pennsylvania FOP Lab have launched an urgent hunt for the FOP gene. Finding this gene will accelerate research and can lead to effective treatments and, hopefully, a cure. It is for this reason that we ask for your help in reaching across the world to identify multigenerational FOP families: parents and children who have FOP and whose DNA holds vital clues. If any health professionals in your area have come across patients with the above features, we ask that they contact Dr. Frederick Kaplan, Director of the FOP Lab at the University of Pennsylvania. His e-mail address is Frederick.Kaplan@uphs.upenn.edu. Your assistance might also help advance research that would benefit other well-known diseases such as osteoporosis, arthritis, and heart-valve disorders. We urgently seek help in spreading the word around the world about FOP. Not only is it important to find multigenerational families, but also it is important

to find anyone with FOP so that we can assure them
that they are not alone.

)

AT FIRST WALT and I believe it's a mistake to fight his alma mater,
to prolong indecision. The Stanford letter states staunchly: "Our
admission decision is final and there is no appeal process."
     I ask Vincent if he wants to appeal. He does. We will. But I
warn: "We can only battle this if you start looking into your other
options." Contradictory advice, I realize, but I don't know how else
to go about this.
     I write to the university's provost, the vice provost, the president
of Stanford. "We could even write to the president of the United
States," I say at dinner that night, realizing I'm getting a little
over-the-top.
     But in some ways it is not so over-the-top. During this time, when
I happen to be researching a Latin American writer, I stumble across
something in a *Guide to the Fernando Alegría Papers, 1924–2000,*
linked to Stanford archives. In this guide to the correspondence
of a Stanford professor and family friend, I find a list of names
including Nobel laureates Pablo Neruda (Box 5, Folder 8), Thomas
Mann (Box 4, Folder 44), Linus Pauling (Box 5, Folder 35), and
the Chilean president Salvador Allende (Box 1, Folder 15), among
others. But one name in particular impresses me the most, in Box
7, Folder 23: Vincent Patrick Whelan. I have no idea how my son
ended up in these archives. I can only think that Alegría's family
culled his papers to donate them to Stanford, and there happened
to be one with Vincent's name on it, perhaps in a letter from or to
my mother. Maybe it was even something like Alegría remembering
how a three-year-old Vincent sang "Guantanamera, Two-tanamera,
Three-tanamera," when he heard me on the guitar. In any event,
it seems that Vincent is already at Stanford, in a list that includes
Nobel Prize winners and a president.
     Instead of writing to Bush again, I ask Dr. Kaplan to resend his
original letter, which has also—curiously—placed Vincent in a list
of prominent names. It begins:

Dear Dean:

Charles Steinmetz, Helen Keller, Stephen Hawking, Franklin Roosevelt, and Vincent Whelan—all brilliant people, all disabled, and all involved in a lifelong struggle to endure, to triumph, to prevail.
    You know about the first four individuals. Let me tell you about the fifth. The world does not know Vincent Whelan yet as he is still in high school, but they will come to know him well in his lifetime. I can imagine what the Encyclopedia Britannica entry will say about Vincent Whelan . . .

I am betting Stanford's "no appeals" warning operates the way NO SOLICITORS signs work. So right now there must be a pile of pleas mounting up alongside ours in the dean's office. We need a strategy. I call Brian in Italy. His friend who fought an admissions decision gets on the phone and tells me across the Atlantic: "You get your high school counselor to contact them." Ah.

"Stanford requires a basis for an appeal," says our guidance counselor. I am on my cell, pulling into the parish school, avoiding orange cones and stopping for mothers shepherding little children dragging backpacks. "You have to have new information, or there has to have been some kind of mistake," explains the counselor. Of course, the mistake was Stanford's, but I doubt they'll see it that way. "We could base the appeal on the fact that our new principal didn't know Vincent well when he wrote his letter," she offers. We both know that sounds lame.

There is something else, however, something no one at any college would even admit to thinking because of disability discrimination laws. I was keeping the question to myself, but my friend Cherie says it out loud today: "Do you think they didn't accept him because of his FOP?" I pose this possibility to the counselor.

"Maybe they decided Vincent has more physical limitations than he does," I explain. "The condition is so rare, practically nobody's ever seen it."

"You want to use that as a basis for our appeal?" asks the counselor.

"What if they thought the expense for special accommodations would be too great?" Stanford is a private university, after all, and the morning after the rejection letter arrived—of all days—an alum friend called Walt to ask for a donation to the university. Walt gave him, instead, a description of the little plane with the banner.

"Hmm," says the counselor.

What if, when push came to shove, with space and funding ever tight, Stanford decided not to take a risk on a boy with "a ghastly condition," as Dr. Kaplan describes it? Might they not think—mistakenly—that a progressive disease like FOP could impact "significant potential to achieve at a high level during the undergraduate years," a requisite listed in the letter? If it all arose from a mistaken impression, we could correct it.

The counselor seems to think I may have a point. "I'll talk to Stanford," she says. But she isn't optimistic.

I cannot concentrate on anything else, so instead of correcting midterms during this Easter break, I take a van full of fighting little girls to see a movie I must yank us out of, which makes everyone fight harder. My karma and its immediate radius are shot: an elderly driver near us backs up into traffic, and a middle-aged man emerges from another car, yelling at him, "Why did you go into reverse?!" *Why?* I can explain: *For the same reason my son didn't get into Stanford; for the same reason my son has a pain that can take away movement if we can't stop it with horrible medications; for the same reason little kids have been fighting in my backseat for fifteen years . . . That's why he went into reverse. The whole universe is going into reverse.*

I receive an answer from a Stanford administrator who has forwarded my appeal to the dean of admission. The dean of admission is not likely to go into reverse for no apparent reason. This administrator tells me cordially in reference to my son that there is "no doubt that he will be successful." But when I think about FOP and Vincent's success on a campus with hills, or at a school where he might expend precious energy on bureaucracy, or getting to medical facilities, I think, *Yes, this kind prediction is correct, but no one can begin to understand what it might cost my son somewhere else.*

Our high school counselor reports back. We cannot appeal.

"I have a feeling we shouldn't fight this anymore," says Vincent.

"If that's what you want," I say. He's right, and, as always, begins to accept loss with a grace his mother doesn't have.

Secretly, I write snail mail, e-mail, toss messages in bottles into the irrigation canal, find carrier pigeons, do everything but fly a little plane around Palo Alto. "We'll dig up old Leland Stanford himself, if we have to," says a friend.

During Lent, Walt and I go to see *The Passion of the Christ.* As I watch Mary stand helplessly while her son falters with the cross, I have to choke down sobs. And as for my own son's Via Crucis, I find there are times when all my efforts to divert his path leave me standing by helpless. There's a reason, I believe it. I don't know what it is, and from here, today, it is impossible to guess.

I am still unable to guess after reading a personal response I receive from Stanford's dean of admission.

The dean tells me she is sorry she cannot relay good news. (*She's not sorry, not one bit sorry, not even 1 percent sorry!* I want to rant, borrowing from Isabel's friend Rachel.) "I want to be clear," she writes, "that Vincent's illness did not play a role in our decision, either positively or negatively."

Vincent was evaluated as if FOP didn't exist.

There is a psychotherapist in Berkeley, Rhoda Olkin, who founded an organization for families coping with disabilities, and she casts disability as "a minority experience rather than a medical problem." This program founder, who battled polio, addresses the practical, social, and legal constraints on the daily lives of those with disabilities. As she explains in a description of a book she has authored: "I never, now or in the past, entertained the question of who I'd be without my disability, how my life would have been different, or how great it would be to be able-bodied. To me, that's what 'living with a disability' means—refraining from or ceasing to ask those questions."

The dean refers to FOP as an "illness." FOP is, unfortunately, a feature of my son's life and it has shaped a part of his personal history. It is in the "hard-to-quantify personal qualities" Stanford would seek. But the dean's response seems unaware of what a Rhoda Olkin would tell the world. It could even be wrong from a legal standpoint. Walt tells me a new discrimination case in Michigan has rendered a judgment that allows for challenges like disability to be factored in—like any minority experience—for consideration in a candidate's profile.

But I know what legal battles mean. *Time to stop fighting.*

)

I AM TRYING to be philosophical about conceding defeat, but it will take a while. "I know what Stanford did was part of a greater Plan." I say to Walt. "But that doesn't let them, personally, off the hook. Like with Pontius Pilate."

It's a clear spring day, and I've just come back from a run. Walt is scrambling eggs for the girls' breakfast and gives me a half-indulgent, not-this-conversation-again look. "You're comparing Stanford to Pontius Pilate?"

"Kind of."

"You're going to have to let this go." But Walt has that fond look he gets when he stops to consider my analogies.

"Why not? Authority washing its hands of a decision that causes suffering and shifts history—but all part of a greater Plan." This makes my head hurt, when I think of the bizarre relationship between free will and divine intervention.

My husband shakes his head, takes the skillet off the burners, and pulls down plates from the cupboard.

It is so hard for me to *let it go.* I am still waking with headaches, jaw clenched, *biting the bullet*, grinding my teeth. My dentist makes

me a fancy new appliance. The appliance makes it look like I stuck
a wad of gum on my two front teeth. It helps, but it doesn't get my
son into Stanford.

And then, right before Good Friday, with what in Spanish you
call a Good Friday face, I pick up the mail as I am leaving the house
and stop to look through it before going into Vons for groceries. I
find a card from a friend I have not seen in ages, and it says:

> *Dear Carol,*
>
> *It's been such a long time since you and I have had the
> opportunity to visit. I wanted to let you know that you
> are in our family prayers every day. We ask God to bless
> and honor all your needs and intentions. Carol . . . I'm
> amazed at your courage, stamina, and grace. May the gift
> of Easter joy fill your heart during this Holy Season.*
>
> *With love—*
> *Theresa*

I sit in the car with my friend's card in my lap, sobbing until I
have a washed-inside feeling. Because I have not felt any courage or
stamina or grace, my friend has just given them to me. And when
I walk in the door at home, the table is set, and there are little cartons from Panda Express, and we eat broccoli beef on paper plates,
the whole family, with Vincent and Lucas's friends Peter and his
redheaded brother Zachary, and we all play a writing game and we
laugh so hard the world looks shiny again.

Walt's rose garden is in bloom, all the graceful, proud-looking roses,
circles of them, in *Fantasia* colors: the orange and pink Rio Sambas,
the crimson American Heroes, the Lemon Spices; one red rose by
my window called Love. They are like a famous dance troupe, here,
right here, performing in our backyard. And in the air is a scent of
spice and soap and water and little miracles.

11

NOBEL LAUREATE
PARKING
APRIL–MAY 2004

I wanted to be able to go around school like normal and
not worry about kids looking at me. I was never made fun
of (actually my brother, the non-FOP child, was). It was a
very difficult age and sometimes it was not FOP that was
bothering me. I know that it may not have been what I
didn't like about FOP but how I felt from worries in school
and such. . . . My family has always taken it day by day and
adapted if we didn't have something we needed at that time.

—AMIE DARNELL, twenty, diagnosed at age
four and a half, Redondo Beach, California

PLAYDAY FOR FOP took place in May 1997, at Celine's preschool, Nosworthy's. It was our first FOP fund-raiser to raise
support for research at Dr. Kaplan's lab. We had a magician turning
children into rabbits, strolling minstrels, raffles, games, prizes, a trip
to Disneyland, and vats of punch from McDonald's. It was the first
time I understood the solidarity of a community in support of my
child; a suffering that had been private up until then was relieved
by so many coming together.

Blanche's Playday for FOP led to another fund-raiser, Starry
Night, in September 1998, featuring Valley artists and writers, and
put together by another Nosworthy's mother, Jackie Thornton.
Because of Jackie and Blanche and all the friends who came to Starry

Night, there would be a miraculous coincidence in September 2002 involving a little boy with FOP and a young nurse.

The event at Blanche's also led to letter campaigns to raise FOP funds at Peter's house, where Cherie has gathered mothers and daughters together regularly over the years to fold, stuff, address, seal, and stamp fund-raiser letter mailings. Because of these mailings, I routinely see long lists of names, familiar and new, donating "In Honor of Vincent Whelan." On that list I have found friends from my childhood and youth, family, relatives in Argentina, professors from my alma mater, friends from graduate student days, Fresno State colleagues, parents from my children's schools, doctors and nurses, dentists, teachers, neighbors, friends of friends of friends I have never met. To add to this fund, Vincent's cousins on the East Coast, Nicole and Natalie, have sold their art and jewelry, and in California, cousins Joe, Blaise, Bianca, Bede, and Vincent's uncle Chris and aunt Linda have all made special efforts. There is no feeling quite like it, to be reminded routinely that there are so many people in the world who stand behind your child, your family.

AFTER THE FAILED prednisone treatment, we were desperate to try another medication. FOP kept attacking Vincent's neck and back. And when Dr. Kaplan and a colleague, Dr. Deanna Mitchell, a pediatric oncologist at the University of Michigan, began setting up an experimental drug trial, we were among the first to sign up. This trial represented a little star of hope, a protocol established to make new use of an old drug. Dr. Henrickson took the project to our hospital board for review, asking for permission to participate.

The drug to be used was thalidomide, a name that can still raise eyebrows in people old enough to remember its notoriety.

Thalidomide was widely prescribed as a sedative in Europe in the 1950s and used to control morning sickness in pregnancy. But in 1960, a connection was made between tragic limb abnormalities in newborns and thalidomide use during pregnancy. General consumption was banned, though today the medication has orphan drug status and is a tightly controlled substance employed to suppress immune and inflammatory response. In 1998 its limited patent was granted by the FDA to Celgene.

The proposed thalidomide trial's investigators were Dr. Deanna Mitchell at the University of Michigan and Dr. Fred Kaplan at the University of Pennsylvania. If our hospital gave the go-ahead, this study would be directed locally by our rheumatologist, Dr. Henrickson at Children's. The trial's objectives, as outlined, were:

3.1 To determine the potential efficacy of thalidomide during active disabling flare-ups, characterized by pre-osseous fibroproliferative masses in patients with fibrodysplasia ossificans progressiva.

3.2 To determine the maximum tolerated dose of thalidomide.

3.3 To determine the acute and chronic toxicity of thalidomide in patients with fibrodysplasia ossificans progressiva.

Our hospital approved participation in the study, but then the question became—would we? After our initial enthusiasm, could we go ahead and enroll our child in the Phase I Trial of Efficacy of Thalidomide for Treatment of Fibrodysplasia Ossificans Progressiva?

It was the last part of the Phase I Trial objectives—"To determine acute and chronic toxicity of thalidomide"—that reversed our enthusiasm. My greatest concern was the threat of transient or permanent neuropathy, loss of sensation in the extremities.

Walt, the risk taker, finally decided we should go forward. I, the worrier, was—worried. We were at a stalemate.

We learned that in 1960 the mechanism behind thalidomide's tragic side effects had been a mystery. But the thalidomide study initiated by Dr. Deanna Mitchell was based on more recent evidence that thalidomide short-circuits angiogenesis, the formation of blood vessels that feed new tissues, a process vital to fetal development. Because of its impact on blood vessel formation, thalidomide, Dr. Mitchell hypothesized, might act as a retardant to FOP's bone-making process, because FOP heterotopic bone—normal bone in abnormal locations—depends on the creation of new blood vessels: *angiogenesis*. Dr. Mitchell's study posited that if we could halt the formation of blood vessels feeding the tumor-like masses of FOP, then we might also short-circuit the FOP process. The goal was to stop muscle and connective tissue inflammation at its outset, before it could produce masses fed by new blood vessels, masses which, in turn, would form cartilage maturing into solid bone. If thalidomide could halt or hinder the initial stages of this inflammatory process—tied, mysteriously, to the immune system—then, perhaps, it could retard FOP's advance.

We remained undecided. Walt still wanted to proceed with the thalidomide trial. I still did not. We called a valued doctor friend for advice. "I wouldn't give it to my kid," said our friend when I read off the study warnings.

But our friend's child didn't have FOP, Walt pointed out. "We need to do this," Walt said, finally. I have always trusted my husband's instincts through the years, but it was the continuing ripple of pains on Vincent's back that ultimately convinced me to sign the papers.

Vincent's involvement in the Phase I thalidomide trial would last a year, starting in January 1999, and would require periodic blood tests, a baseline nuclear bone scan, a follow-up full-skeleton scan at the trial's conclusion, and regular report questionnaires filled out by a parent. He could take the thalidomide capsules at home, without hospital monitoring. If a single one of the study's requirements was not carried out to the letter, however, the trial could be terminated at any time—and almost was, one day, due to a communications mix-up. Our son's medication would be funded by the study.

The thalidomide packaging was somewhat forbidding in and of itself—vacuum-sealed blister packs with bold lists of side effects and warnings forbidding use in pregnancy. Each individual capsule came with the black silhouette of a pregnant woman inside a slashed red circle. On the individual packets was a photograph of a thalidomide baby, with arms and legs tragically stunted. We were to submit a monthly survey confirming that Vincent had not shared his thalidomide with anyone, nor donated blood products. For adult patients the survey involved questions on sexual activity.

One of the first challenges of the drug trial was discovering which dose would avoid side effects. We started out with doses low enough that they appeared to have no impact in any direction, and then went to doses that seemed to put Vincent in a trance all day. There was an alarming episode one afternoon when our son fell into a deep sleep on one of the family room sofas, and for a few panicked moments I couldn't wake him. We lowered the dose, and Dr. Henrickson suggested we give the capsules only at night. Another time Vincent felt pins and needles on his forehead. We suspended the drug and then lowered the dose. Another time he felt pins and needles in his hands. We halted the treatment, changed the dose. On a few occasions, Vincent was unable to add and subtract numbers on math exams. Math genius that he is, this was one of the most alarming symptoms (an effect from the sedative properties of thalidomide). We changed the dose. We rescheduled exams.

Did the thalidomide affect the FOP process? It was difficult to tell, because the flare-ups continued, creating a wing of bone on Vincent's left shoulder blade, leaving ridges of bone on his back. But he no longer woke at night in pain; he had more stamina, seemed hardier. Instead of tidal waves, the FOP flare-ups seemed to come and go like relentless ripples, still there, still alarming—but somehow different.

"We have no clinical proof it works," said Dr. Kaplan to me one day, when I asked how other patients were faring on thalidomide. Our study was almost too small to be called a study, considering just a tiny fraction of the two hundred identified FOP patients in the United States were on it—not even enough to divide into control groups. And with FOP, you could never tell if the disease simply retreated or lost intensity on a whim.

So when the time came, a year later, for the follow-up bone scan, I lamented the fact that Vincent had to go through the procedure of a radioactive isotope injection all over again, just so the gray films could show us what we already knew: the FOP had advanced.

But the shadows of films on lighted panels would show Walt, our rheumatologist, and a radiologist something I didn't know, something a little astonishing.

APRIL–MAY 2004

WE ARE ON Highway 65, headed south to UC San Diego. Walt is driving and Vincent dozes in the front seat, a better spot for his long legs. "Fields of Gold" plays on the radio like a soundtrack for stretches of wheat rolling past. On the fields are cows, brown and gold, heads down, always static, as if they were painted onto the backdrop of the land. We pass orange groves on the other side and I roll down my window to breathe in their jasmine scent.

Sensible families, the ones who do things on time, visit colleges a year before deciding where to apply. They don't start touring a week or two before sending registration fees. But because we were so *sure* Vincent would make it into his dream school, running around the state to different campuses seemed to me a superfluous act.

Now, the project is taking on life-and-death dimensions.

The gold stretches of wheat and the orange groves give way to oil fields, and instead of trees there are oil drills, bowing and rising like giant birds. Past those is the Mojave Desert, beyond the Tehachapi Mountains erased in the bad air of the basin. We reach the Grapevine, where the mountains are desert rock, with a scorched stretch of chaparral and charred yucca like flashes of black lightning. Overhead, a jet cuts a white path in the sky, pointing us south.

I look down at a pamphlet from Claremont McKenna, where we will stop after UC San Diego and UCLA. The brochure shows greenery, stately buildings, and happy students on their way. It has gotten hard to tell one school from another thanks to all the college promotions mailed en masse. The only letter I really remember, the most ingenious pitch of all, went to Vincent's best friend, and it started off, "Dear Peter: Blah, blah, blah, blah, blah, blah . . ."

A good while later, we are passing Magic Mountain, and I see

Goliath, the green roller coaster, with its white scaffold hills. In one room of my memory it is yesterday that Vincent was thirteen and we rode a spinning wheel—and college was as distant as the future. And in another room of memory that time is as far away now as Vincent leaving home was then. "Keep an open mind," Walt is saying to Vincent about the five colleges he will visit in the next two weeks.

To San Diego from Fresno is far, *very far, too far,* I am thinking, *for any kind of urgent need,* even with flights from our remodeled little airport with its alternating acronyms, FAT/FYI. We go from freeway to freeway, each as congested as the next, driving, driving, driving.

Then there is the seduction of ocean air and palm trees along the highway, whole groves of them. We pass San Juan Capistrano and its blue fence of ceramic swallows. The real swallows arrive from Argentina every March nineteenth—Celine's birthday.

A silver Honda with a yellow surfboard on its roof goes by. This is the California of postcards.

The UCSD campus is rustic and sprawling, with more grass and trees than buildings. Vincent takes a tour while Walt and I attach ourselves to a group on its way out of the Price Center, where there is rock music blaring under eateries and theaters. You can tell this school is close to the beach: kids in flip-flops, lots of bleached-blond heads, surfers, skaters, bikini tops. *We aren't in Berkeley anymore, Toto.* It's crowded and loud and festive, and I'm already worried about Vincent keeping safe in the throngs.

Leading our line is a young woman in jeans and T-shirt, with exotic eyes, dark hair, and a badge. We follow her down Library Walk and stop at spots where she recites lore and academic facts, ticking off a list for "where to get your grub on." She enunciates with her entire body, palms sloping up and down gracefully, and she has a flamenco look to her. Her name tag says SOLEDAD.

Soledad is as lovely as her name, *but I don't like it here.* For one thing, the buildings aren't so great: functional, drab—and I see stains. This campus has nothing like the grandeur of Berkeley's neoclassical temples or the glamour of UCLA's brick palaces. And it's too far. *Did I say Berkeley?*

We are on a sloping path to the library, which is, I must admit, a triumph of geometry and glass. "This building was in *Attack of the Killer Tomatoes*," Soledad is saying. It's quite a monument, but standing right under it and looking straight up, I can see cobwebs.

Soledad leads us past a Singing Tree. "These eucalyptus recite poems," she offers, explaining the little forest's history. We never had poetry-reciting plants at my school. Huh. But then a young man with long brown hair and a backpack slung over one shoulder goes by, surveying our group of kids and parents. "This place sucks!" he calls out, jocular. "Don't go here!" He's right. *It's a sign.*

In the middle of a sunken courtyard at the Education Abroad Program office, Soledad tells us, "My family's from Argentina." *How many times have I heard myself say that!* This lovely Argentine girl moves us on, up and down sloping paths, pointing out the wooden army barracks turned into university buildings a few decades ago. "I want to show you these cool retro buildings," she says to our group. Huh.

When it's time to leave the tour, I tug on the sleeve of my Argentine leather jacket and exchange a few words in Spanish with Soledad, who makes me realize UCSD is not so bad at all. Walt and I shake hands with her before jogging back to the Price Center, where we separate for a search, and I spot Vincent at the edge of the crowd. But there are multitudes, and he disappears behind a group of girls in tank tops. *The throng is so thick, the music is so loud, this campus is so big.*

I elbow through backpacks, up stairs, and finally find Walt and Vincent by a student union movie theater. Vincent is animated. "I liked my guide!" The young man who led him around on a golf cart was a science major. "What did you think?"

"It was all right," Walt says. I make a few sounds, trying not to influence. But as we trek back to the administration building, I can't help it. I rattle off unacceptable features: distance from home, campus size, hills, slopes, *distance from home*, too many beach types, *distance from home,* housing shortage, *distance from home.* I don't say anything about architectural style.

Walt refutes every one of my points. *Whose side is he on?* And while Walt goes off to find the car, Vincent and I wait across from Administration, where a group of students is preparing for a protest and a newswoman is positioning herself for a cameraman. Kids are holding up signs that read DON'T RAISE TUITION. There are no more than twenty students, objecting tamely enough: *We will be back and we will be better. We will be back . . .*

"What's that supposed to mean?" Vincent says. The students file off, the uprising over almost as soon as it began. *Nothing like a Berkeley protest.*

"My guide told me they never have protests," says Vincent. "He's a physics major, and one of his professors is Sally Ride—the astronaut. All she has to do is push a button to take a satellite video of the earth that will show up instantly in her office!" That seems a better reason to pick a college than what the buildings or protests look like.

I wish I could share my son's enthusiasm. I haven't seen him this animated since before the Stanford letter. "That's great," I hear myself say, trying to mean it. "But keep an open mind." We still have four more colleges to go.

"You just want me to go to Berkeley," says Vincent. He is looking in the direction of the straggling protesters. *Do I?*

"That's not true." *Is it?*

And as we examine dorms that look cramped but seem splendid to Vincent, and as we drive away from the shaded rural paths, I think Vincent *will* go to UC San Diego. And it won't be because the world-class science program has an astronaut, or because there is beach air and a medical school hospital, but because an Argentine girl called Soledad led his mother to a forest of eucalyptus trees and poetry. *It's a sign.*

)

WE ARE HEADED to UCLA to show Vincent the campus and revisit Rolfe 3112, the classroom were I was a TA and Walt was a law student and I pronounced his name for the first time from a roster.

Vincent's mind is made up about UCSD, so our visit to UCLA is a formality. On the way past the palms on the 405 out of San Diego, our son is happier than I've seen him in a long, long time. "I guess I'll just hop on a plane to visit," I say. Vincent smiles to himself.

"Keep an open mind," says Walt as we near UCLA. We drive down Westwood Boulevard, past opulent new additions to the medical complex. "That's the biggest building in the world," I point out proudly. There is a big-city energy near this complex: lots of traffic, working people—intense, busy—bustling past the rising structures. It is all making UCSD look like a day at the beach. *And I love it.*

"I don't have the same feeling here that I had at UCSD," Vincent is saying. His tone of voice is the equivalent of folded arms. We are in an elevator at Royce Hall, the brick palace where U.S. presidents and Hollywood stars have appeared (and where I stepped into a broom closet instead of a hallway after I thanked everyone for my M.A. orals).

From the moment we leave the elevator in Royce and I start scribbling notes at the office doors of old friends, everything goes from bad to worse: I lose track of time, Walt loses his patience; I lose my camera; I lose Walt and Vincent; we lose the chance to go back together to Rolfe 3112, where it all started, where I met a handsome, athletic redheaded law student who wrote the best and funniest Spanish compositions I had ever corrected.

I visit Rolfe 3112 alone, and find it is no longer a language class-room but an office, locked, with a keypad. I wander down the hall and find the same stairwell: linoleum and brick. Downstairs is an old hangout, North Campus, deserted, its tables still bolted to the ground, its stucco drabber than I remember. In another lifetime we filled these tables, students from Cuba, Spain, Mexico, Puerto Rico, shooing away squirrels and pigeons, shouting, laughing, loaning books and cash. North Campus looks smaller somehow, while the rest of my alma mater has grown grander. I don't know what bothers me more, the emptiness of old haunts or the opulent new buildings taking up more of the sun.

I visit the adjacent English department. It is reassuringly shabby, nothing too different. I go down a well-lighted hall, the same pale walls and linoleum—and there he is: I see him through a half-open door, an old mentor, in the same little office cramped with books. He has the same leonine gray hair, the same wireless glasses, and he is looking down at a paper with the same unforgiving air. He does not see me pass, and I hesitate, pulled toward the space in his doorway. But I move on, feeling weak. Everything here, right here, right now, hits me like an accusation. How would I defend myself from this man's questions? Would he understand my answers? Answers about motherhood versus lofty career goals, versus—my life? Have I done the best I could? Have I? Haven't I? I feel like J. Alfred Prufrock, the lame, middle-aged alter ego for T. S. Eliot. *I grow old . . . I grow old . . . / I shall wear the bottoms of my trousers rolled.*

"I don't like it here," says Vincent stiffly, when we meet up on the steps of *my* College Library, the other brick palace, with Spanish tiles and a train-station ceiling. Vincent seems braced for me to repeat, *Keep an open mind.* Instead, I only nod.

"Should we see the dorms?" Walt asks without enthusiasm. The student residences loom far off on the horizon, built up like beehives.

"What for?" The place where we met, where I was a Spanish TA and Walt was a law student, where he sat at the desk behind John Hemingway, square-jawed grandson of Ernest, where there were times the students made me laugh so hard I didn't have air for words—it isn't here.

It is an L.A. day, mild and sunny, with a hazy halo. But I know, already, that I won't be coming back with Vincent as a freshman, and it won't be because he's already chosen San Diego, and it won't be because the steps of Bruin Walk are too steep

"THE AUDITORIUM IS bigger at our high school," says Vincent, arms crossed. We are at Claremont McKenna in a plush little theater. He seems to be applying the Building Appearance measuring stick like I do. You don't need grandiose structures for a college of some one thousand students. Vincent wouldn't have long distances or crowded spaces to cross. This place is perfect.

A portly silver-haired dean appears on stage, and he introduces the school's president, a striking woman with white hair in a white suit. She is professional, knowledgeable, and in charge. Similar to her in style are the students in the quad manning tables, poised and articulate, no kid-speak: I hear them say, "a host of activities," and "a fellow who . . ." These students are younger versions of the president, who just listed everything we could want in a dream school. The campus is modified mission style, with green lawns, pristine, orderly, *flat*, with Southern California weather. Like I said, *it's perfect*.

Immediately, we are provided with a golf cart and tour the little campus together. Our guide is a clean-cut blond from Oregon, a soccer player. "This is where we had lunch with Janet Reno," he says, taking us into a dining room with linen and china. Our guide shows us his dorm, where quarters seem tight, but not as cramped as at UCSD.

The students here all look engaged, deliberate, on their way. I know they come from a score of countries and states, many choosing Claremont over the Ivy Leagues—or Stanford. There is little traffic while classes are in session; in fact, it's like a ghost town. But that's perfect: no throngs.

We are eating a catered lunch of grilled chicken at picnic tables under dorm windows blaring rock. Walt and I are shouting over the music about how great this place is. "It reminds me of Stanford," says Walt. Vincent listens mutely.

"I don't have the same feeling here as at UCSD," our son pronounces. He is staring morosely at the bright students, *flat* grounds, and clean buildings. ("I've never seen such clean buildings," other parents were saying.) "She Drives Me Crazy" is rising in volume from a window above us.

Walt and I both launch into it over our catered lunch: *Give this place a chance. And why is it so difficult with you kids? It's the same old thing all over again,* and Brian did the same before Berkeley—and blah, blah, blah, we might as well be saying.

Vincent says nothing.

Walt rises impatiently from the picnic table. It is, indeed, the perfect place for a boy whose condition can worsen with trauma and overexertion, who stands to benefit as much from the personal care as from the high-powered programs. "It's better than Stanford," we say.

"OK! I'll go here!" says Vincent, his back tensed as he moves off angrily, blasts of music from the dorms falling away as we follow. "But I won't be happy!"

"All we're saying is, keep an open mind," I say lamely, catching up.

Vincent agrees unhappily to visit the science building, which is as elegant and well appointed as the rest of this college. All the floors are carpeted (*safer*) and the walls are maple paneled (*less din*), none of the shabby gentility of UCLA's insides. How could anyone turn this down in favor of the stained edifices at San Diego?

We pass small, orderly labs and peek in through little door windows, see professional-looking student displays mounted on walls. We find the classroom holding a lecture on the science program. The professor in charge, a large man in shirtsleeves, sits comfortably in a folding chair, back to the blackboard, arms crossed over his belly. He doesn't look terribly dynamic, at least not like he will be sparking my interest in organic chemistry. But when he opens his talk he says something that has nothing to do with science, and it is as if he had planted a bug at our picnic table.

"Why pick a small liberal arts college over a university?" he says. "Some people feel right at a place where everyone knows them; some are perfectly comfortable at a school like Berkeley, where professors don't know or care if they come to class or not."

The science professor then asks students where their interests lie. "Genetics," says Vincent.

"We tend not to believe you when you say at the beginning what you want to study," says the professor." How would *he* know? This isn't making any points with my son.

As our speaker gets into requirements, I begin to check out mentally, remembering a young instructor I just saw in the hallway pushing a stroller, two students trailing her into a book-lined office. *Now* her newborn is cooperating in a maple-paneled setting—but just wait, Madame Professor, until you have juice bottles leaking on rare books and you're jogging between classrooms and parking tickets, and you're correcting exams at the pediatrician's and you wind up part time on the mommy track. *Not that there's anything wrong with that.*

"Take my friend who went to Berkeley," the professor is saying. I perk up. "He said he didn't *want* everyone to know him, to know whether he missed class or not, who he was going out with. He wanted to be *anonymous*. And even when he felt bad being anonymous, he liked walking on campus at night, looking up to see a light on in a building, knowing a Nobel Prize winner might be up there working late—and knowing he was a small part of all that."

Walt and I leave the science building, agreeing that the man who gave the talk did not have enough pizzazz. But Vincent interrupts us, excitedly: "See!" he says. "That guy said *exactly* what I've been trying to tell you all day!"

And we realize that Vincent is tired of being known by everyone at small schools as the kid with something called FOP. And we aren't about to argue with that.

)

WE ARE GOING over the Altamont Pass, along hills so green they look artificial, like Astroturf. And there they are, familiar but always alien looking, the white windmills on the bright slopes, row after row, pulling power out of thin air with their oars.

We're all a little weary of the California college blitz. "If we were in Europe we'd have gone through several countries by now," remarks Walt.

Then we are on 580 headed toward San Francisco, passing gold California poppies in clusters on hillsides. "Are we close to Berkeley yet?" asks Isabel. We are on our way to Cal Day, with tours and exhibit tables and balloons and lectures.

"Yup," says Walt.

"How long?" says Isabel. Vincent gives an estimate.

At our last gas station stop, Northern California's geography was folded into maps on display: routes through Marin, San Francisco, Oakland, telling us how far we are from San Diego, where Vincent still has his mind made up to go. Berkeley we can round-trip in one day, that's its great advantage, along with its stellar rankings. But we are going as a formality, to rule it out.

It is sounding sillier than ever to say *Keep an open mind* to our son, when he's heard us ranting about Berkeley on his brother's behalf for two years. Brian is still studying in Italy, so he will not be on campus to influence Vincent one way or the other. ("Vincent should go to Berkeley," he said from Trento. "He'll like the people there better. And I'll show him the ropes.")

We are leaving the dense urban corridor of Oakland and see great trees on either side of the highway, tall pines and eucalyptus forests. Isabel sounds out a word on the sign for the Warren Freeway: "Berkeley!"

"Who calls it Berzerkeley?" asks Vincent.

"Uncle Chris," says Walt. Not that Walt's brother invented the nickname. And I've called Berkeley worse.

"Why do they call the school Berzerkeley?" asks Isabel. Walt explains. Like I said, we're here to rule it out.

At the campus we actually find parking right away near the promontory of Brian's old dorm, Bowles Hall, the stunning historical landmark with a fault line crossing its dining room. "It looks like a Harry Potter castle," says Isabel. And just as dangerous: stairs and stairs and stairs and slick concrete and locked-off rooms and secret passageways, and catacomb portals and washers on one floor with dryers on another and general mayhem, the mayhem of males all under one roof suddenly *free*, duct-taping friends to chairs; sandwiching them between mattresses; launching forks and furniture; setting fires; police banging on doors and half a city stuffed into one building for Halloween. *And that's only what I know about.* No,

Vincent will neither go here nor live here. Still, I am always taken
with it when I look up at the Bowles castle, grand and rakish, like
something out of *Robin Hood*.

We trek down an asphalt path, past a green glade toward the
Campanile, the landmark clock tower with a view of the Golden
Gate, which is shining like a jewel this afternoon. We pass blue "NL"
signs for Nobel laureate parking slots. We take a picture of Vincent
at an "NL" post and he says, suddenly, "This place isn't so bad!"

Huh?

As Walt goes off to find a golf cart tour, Vincent and Isabel and
I visit one of the Cal Day exhibits. We talk about plant genetics to
a student from India wearing a white turban, and Vincent explains
he wants to study human genetics. But the Indian student is so gracious and he smiles so nicely at Isabel that I almost want Vincent
to switch to plants.

I approach the housing booth under a striped tent, where there
are little baskets of blue-and-gold CAL PARENT buttons, but I do
not take one. Instead, I talk to the man in charge, Edward Malone,
African American and warm and interested. I tell him about my
son and he hands me his card. "Write directly to me," he instructs,
to cut through red tape. One of the scariest features of Berkeley is
its bureaucracy. But Mr. Malone has just shaken my hand and given
me his numbers. Too bad Vincent won't be going here.

We take our tour on one of the most glorious April afternoons
ever, under a keen blue sky, the bay brilliant. Our guide is an econ
major, tall and thin, with neat brown hair. He has that intelligent,
alert Berkeley look, and he drives our golf cart to the second-largest
building on campus, Zoology, the neoclassical temple with the
largest collection of seeds in existence and a *T. rex* rising through
a spiral staircase.

We see the Doe Library, another temple, full of pale marble
and the spirits of ancient volumes in the echoes and rustlings and
the silence. The students are too familiar or burdened with it all
to take notice, but that religious feeling, it is here, always, in this
library. I felt it when I was a young woman and I felt it when Brian

first arrived at this school. I am falling in love with Berkeley again. *Against my will.*

Our guide takes us to the oldest building of all, Education, Victorian ornate and made of brick. It is across from Sather Tower, with its venerable green bells, and he points out a curiosity at the entry. I squint hard and find a little bear in repose on a ring carved in the stone moldings, and so does Isabel, charmed. We all stand before Education, looking past it at the blue jewel of the bay and the Golden Gate Bridge, shiny as a talisman.

"Whenever I feel down," says our guide, "I come to the Campanile, go up the tower, and look out at the Bay. And I feel better."

Our guide drops us off at old residence halls full of big sunny rooms, and we visit a computer center with a PowerPoint presentation by a young woman who tells of the miraculous hours everything is open to help people find their bearings. "Berkeley is a gigantic place and a great bureaucracy and students might feel afraid to contact professors—of which there are four Nobel laureates," she says.

A molecular cell biology major explains why she picked Berkeley, confesses she didn't like UCLA, and then ducks in mild embarrassment, aware of her audience of parents: "I don't know why—I don't want to say, I just didn't." Vincent is smiling.

And as we are exiting the high-rise dorm, emerging into the shiny Bay Area afternoon, Vincent muses, "I guess I didn't like Berkeley because I was looking at it as someone who wanted to go to Stanford."

Last, we visit Clark Kerr, a sprawling mission-style dorm with a dining room in Spanish tile, a courtyard with a fountain, all flowers and peace and quiet—more resort than residence hall.

And as we stop at a gas station, filling up for the ride home, Vincent announces suddenly: "I think I'm going to go to Berkeley."

"Really?" we say.

"Yeah, I had a dream I was going to school with Brian."

"You did? When?" says Walt.

"About two days ago; I was in a car with Brian and we were going to school."

"Don't base your decision on that," I offer.

Walt is fiddling with the gas nozzle. "Why not?" he says. "You base your decisions on otherworldly stuff."

"Peter's going to be so surprised!" says Vincent.

"The grandmothers aren't going to be happy," I say to Walt.

"The grandmothers aren't going to college," Walt says.

I'm relieved our son has made a decision, but I can't help regretting he has not picked Claremont, the quietest, smallest, most protective, most high-powered college of all. They have a nine-to-one ratio of students to instructors.

At Berkeley, Vincent will take classes with 1,400 names on the roster. And whereas at Claremont professors give out their home phone numbers, happy to hobnob with parents, the Cal dorm director noted what I knew decades ago and what Brian has learned the hard way: "Berkeley is a *huge* bureaucracy. But it's a great preparation for the real world, kind of like boot camp for life."

Boot camp for a kid with FOP? Good? Bad? I don't know.

12

SILVER COINS

APRIL–JUNE 2004

*From the age of fourteen, I was unable to use the school
bus, as one of my legs was partially bent. So my father
used to drop me off and pick me up after schooling. For this
purpose, he shifted his office and our residence nearer to
the school. During lunch interval, my father used to come
to where I was to render any help or assistance, if required.
Very often the school furniture did not suit my requirements,
and as such my father arranged special adjustable or por-
table furniture to accommodate me.*

— LAKSHMI NATARAJAN, eighteen,
diagnosed at age five, Faridabad, India

WITH FOP, a few things changed in the car. For one thing,
everyone knew not to call "shotgun" anymore on the daily
school race, because the front captain's chair in the minivan was
the most suitable seat for Vincent. For another, everyone had to
learn to tone down games that could escalate into fights. One of the
games in the car that still gives me a headache is Slugbug. Slugbug
starts out tamely enough, with someone claiming a Volkswagen on
the road. There is tapping involved, and then someone else will say,
"*Slugbug,*" a little louder, and tap again, but the taps get progressively more forceful and can turn into slaps and punches if there is
any confusion over who called it first. And then I have to pull over
and yell. But of course, with FOP everyone learned to refrain from
tapping Vincent. Vincent—as would any kid—sometimes took

advantage of this protected status by saying or doing things nobody could hit him back for.

Vincent has always been the one to explain some of the rules of childhood to me, and this has—sometimes—helped me intervene when necessary. I remember the morning I had just parked by a Sports Authority to buy my first grader soccer cleats. "Celine, what size did we say your shoes were?" I called over the seat. No answer. "Celine?" No answer. I turned to look at my six-year-old, sitting mute, her lips puckered inward. "Why aren't you saying anything?"

"She's jinxed," Lucas said.

"She has to be unjinxed," said Vincent.

The jinx game was, no doubt, a brotherly plot to silence a little sister. Fights had been started over Celine trying to speak over the brothers singing "Never-ending sto-o-o-r-y-y-y-y-y" and Lucas announcing, "We're the sarcastic singing crew!"

Celine sat with her lips glued together. "*Unjinx her!*" I looked at Lucas, unbuckling Isabel from her car seat.

"Lucas can't unjinx her," Vincent told me. Celine remained mute, looking like she would readily answer any questions, if only she could.

"You're unjinxed!" I stirred my arms in an abracadabra way.

"That's not how it works," said Vincent. Celine's lips were still concave. Vincent carefully outlined the procedure for unjinxing and went ahead with whatever ritual it required. Celine promptly let out such a sigh of relief, it was as if not just speech, but the air itself had been trapped inside her little body.

If only we could unjinx ourselves of FOP so easily. *Someday.* In the meantime, we have the rituals of experimental efforts.

Vincent's Phase I Trial with thalidomide ended in January 2000 and Walt took him to the required follow-up nuclear medicine bone scan at Children's. Because we had seen FOP's advance with our own eyes—more stiffness in our son's neck, ridges and knots of bone along his back and shoulder blades—I didn't need fancy X-rays to confirm what we knew: thalidomide had not prevented FOP ossification. It *seemed* to help with pain and stamina, but Dr. Kaplan was right, there was no clinical proof it worked. So a nuclear bone scan was an unpleasant formality, and I was happy to let Walt take care of it. I had had it with X-ray facilities.

"I forgot to tell you," said Walt, one night in January, on the day he and Vincent had gone to see Dr. Henrickson for a follow-up. "The radiologist found something unusual in the bone scan."

I was standing in our room, toweling four-year-old Isabel's damp curly hair before bedtime. I tensed. As I said, because of their steadiness, Walt and Vincent's voices don't offer preamble clues: car breakdown, lottery win, no way of knowing what's coming from their tone.

"A small area on the left sartorius muscle had been calcifying a year ago," said Walt. "And it was gone." This was news in the direction of winning the lottery.

"Are they sure?" It was hard to believe, considering all the FOP activity we'd seen. Walt nodded, looking as hopeful as I felt. I shooed Isabel off for a toothbrush and sat on the edge of the bed, a damp towel on my lap. "How big?"

"Like this." My husband curled his thumb and forefinger together around a dime-sized space. "The radiologist put the bone scans next to each other," he went on. "The white spot, the calcification, was in his left leg in the first one, but not on the scan they just took."

"They're *sure*?" I repeated. "What did the radiologist think?"

"That it was something."

"And Dr. Henrickson?"

"The same."

I felt, instantly, the way you do right after you've laughed or cried very hard.

As it turned out, the absent white blotch on dark acrylic was not clear-cut proof that thalidomide could retard FOP. When Dr. Deanna Mitchell presented her thalidomide study's results at the 2000 International Symposium on FOP in Philadelphia, she included Vincent's bone scans, and the absent white space was interpreted differently by different researchers: it meant something, it meant nothing.

Thalidomide had appeared to ease FOP symptoms for some patients, but not at all for others. It was very difficult to measure treatment efficacy in a disease that could retreat and advance at random. So Dr. Mitchell's most compelling evidence was what she flashed in black and white on a screen in a hotel ballroom in the form of quotations: *he was able to play (modified) soccer again, his elbow unlocked, he could sleep better, her pain was controlled.* But that data was "anecdotal," and the word *anecdotal* in medicine seems to carry as much scientific weight as *abracadabra.* There was some disappointment as FOP parents filed out the door after Dr. Mitchell's paper. We had all hoped that the data cited by the slender, fair-haired doctor in a dark suit would prove *something could really fight FOP.*

As we were leaving the hotel ballroom where Dr. Mitchell had spoken, where high-powered scientists from places like Harvard and Berkeley shared their impressions with other scientists and FOP families, I caught sight of a mother from Bosnia, pushing her child with FOP in a wheelchair. Her little boy had been airlifted out of their war-torn country in a helicopter, and she looked over at me and said defiantly: "I *know* thalidomide works for my son."

With Dr. Henrickson and Dr. Kaplan, we decided Vincent would take thalidomide for flare-ups, whether there was solid clinical proof or not. We went with the same gut feeling the mother from Bosnia had expressed.

Thalidomide had been free of charge during the study. It wasn't until the day our insurance company balked at covering the drug that we discovered thalidomide cost three thousand dollars for each prescribed course.

Dr. Henrickson wrote a letter and Walt had a talk with an insurance rep.

One dark afternoon after the Phase I study had concluded, when Vincent had started a major joint flare-up, I called the hospital at the University of Michigan to speak to Dr. Deanna Mitchell. Dr. Mitchell's youthful, slightly grainy voice had become a comforting sound through the course of our thalidomide study, and her own work with desperately ill children in oncology seemed to lend her a calm that lost none of its reach across time zones. During our talk that desperate afternoon, she mentioned a new Harvard study on thalidomide combined with an anti-inflammatory drug that had reduced tumors in mice by hindering angiogenesis.

"But it hasn't been tried on people," she told me firmly, when I asked if we could use the same combination for FOP. The drug employed with thalidomide in the Harvard study was a nonsteroidal anti-inflammatory called sulindac.

"It's only been successful in limiting angiogenesis in *mice*," stressed Dr. Mitchell. As a pediatric oncologist, Dr. Mitchell was accustomed to the cocktail approach to treatments, using not one but a combination of drugs to attack a disease process synergistically—the components together becoming greater than the sum of their parts. Still, she was reluctant to recommend this particular mix.

That desperate afternoon, when I was in mortal fear my son would lose more arm motion, I posed to Dr. Mitchell the same question I had asked Dr. Glaser that summer of 1997 when FOP hit for the second time: "Could the side effects be worse than FOP?" And I asked Dr. Mitchell, who is also a mother: "What would you do if it were your child?"

Dr. Mitchell prescribed the sulindac, with the caveat that we would run the medications past Drs. Henrickson and Kaplan. The resulting cocktail, thalidomide, sulindac, and prednisone, is now our mainstay for FOP flare-ups. While we have become used to the measure of relief it offers, we know that its work is imperfect. I stress the word *imperfect*, because the drugs are not consistently effective and they do not perform in the same way for everyone with FOP. Finally, our son continually braves side effects and long-term risks both known and unknowable.

)

As there are natural laws, those that govern the body and its responses to illness or medication, then there must be—*I'm sure of it*—laws with hidden mechanisms all their own, and they come, sometimes, in the form of coincidences, little or big. "In the designs of Providence," said John Paul II, "there are no mere coincidences."

An example of a tiny stitch in Providence's designs: After Playday for FOP in 1997, it had taken me weeks to get to a bank to change funds into a cashier's check to mail to the IFOPA. I was berating myself for lateness as I sat in the car, finishing my list of donor addresses for tax purposes to mail off ASAP. The last loose end was an address I didn't have: missing was the contact information for Captain Magic, the magician who had given our little event its glamour, with his movie-star looks, top hat, and disappearing rabbits. Resigned to my usual delays, I waited in line at a Bank of America, one far from our house but close to Celine's preschool—a bank I had entered three times in my life. When I got to a window, I shook out my envelope full of cash and checks, made small talk with the teller—and recognized a voice to my right, at the next window. There was the handsome profile of a man who had appeared in a Hollywood movie and turned a child into a rabbit at Playday for FOP: *Captain Magic*. I had never run into the magician before and have not since. The coincidence was a strange one and I like to think it meant that no matter how late I was at doing what I was doing, this particular time, I was where I was supposed to be—at the right time

"I needed to see exactly you, exactly now," I said to the magician. We both laughed at the timing; he gave me his address and I mailed off my package of donations for FOP research.

An example of a more elaborate stitch in Providence's design:

Two Junes ago, I was stopped on my way out of the house, four kids in tow, by a ringing telephone. Normally I would have let the machine catch the call, but my hand happened to be right on the phone when it rang. A stranger's voice with an accent asked to speak to me, and I identified myself a little impatiently. "I am Prisco Ramirez," said the stranger. "We just moved to Fresno, and I found you from your *Newsweek* article. My daughter has FOP."

I put my purse down and told five-year-old Isabel to close the door. The *Newsweek* piece from 1999 was the one I wrote to raise FOP awareness. It had elicited cards from people around the country, donations, and messages from alternative health practitioners, but nothing like this phone call . . .

If the odds of FOP hitting an individual's genetic code are one in two million, then the odds against two people with FOP living in the same Valley town have to be even more astronomical.

Suddenly, Prisco Ramirez was no stranger. The details of his family's life might differ from mine, but I could recite his sorrows by heart: a child healthy at birth, a perfectly normal life, until one morning—a persistent pain, a mysterious swelling. A quest for a diagnosis. A quest for a cure. And in between, countless hours of helplessness, the suffering of seeing your child lose the ability to put on shoes and ride a bike.

Prisco told me his family had just arrived and was from the Philippines. I learned that his daughter Charis would start college, and that the family had no doctor, no health insurance, and none of the medications we use to try to slow down FOP. Charis had just started having to sit after walking a few steps. She had had a fall, and, of course, I knew what that meant.

I went to visit the Ramirez family. Prisco and his wife, Babette, both nurses with green cards for work in California, lived with their four children in an apartment off a well-transited avenue not far from the freeway. I wasn't prepared for the strong emotion that took me the moment I entered the little apartment and saw Charis Ramirez. In this lovely young Filipina I saw my own son so patently, tears stung my eyes. Her rigid upper body, her delicate shoulders and stiff neck told me she shared the same personal history of loss and pain as my son. And she had the same sweet clarity in her eyes, the same dignified bearing in her difficult gait. And when I met Babette, I saw myself.

After we embraced, Babette offered a Kleenex box, and we both wadded white tissues in our hands as we talked on the metal folding chairs of the little living room, for which Babette apologized unnecessarily.

"Charis has your picture!" Babette remembered. She shuffled through a stack of papers on a tiny table and produced a photo—in the center of a page torn directly from the July 12, 1999, *Newsweek*—of Vincent and me at Children's. "A friend sent it to us when we were living in the Middle East," said Babette. "When we came to California, Charis said, 'Maybe we can meet them!'"

The thought of the family studying and saving our story on the other side of the world, finding themselves a few years later living in our town and hoping to meet us, made me reach for another tissue. "We found your name in the phone book," said Babette simply.

Babette then traced a long livid scar down her daughter's left leg. "From the surgeries," she told me. Like so many FOP children misdiagnosed with cancerous tumors, Charis had withstood early treatments that did nothing but accelerate the furious bone formation.

Pressed for time, I hurried to give the Ramirez family the names of doctors and medications: I explained the experimental use of thalidomide, about the capsules with the silhouette of a pregnant woman with a circle and slash. We talked about hot pools and herbs and prednisone and prayer.

Without being able to say everything that needed to be said— even with all the time in the world—I looked down at my watch and rose abruptly to hug the family, late on my way to collect my kids.

I was a little distressed by our language barrier, which was miraculously lifted when the first pharmacist I called for the family was a Filipina who spoke Tagalog—and helped with Medi-Cal forms. And a few weeks later, Dr. Henrickson called me with an Asian medical resident who had—coincidentally—just asked if he knew anything about something called FOP because she had diagnosed a case in a rural Valley town. The resident went on to make house calls for Charis, and Dr. Henrickson enrolled his second patient in the thalidomide study.

I wish I could say we saw the Ramirez family frequently after that first encounter, but life—and FOP—got in the way, and I started to wonder if perhaps my "help" had been intrusive.

But the Ramirezes and I met again by sheer coincidence not long ago, when Vincent and I stopped off at a Target, right after a checkup in Rheumatology, where I had asked Dr. Henrickson about Charis Ramirez. I was standing near the shampoo aisle when I heard someone call my name. There were Babette and Prisco, on either side of a red shopping cart. "I thought that was you!" said Babette with a great hug. And it was like no time had passed, and there was so much gladness and love in the couple's eyes that I knew our bond was something that required no excuses or explanations and none of the usual formulas of friendship.

There is a line from my favorite writer, Gabriel García Márquez, one that summarizes the everyday magic of all of the above: *No one would have believed that real life could help itself to so many coincidences forbidden to fiction.*

APRIL–JUNE 2004

VINCENT IS NO longer sure he wants to go to Berkeley. Right now, days before the deadline to file the intent to register, we have a three-way tie between Berkeley, UC San Diego, and UC Davis. So we are contacting university offices that assist disabled students on the Northern, Central, and Southern California campuses. We have to break this tie, and we have four days to do it before the deadline.

At Cal, if you need information on special-needs assistance, you call the DSP, which stands for Disabled Students' Program. At UCD the same kind of office is the SDC. At UCSD, it's the OSD. None of them has ever heard of FOP. The acronyms alone are making me grind my teeth at night.

I find out from the SDC at UC Davis that Vincent would not be allowed a golf cart until a committee could decide if golf carts were feasible between classes and waning phases of the moon. So scratch UCD and its SDC. That easily narrows it down to Berkeley versus San Diego. (Did I say *easily?*)

At Berkeley's DSP I become old friends with a counselor who sends students off to scope out facilities for us, calls a paratransit company, investigates shuttles and note-taking services, and determines that a medical scooter would be safest in the hallowed halls when *they gallop out of classes,* as she puts it. All that information represents many, many, many phone calls, answering-machine messages, voice mails, and not a few e-mails. No matter; Berkeley wins.

I tell Vincent about all the assistance and fantastic facilities at Berkeley. "I still like UC San Diego better," he says.

Of course, this is not *my* decision. So I put in a call to UCSD's

OSD; I have flashbacks to a kid in a Hawaiian shirt manning a desk and tell the young voice on the line to *take me to your leader*. No superior is available, but one calls back. She is amiable and professional, but she is not my best friend like the Berkeley counselor. I tell her something to this effect—in a more factual way.

"Berkeley is *king* and *queen* of disabled students' services in the UC system," she concedes, describing the phenomenal aid Berkeley is able to pull up. She's right: Vincent should go to Berkeley.

This UCSD counselor, however, confirms that golf carts on the San Diego campus are plentiful and punctual, so Vincent would not need a medical scooter for distances. She also notes that, as a larger campus with fewer students than Berkeley, crowds are rarely a danger. And the dorms are smack-dab in the middle of everything. She gives me the number for UCSD's housing director, and I'm almost positive the acronym I am told to write down is LSD (*that can't be right* . . .).

The director from the last acronym is very efficient, and by the time I learn Vincent can ride a golf cart, have a single room in a suite for four years, and live across the street from a research hospital and the beach, I'm sold.

When my dad drops by, he and I sit at the kitchen table, and I tell him excitedly about UC San Diego and he listens and then says, puzzled, "I thought Vincent was going to Berkeley." So I list more UCSD marvels, and my dad says, "Well, then I'll be passing through San Diego on my way to the bullfights!" (When my brother, Martín, and I were small, he would stage mock bullfights for us with toothpicks and a little rubber Argentine cow.)

Vincent appears in the kitchen and says to us, as if on cue, "I think I'll go to Berkeley."

"You don't have to, just because you think I want you to!" I say, and sum up my conversations with the San Diego acronyms. He looks pleased. *So it's settled: UC San Diego it is.*

And, then, after opening and closing and the refrigerator door, Vincent says, "But I like the Berkeley students better."

I call over Lucas, who is listening from his station at the computer. Lucas may be only fifteen, but he has a knack for getting to the heart of things. He sits next to his grandfather at the kitchen table, and we watch Vincent fill in blanks on a scientific grid. He lists the colleges vertically: UCSD, UCB, UCD, and horizontally lists categories: science, friends/family, distance, housing, transportation, safety, library, disability services, weather, all to be ranked one to three for best to worst. Including every possible feature, Berkeley's total comes to twenty-three and UCSD's comes to twenty-five. Berkeley "wins." Vincent looks skeptical.

"My World Cultures teacher said today that it doesn't matter where in the world you are if you're with people you like," says Lucas. "So you should go to Berkeley," Oddly, this argument changes Vincent's mind back to San Diego.

I stand in front of everyone at the kitchen table as if I were teaching a class and announce: "Vincent *would* have it *easier, funner, freer* at UC San Diego. Berkeley would be *harder, less safe, more challenging* physically, and he would have to ride a medical scooter rather than be driven around on a country club golf cart. You pick between a school that's a legend, like Harvard, difficult and challenging, and a school like UCSD that's prestigious and you'll get just as great an education—"

"You don't believe that," Vincent interrupts.

"I do!" I say. "And you would have more fun and everything would be easier and you would probably be safer."

"Jeez," says Lucas. "All of a sudden, you make Berkeley sound terrible!" My father, wisely, says nothing. (He could remind me that in Latin America you just go to the college near your family.)

"OK, then," I say, losing my cool. "This is how we decide." I take a quarter from my purse. "Tails: San Diego. Heads: Berkeley." I stand at the end of our long maple table, toss a quarter, slap it on my wrist. It's the eagle. San Diego. Vincent seems happy.

Lucas looks doubtful. My dad is fine with it. I'm clenching my jaw.

"OK, let's do this two out of three," I say, tossing the coin before anyone can stop me.

Tails again. San Diego.

"Let's do *five* tries." Nobody protests as I toss the silver again, slap it down: George Washington. Heads. I toss two more times: George: three in a row. "Berkeley!"

I can't tell if Vincent is happy or not.

Of course, that's no way to decide. Is it? "Close your eyes, Vincent," I say. "Where do you see yourself?"

My son assumes a look of meditation behind his wire-rimmed glasses. We all wait. "Berkeley," he says finally, opening his eyes.

But then, after dinner, Vincent is on the family room computer comparing college rankings; I look over his shoulder. "Ha! Way lower than Cal!" I say.

"You've just wanted Berkeley all along!" says Vincent. He doesn't look like he wants Berkeley very much right now.

"No, I haven't!" *Have I?*

And now Vincent is calling Brian in Trento for advice.

This isn't going very smoothly.

Tomorrow I keep my mouth shut. And no more calls to DSP, SDC, DSO, or UC anything.

TODAY WE ARE on our way to the outskirts of town. We are only an hour and a half late for a graduation party at a friend of a friend's in a rambling California ranch-style house. When we arrive, we are generally introduced and ushered into a kitchen with food on every available surface, a television going, kids swimming outside, and lots of unfamiliar faces. I am not up for this today, and it is all I can do not to turn around and leave, but the event is in honor of the son of good friends, so I steel myself for an afternoon of chitchat with strangers.

Celine and Vincent and I settle in the garage, where a group of parents and kids is playing pool and my friend who invited us is part of a little semicircle. I'm in a flowing red dress with flowers, not an outfit for the garage, but I pick a chair with a paper towel on its seat and somehow get into a conversation about a rental-house garage with spooky noises. Then my friend says to me jovially, "You know, this house is haunted. *Lori sees dead people.*" Lori is the hostess, and she breeds horses.

A lovely blond woman in our semicircle adds, "And one season she dreamed every night the colors of one of the foals and that's exactly the kind of horse that was born."

"Wow," I say politely and reach for a beer in an ice chest nearby.

My friend who has invited us is from the Midwest and works in a lab; her husband is an accountant. Both of them are sensible, grounded people, so she is goading me when she repeats, "This house is haunted."

In response, I call to the hostess: "OK, let's have it, a full report on your ghost situation." Who doesn't like a good campfire story?

Our hostess is going past, a cigarette in one hand, beer bottles between fingers. She is a handsome woman, Italian, dressed in a gauzy pink shirt and jeans. My question stops her and she looks over at me. "Would you like a reading?" I put up my hands in a *halt* gesture, shake my head no, and she shrugs, disappearing into the house. I do *not* want to know the future, forget it, not to mention it's against my religion. It's one thing to decipher coincidences, another to have your destiny read.

But our hostess is back in the garage, the door to the house slowly closing behind her on a bicycle-pump hinge. She picks our conversation back up. "I have to keep the door in the back room locked because it gets haunted," she explains matter-of-factly, like someone complaining about mice in the pantry. "The temperature drops suddenly. And I get stuff moved from one place to another."

This is certainly good chitchat, but it's sounding a little scripted. "Like *The Sixth Sense*?" I say.

"I told my husband when we saw that movie, 'That was *right on, right on*; they nailed it.'" Our hostess takes one of the plastic chairs to join us. "Are you sure you don't want a reading?" She looks at me helpfully.

"*No!*" No, no fortune-telling. The idea that someone at a graduation party might possibly know something about us or our future via supernatural channels is making me nervous.

I can hear the squeals of the kids off in the pool in the backyard, which sounds very far away right now.

"People from the other dimension are in every house," our hostess
goes on, takes a drag on her cigarette. "Sometimes it's just energy,
the memory of a being who lived at some time in the place." And
then, without any preamble or gear switching, she announces, suddenly, just like that: "Like they're here now. You have three behind
you," she gestures to me. "He," she nods to Vincent at my right, "has
seven, and she," she points at Celine to my left, "has two."

Uh.

This last bit doesn't sound so scripted. I've always said Vincent
is surrounded by guardians. Right now, a few centuries of Latin
blood kick in like a compulsion, so of course I *have to ask*: "Can you
tell me what one of them looks like?" I nod toward Vincent. I've
sometimes wondered who has been sent to protect him so fiercely
and in response to so much prayer all these years. Then again, this
is just a parlor game.

Our hostess looks over Vincent's shoulder and I follow her gaze,
seeing nothing: "It's a lady with gray hair; she's wearing a blue dress,
and she looks like you. She's plumpish; she's like you, only you're very
thin," she adds. "So she would be like you with about thirty more
pounds. And I hate to say it, but she has a penchant for sneaking
brandy on the sly."

"My grandmother drank vermouth in the kitchen so my grandfather wouldn't catch her at it," I hear myself explain. I say this
half-amazed, half-doubtful. She shrugs: "Brandy, vermouth, sorry,
but she drank it on the sly." I can almost see my grandmother in her
dark dresses and natural pearls, taking the cut-glass decanter and
pouring herself a tiny ladylike drink. She was no alcoholic, she just
liked her vermouth. My grandmother was always my accomplice in
laughing at whatever went wrong. And I look like her.

The hair is rising on the back of my neck. "There are lots of
doctors around him," adds our hostess, looking at Vincent. "Are
there doctors in the family?" Yes, I tell her. My arms are turning to
chicken skin: there were a good number of doctors in Argentina
on my grandmother's side.

"What about me? Who is with me?" I have to ask. *Why am I
doing this?*

"You have a child with you," she says, looking above my shoulder, to my right. "About nine or ten, brown hair, brown eyes; he looks like you."

I feel my throat tighten. I had a brother who passed away in Argentina. I don't remember him and I've never even seen a photograph. "My brother?" I say. "But he died when he was a baby."

"He had something wrong with an arm?" she asks. As she is talking, she's very casual, smoking, pulling on a Bud Light.

"My brother had something wrong with his heart." Our hostess shakes her head no, it was an arm.

Later that night, I will go over this singular conversation. What if in some strange time-space continuum, our hostess might have been seeing Vincent at age nine *and* age ten when FOP attacked, robbing him of arm motion? He looked like me as a child, brown hair, brown eyes, same face shape—and he is always "with me." *Am I losing some more marbles?*

"And you have a very tall, very thin man standing behind you. With a beard."

Don Quixote? Cervantes?

"He's carrying a doctor's case. He's a doctor. He's in a '30s suit. Very distinguished."

"Well—it could be another doctor on my grandmother's side," I say doubtfully. What if he's the ancestor the Filipina healer was trying to tell me was responsible for the FOP?

I'd rather it be Cervantes.

But our hostess has suddenly turned her attention on Celine, whom she seems to like best of all. "You have two angels with you," she tells her, smiling. "She's very strong," she says to me. Don't I know it—another future lawyer. When I went to pick Celine up at a raucous pool party last week, a classmate's aunt said, admiringly, "She looked like she wouldn't take no crap from nobody." It doesn't take a psychic to see determination in those blue green eyes.

"Androgynous angels. Beautiful. With long blond hair," the hostess is saying.

I guess Celine doesn't need as many guardians as the rest of us mortals.

"You're going to be wildly successful," the hostess predicts. "President of something. In politics."

Celine makes a face. "I want to be an actress." Well, *acting—politics*, I don't have the heart to explain, but Celine comes up with a formula herself, when she considers the governor of California.

"You'll be *very successful*. And make lots of money. Will you take care of me?" jokes the hostess as she takes another drag on her cigarette.

"Who's the third spirit behind me?" *What is wrong with me?*

"An elderly hawk-nosed Native American woman." Doesn't everyone have a Native American spirit guide? And she's a medicine woman. Please.

I don't know how much our hostess knows about us from my friend, who must have told her about FOP and our medical quest.

But Lori looks to Vincent again and starts to make a prediction. "*No future predictions!*" I say, holding up my hands.

"But it's good!" She smiles a little mischievously. "I never tell bad futures." Vincent looks interested. "You're going to go into research," she says. "But you won't like it; you'll be more hands-on." She tells Vincent he will be a great doctor because he'll be able to know what's wrong with people. I could predict that myself, of course.

The one Bud Light I've had is making my head light. I leave the dark garage for the sunny driveway and find Walt at a card table talking to a good friend who is Chinese. Walt shakes his head over the garage goings-on. Our friend only wonders if it's not too early for this kind of thing. "Isn't it better to wait until nightfall?" he asks.

From the driveway, I can hear Celine asking for a dream to be interpreted, so I march back to put a polite stop to things. Luckily, the dream stumps our hostess, who shrugs unknowingly. Time to go.

But there is one last thing I can't keep myself from asking: "Who put out a hand to steady Vincent on the steps of the Supreme Court that day?" Our hostess looks down, trying to remember. "Are your parents still with you?" she asks. Mine are, thankfully, but Walt's father passed away of a sudden heart attack in Walt's youth. "It was him," she says with sudden conviction. "He's a very strong spirit who can move between both worlds the easiest of all. He was here earlier. He didn't like me at first, but then he left because he figured I was OK."

Walt's father was a medic in World War II, honored by the armed forces for bravery on his battleship. We have a portrait of him on our piano, in his Navy uniform: dark, Irish, movie-star looks. A young cousin, Joseph, said, "Brian?" when he first saw his grandfather's photograph, as the resemblance to our oldest in features and clear gaze is uncanny.

I feel disoriented.

On our way to the car I admonish my daughter, "Don't tell your dreams to strangers!"

THE CONVERSATION IN the dark garage dogs me into the next day, when we are visiting Walt's sister Joan and her family at their brick ranch house overlooking distant orange groves that are like green corduroy from the top of the hill. Joan and Walt's mom and I are in the kitchen. June is like a second mother to me and Joan is one of three sisters (Junie and Jennifer are the others) I never had, so in Latin fashion, I go ahead and interrupt their stories with the tale that is bothering me.

It is noon, hot and sunny, and you can hear the Cochin rooster and chickens down the hill. The birds, all breeds, belong to cousins Bianca, Blaise, and Bede to raise, and they are mailed to the town post office. The rooster crows, and I see steam rising from a big pot of corn set to boil on the center island. Joan is frosting a vast chocolate sheet cake and returning cubes of margarine to the fridge. Her bright, orderly kitchen of maple and white tile is a stark contrast to yesterday's dark garage.

My sister-in-law and mother-in-law listen to my tale of guardians and futures with good humor, and when I'm done, Joan, with her Celtic, Catholic blood, says dismissively: "Some of these people, they just read your mind."

13

9 DE JULIO

*One of the tasks we set for ourselves was to look for and
make contact with FOP families in Argentina, as communication is the best way to face FOP. And after reading about
the hunt for multigenerational FOP families, for DNA
research, we realized that this search was a task we could
carry out in our own country. We found ways to spread
information in popular and medical publications. Sharing
information was a way to help others avoid the long and
difficult process of arriving at a correct diagnosis.*

  *In 2004 we helped Dr. Kaplan find a multigenerational
FOP family in Korea, and a fifteen-year-old girl in Argentina correctly diagnosed herself when she read the first article
that appeared on FOP in one of our national newspapers,
El Clarín.*

—MOIRA LILJESTHRÖM, mother of Manuel, eight,
diagnosed at age four, Buenos Aires, Argentina

I SPARED MYSELF BOTH worry *and* relief by shoving the FOP
guidebook in a sock drawer. But for years I thought I might have
spared my son the first disabling blast of FOP if I had researched the
disease with my usual persistence—and if I hadn't been late picking him up at summer school one afternoon. All we knew in the
summer of 1996 was that trauma was bad, but we had no idea *how
bad* trauma *could be* or *how bad* trauma *had to be* to cause trouble.
Trauma, as we understood from the visiting UCSF specialist early on,
meant something like contact-sport injuries. To be on the safe side,

we put Vincent in a sedentary summer program of science, ceramics, and public speaking. And as the well-intentioned psychologist had advised, we did not tell the school about FOP, so that Vincent wouldn't feel like a victim.

The day of the accident at summer school, I arrived fifteen minutes late. And what played on and off in my head for years thereafter was: *If only I hadn't been organizing the house; if only I weren't chronically late; if only I had read the FOP Guidebook for Families; if only if only if only* . . .

In the third trimester of every pregnancy—except for my first, when I was on bed rest—I've been seized with the so-called nesting instinct. This was going on the fateful day I arrived later than usual at summer school: I was throwing out papers, sorting clothes, tossing toys, dusting books, rearranging closets, sweeping floors, and alphabetizing videos. (In a nonpregnant state I don't care for this kind of thing.) While I was organizing the house, my nine-year-old was hopping across concrete benches on the other side of town.

"He's in the nurse's station," someone said, when my ninth-month belly and I rushed into the summer school office, not having found everyone at the usual pick-up spot. Vincent had just been injured.

"My son's not supposed to get hurt!" I cried to a young woman behind a desk. She must have been thinking, *Well, who is?* She waved me to a tiny side office with a cot, where Vincent sat, looking intact, while a motherly nurse applied Band-Aids to a leg that looked perfectly fine. "Just a little scrape," she said pleasantly.

"You OK?" I asked, hugging my son. Vincent nodded.

"We *saw* him jumping around the benches," said an older secretary at her computer. The office wall was half windows, so she, they, everyone in charge, had had a clear view of the jumping and the falling. And plenty of time to intervene—had anyone been warned ahead of time that trauma was bad, bad, bad. *If only I had used common sense and ignored that psychologist's advice* . . . *if only, if only* . . .

But Vincent looked fine, even though he admitted the side of his head hurt a little from hitting it on the bench. I checked for swellings, saw none under his short brown hair, and rounded up my other kids to drop them off at a friend's for swimming. An hour later my friend, a nurse, called to say, "Vincent just threw up—and he says he has a headache."

"It's a concussion," said our pediatrician in the little room with a long mirror over the examining table, colorful stickers on the walls and a bin of toys under the baby scale. "Keep an eye on it, wake him at intervals, and make sure he doesn't start talking about pink elephants." This was young redheaded Dr. Sumrell, our new beloved pediatrician alternating with Dr. Weinberg. We chose him when Dr. Weinberg retired because Dr. Sumrell shares the same diagnostic insight, generosity, and calming manner. (Dr. Sumrell has been our rock all these years.)

Four kids, twelve years concussion free—until now—and the kid who isn't supposed to have any trauma at all gets a concussion.

To keep Vincent's records up-to-date, I called Dr. Kaplan, who had confirmed the diagnosis back in January. I had never actually spoken to Dr. Kaplan, as I was following my rule of having only Walt think about FOP until I safely gave birth.

My first conversation with Dr. Kaplan was very different from any I've had with him since. On a regular basis, Vincent's University of Pennsylvania specialist quells my fears with medical advice, humorous anecdotes, and news from the lab. But our first exchange was not exactly that.

"He has a *concussion?*" There was so much alarm in Dr. Kaplan's tone I thought I heard his voice crack.

I could feel my vast belly stiffen. At least if I went into labor it wouldn't be premature, since the baby was due any day.

"FOP kids can respond differently to head trauma," Dr. Kaplan was explaining. His voice was young and pleasant—and urgent. Even so, he was trying to calm me down and relay medical information at the same time, two things at odds with each other just then, and in competition with a baby elbowing my insides. It helped to write everything on my palm: FOP children—nobody knew this—could be more susceptible to ruptured blood vessels at the site of the injury: hemorrhage. *Dear Lord.*

I called our pediatrician, who immediately ordered a CT scan.

Walt rushed home from work, drove Vincent to Children's. I took a walk around the neighborhood, hanging on to my rosary with one hand and my belly with the other. It was infernally hot, but I don't remember feeling much, and I walked and walked and prayed. When Walt's little white car rounded the corner, I was right at the entrance to our neighborhood.

"He's *fine*," called Walt, rolling down his window. Vincent was in the backseat, looking fine. The CT scan was normal. *Thank God.* We rented a stack of videos and Nintendo games. Everything would be OK.

But everything was not OK a few weeks later. A few weeks later FOP would never again be an abstract. And though with such a rare, mysterious disease, it is possible FOP appeared for no reason, out of the blue—after a year of quiescence—it is also *possible*—"though probably not," said Dr. Kaplan—that the concussion triggered that first major flare-up of 1996, right after Isabel was born.

If only I had warned the summer school about FOP played and replayed the tape in my head for years after. These days we are so scrupulous spelling out FOP, in letters and pamphlets, with lists and restrictions and updates, wherever Vincent goes. If I had known in July 1996 what it seemed I found out the hard way, our son would not have been jumping across benches, there would have been no concussion, no flare-up, no heartbreaking loss of mobility. *Maybe.* With FOP we learned, however, that lumps and bumps do not necessarily spring from the site of trauma. And the flare-up on the heels of a concussion *could* have been a coincidence, I know that. But whatever caused or didn't cause that first terrible blast of the disease—*which can be triggered by trauma, by no trauma, or remain quiescent, trauma or no*—I finally understand (and it has taken me years to realize) that it makes no difference *what* triggered FOP. The flare-up was—I do believe—somehow inevitable, on some level, part of an inexplicable order, like Isabel's birth, which marked the end of FOP's yearlong truce and blunted its impact in the months to come.

It continues to amaze me that I have been pregnant and given birth five times, especially after my first baby came with premature labor, bed rest, toxemia, and the crash C-section. "You have such difficult pregnancies," scolded a nurse midwife at my Santa Monica medical group, even though she had just suffered through my first child's gestation. The pregnancies improved, but the labors were, all of them, unnaturally long and hellish. Isabel's arrival in 1996 was no exception, though that labor was streamlined to thirty-six hours with Pitocin, which acts like a hormonal pitting device. "Are all your babies this stubborn?" asked my Fresno obstetrician, Dr. Peters, patient, wonderful man who wound up waiting it out for three of our kids. "You're not setting any speed records," said Dr. Baldwin, my uncle-doctor, who brought Vincent into the world and sent me out to walk around Stanford's shopping center during labor. That was where I made clerks and cars wait for a contraction to pass so I could let go of a credit card or finish out a crosswalk. In Fresno, I didn't get to shop through labor, but I was given something called Stadol. Stadol made my belly, my baby, and the doctor seem very far away, off in another hospital. "I must be in a lot of pain right now," I would say breezily to nurses, while Dr. Peters rearranged the baby or my insides.

The night of Isabel's birth, Argentina's Independence Day, brought jubilation and relief. After she arrived, siblings and grandparents stood in a reverent semicircle in a room with country decor and a wooden rocking chair. The boys ate all the fries a nurse brought in to me on a tray. But I wasn't hungry: we had just been given our fifth miracle, a joy that would sustain us, somehow, through FOP's first real visitation a few weeks later—an unusual "schedule," since FOP stayed away through my pregnancy. (And in swearing off worry to protect the pregnancy, taking walks instead with my rosary, I think I began accepting FOP through a process that evaded conscious thought.)

During the year of FOP's first appearance, I befriended the father of one of the children in Celine's class. This father was in a wheelchair because he had dived into a shallow river when he was a teenager and lost most of his mobility; he was able to maneuver himself only with the side control switches of his chair. I remember watching him speed through the neighborhood, his small son riding shotgun on the wheelchair; they both looked so free and joyous in this routine. The days he and I went for walks around the preschool, I wanted to bring up the subject of disability, but was nervous about offending in some way. We talked about kids and political personalities and current events and the book he was writing. He also believed in coincidences as little traffic signs from an order we couldn't see. One day I gathered the courage to ask him how he had coped with his catastrophic loss of mobility, if he had been angry at God, enraged, depressed.

My friend thought for a moment, almost as if the question had never been put to him, and his answer surprised me: "Not really," he said, and his face was so untroubled and his voice so clear that I found his answer both believable and unbelievable.

I can only say that this phenomenal man had an extraordinary outlook, and it is possible his journey and nature were different in every way from mine or Vincent's, or that his life circumstances were such that he was able to accept his cross without the torture many of us feel through far lesser difficulties. It is equally possible that he did not want to share these past agonies with me, the mother of a boy with a disorder such as Vincent's—or with anyone else. He had moved on—in every way—from the point where he had lost his motion, and it served no purpose to go back. But I will never forget feeling hopeful over his answer, that this man who could move so little of his body could have given me such an answer with such honesty and peace in eyes the color of the sky.

AT THE AGE of ten, Vincent raged against the FOP, the pain, the sleepless nights, the sudden limitations, and when he was left stranded at home while a neighbor and his brother went off on two-wheelers, he sat miserably on the stairs, saying, "Why *me?*" *Why you, indeed, precious child?* There can be few greater sorrows than for a parent to stand by powerless as a child asks this reasonable question. I had no reasonable answer. And thinking back on the friend in the electric wheelchair, limited mostly to the movement in his arms, I realized two things. One was that the acceptance of a catastrophe that occurred in increments had to be very different from the acceptance of a disaster that happened all at once and was "over with." How could you accept both what was happening and what might happen—or not—at the same time? You couldn't, could you? Maybe the friend had blocked out his own youthful *why me's*, maybe not; everyone has his or her own individual program for coping with loss, just as every *body* has its own healing schedules. The second thing was that I began to see, on alternate days, in my own son, some sort of emotional "anesthesia" blocking out the brutal threat of FOP. Though pain and frustration led to sadness and outbursts of anger, even withdrawal, in all of us, in some form or another, *these came and went relatively quickly*. Most of the time Vincent seemed to begin to want to ignore the FOP, to not talk about it—though of course, I worried that this was not so good, either. We saw a child psychologist to help him and us articulate our pain, and she said one day: "Denial is underrated." There was nothing wrong with ignoring FOP judiciously. And she noted how we all went up and down in this journey to acceptance, back and forth, until one day we said, "OK, this is my life," and went on to move forward. I think that maybe Vincent got to that point much sooner than I did. In any event, I have heard from FOP adults that FOP is, in some ways, harder on parents than it is on the children. And again, I remember the untroubled look on the face of the father in the wheelchair, and that gave me peace—*and it continues to do so*.

At the onset of FOP's devastation, Vincent asked, "Why did I get FOP instead of Brian? He's the oldest." I suppose his nine-year-old logic was that the oldest got everything first. The only answer I had was, and still is: *I don't know why you got it at all, my beloved son*. I could only say with certainty how sad and mad it all made me, too, and that it was OK to be sad and mad. I even gave him magazines to rip up, as a friend whose son has diabetes had done for her boy. But I didn't know if what I was saying or doing was right or not, and it all felt like one of those dreams where you arrive at school in your pajamas for a test you foolishly take even though you haven't studied, or a recurring nightmare I've had since high school drama:

I'm onstage in front of an audience and I don't know my lines, who I'm supposed to be, or what play I'm in. (I must add that I later found direction from adult friends with FOP.)

Right after Isabel was safely born, her demands—along with the needs of four other kids—kept me so busy and tired I didn't have much time to wring my hands over FOP. Our fifth child was a happy little soul, seemingly unaffected by FOP's first visitation. She was content to be passed from lap to lap, even though I held on to her most of the time—and this was how she turned into our only nursing baby who refused any type of bottle. I could never leave the house for long because she got enraged with any hapless family member trying to trick her with latex. But my father, the engineer, hit on a system: someone would install Isabel in a mechanical baby swing. For some reason, she wouldn't rock back and forth and cry for food at the same time, so my mother called our method "the swing diet." I would come home from teaching a night class to see Isabel rocking back and forth pacifically, her fat little feet tracing an arc in the air, her brothers right there, doing homework at the kitchen table, my father and Celine watching *Telemundo*.

One thing I knew to do after Isabel's birth in July 1996 was to give detailed instructions regarding FOP precautions for Vincent, since he was no longer just a kid with a limp: he was a kid with restrictions in his right arm, and we had to keep the rest of him intact. I remember that Friday in fifth grade, when Vincent was an altar server at a Friday Mass. He wore the long white robes, a belt of thick rope around his waist, and he sat on one side of a makeshift altar in the parish hall. Father Ray, the pastor, asked a rhetorical question during his sermon, and Vincent raised a hand along with everyone else. It hit me that day that he was signaling with his left arm because he couldn't raise his right hand. And I remembered he had said he might like to become a priest someday and asked, matter-of-factly, "But what if I can't open my arms for the Consecration?" My ten-year-old seemed concerned, mainly, that he might not meet one of the job requirements. *You will, Vincent, you will*, I answered, knowing in my soul that God would see this boy's arms span the width of a cathedral.

A few years later, one summer school made a singular effort to keep Vincent protected. Whenever he began a new summer program, we had to start all over again with FOP information—articles, pamphlets, letters—for teachers and principals. When Vincent was twelve, we signed him up for a quarter of magic, Italian, and rocketry. Vincent and Lucas, ten at the time, took the classes together, and it was Lucas who mentioned the brewing trouble:

"There's this kid in magic class, and he keeps bugging us," said Lucas. We were standing in the door of a ceramics class, waiting for Celine and watching a teacher scrape clay off a silver wheel.

"What does that mean, exactly?" I said. I could see Isabel was restless in the umbrella stroller, trying to walk with it on her back like a shell.

"He calls us names and stuff," said Lucas.

" 'Stuff'?"

"Today he was throwing rubber bands at us," said Vincent. "And his friends were doing it, too." Isabel was still trying to stroller-walk.

"Anything else?" Isabel had gotten herself released from the stroller and was standing reverently by a table of figurines, with Celine holding her hand.

"Sometimes they throw paper clips," added Lucas.

In response, the teacher could only face the class and call out, "Stop."

That does it.

"And he's older, and he wears, like, chains," said Lucas.

That does it even more. The kid and his gang could start getting physical. Time to contact the principal again.

I rolled Isabel in her umbrella stroller over to the summer school office the next day, wound through corridors, and met the principal, a middle-aged man with a gray mustache who knew me from my calls and letters and listened carefully to my complaint.

"Can you kick them out, please?" I concluded.

The principal sighed. "We can't do that." *What? Why can't they?* There's no law that says people have to go to summer school.

The principal explained he could not kick kids out, for some reason I found unreasonable. "But we can do something else," he said.

Some ineffectual bureaucratic gesture, no doubt. I started to calculate moving the boys to a safer class, one more hour of rocketry maybe.

"We'll put an aide in there," said the principal.

I'd seen aides: somebody's grandmother or a friendly college girl, powerless against teenage boys.

"OK," I said lamely. "Thank you." Isabel looked up at me, with her beautiful brown eyes and Shirley Temple curls. *You lost,* said her little face. I could always pull my sons out of magic.

The next day at my punctual summer school pick-up, Vincent announced: "We got a teacher's aide in magic."

"Oh?" I didn't want to let on that it was my doing. Vincent was already getting weary of my interventions.

This aide, I was told, had instantly kept the dangerous kids in line, and not a single rubber band or paper clip was set off that morning. *Good work, Mom.*

"He's pretty tall," said Vincent.

He? I hadn't pictured a male version of a teacher's aide. Well, this was a good idea, something like an FOP bodyguard.

"When those guys were acting up, he said, 'You're laughin' now, little brother, but I'll be the one laughin' if you end up in the Big House.'" Lucas made him sound like a cowboy.

The Big House, in this context, I learned, also meant the slammer, the joint, jail, prison. A new kind of child psychology seemed to be in effect.

"He's an ex-con!" said Lucas, in the same tone any other ten-year-old might use to say *astronaut* or *secret agent.*

I was pulling out into traffic and checked both my sons in the rearview mirror. They couldn't be happier. *But what had I done? I had gotten the principal to install a criminal, maybe even a convicted felon, in my children's magic class.*

Surely the man hadn't been guilty of murder—or worse. "Do you know why he was in prison?" I kept my voice nonchalant.

The boys shrugged. "Mom! You worry too much! He's a good

guy!" I could see the wheels turning in their heads: *That's the last time we tell her anything.* "And he's keeping those other kids in line!"

Keeping the other kids in line was key. Even so.

I let a week go by, meaning to ask the principal about the teacher's aide's credentials. Every day that week, the boys got in the car happy to recount his tales about the Big House. The teacher's aide had even started in on some ghost stories, something about noises at an aunt's, a haunting, and about how you never want to mess with a Ouija board. As it turned out, he had served time for drugs, but had been scared straight at the Big House. And from all accounts, the kids with chains and paper clips and rubber bands had been completely neutralized.

"They don't want to end up in prison," explained Lucas.

"Aren't you learning any magic in that class?"

"Card tricks," said Vincent.

I wanted to visualize this teacher's aide as another *Shawshank Redemption* inmate, a guy, who—if it turned out he hadn't been falsely accused—had the excuse of being raised by a distant relative in a haunted house, with a Ouija board telling him to make some bad choices in life. But he was doing his best to rehabilitate himself, setting youths straight on drugs and the Big House and protecting a boy with a rare disorder. *On the other hand . . .*

One day after a rocket demonstration, the boys pointed their magic aide out to me proudly. He was on the other side of the corridor, a mountain of a man, towering over a group of students keeping a respectful distance. He had a no-nonsense voice, and it sounded like he was reprimanding a couple of boys for something they had said or done. The man had a regal presence, and it was clear nobody would dare defy authority on his watch. He looked like the best bodyguard in the world.

The last week of summer school, I rolled Isabel in her umbrella stroller back through the corridors of the campus's office to give the principal another article on FOP. "Are things going better in magic?" he asked.

"Yes! Yes, they are, thank you," I told him.

"You know," he said, looking thoughtful. "I've noticed it's good to place certain aides with certain classes."

Amen.

(Two days before finishing this book, I found myself at the summer school site where Vincent fell before we told the world about FOP. I was there for Celine's basketball team, and it had been years since we had gone back. The concrete benches were smaller than I remembered, and seeing them gave me a pang. I started to fall back into what-ifs—but just then, my cell phone stopped me. "Mom?" It was Vincent, calling from college. "I got 114 points on my biology midterm!" I heard myself give a whoop so jubilant, it echoed off the benches and filled the empty school.)

APRIL–JULY 2004

VINCENT IS AT a California Scholarship Federation Life Membership banquet, where students are awarded gold pins and announced individually on a little stage. For Vincent's student memento display we have brought plaques and certificates, photographs of proms and band, where Vincent stands with his silver trumpet, wearing the blue and red marching band uniform with gold brocade and a tall red hat with a white plume. In the box we include Berkeley's letter of acceptance, which is lavish, constructed as a gateway, glossy blue with the Campanile in silhouette. Gold letters read: "Welcome to/ University of California/Berkeley." When you open the card-stock "gates" there is a crackling sound from Velcro. Inside is a Sather Tower sunset, the university seal, and the letter, which says:

University of California
Berkeley

This is what you've been waiting for, the good news. You've been admitted to Berkeley. The sound you hear is the world opening up at your feet. It's the sound of

*ideas popping. Of every language, every point of view.
Of conga drums, carillons, and a thousand things you've
never known before. There truly is no place like Berkeley.
Anywhere. And you've earned a place here. We think you
can take this excitement and make it your own. Take the
world's ideas and forge new ones.*

*Learn. Imagine. Experiment. Create. Change the
world.*

We congratulate you, Vincent Patrick Whelan. *
You can do it and you can do it here.*

We know you can.

Please join us at Berkeley.

If Vincent doesn't pick Berkeley, *I'm signing up.*

At the CSF event, Vincent and I prop up the gates from Berkeley
with his other letters of acceptance. He still has not told us which
school he wants, and we are staying out of it. So when CSF students
go up one by one to receive their awards and announce their college,
I suppose we will find out.

The evening has speeches and a little talent show and bright
young adults I can still see bounding out of Room 1 with missing front
teeth and soggy shoelaces. I watch the proceedings with an ache of
pride as Vincent crosses the stage to hold one side of a trophy with
his friend Jared on the other side. And when it is his turn to take the
podium, Walt, Peter's parents, Vincent's science teacher, Mrs. Carter,
and I ignore our Cornish hens on fine china and sit suspended over
white linen waiting to see which college he will name.

On a screen behind the podium is a slide show for each student.
We see Vincent's image as a little boy, with all the grandparents; as
a round-faced infant extending his arms like a little pope; then fifth
grader Vincent with Peter, fists triumphant over a science project;
then my high school son, tall and handsome in a black tux with
his friends. My eyes are stinging.

Vincent leans soberly into the mike. "I'm going to be attending UC Berkeley in the fall," he says. The audience applauds and

Vincent steps down. Walt and I look at each other. I rub a finger under each of my eyes.

Now I can stop grinding my teeth.

)

VINCENT'S GRADUATION IS here, and so is all the family: grandparents, aunts, uncles, cousins saving seats in a long row at the Saroyan. We watch our 2004 graduate, tall and serious, in his royal blue robe and mortarboard, seat himself at a grand piano upstage—a stage where one of the three tenors, José Carreras, sang once. I feel that ache of gratitude as Vincent begins the opening ragtime notes he's practiced all month behind the French doors. Girls in glossy red togas and boys in shiny blue robes stand on tiers with CLASS OF 2004 on a banner behind them, to chant the senior farewell song as our son plays "You've Got a Friend in Me."

)

IT LOOKS LIKE I stopped grinding my teeth too late. I am at the endodontist's getting checked.

"This is all Stanford's fault," I tell the doctor, a handsome young Armenian with kind eyes. "You can send them the bill." I explain the tooth-grinding process of visiting schools, memorizing office acronyms, and *trying* to stay out of my son's way. All of it—including the tooth grinding—could have been avoided with a little yes from a certain school.

"So my son is going to Berkeley," I conclude.

The endodontist nods, checks me for pain tolerance, and then stops and puts a hand on my arm. "About your son not getting into Stanford," he says. "There's a reason."

I try to sit up and pull off the paper bib to listen. The endodontist helps me.

"There is something your son will find at Berkeley, doors that will open for him there that would not have at Stanford," says the young dentist. "There is a *reason* he should be at Berkeley." Then he goes on to tell me that his life's dream had been to go to UCLA, that he ranked first in his high school class. And UCLA denied him admission. "We appealed, and called, and wrote—everything," he explains, the trace of an old feeling in his eyes. "It got ugly." *Don't I know it.*

"Finally, I gave up," he says and shrugs. "I settled for another college. Lower ranked. But at the smaller school I was able to take all the science classes that were impacted—filled to capacity—at UCLA. And I was the youngest to graduate in my program, with the highest recommendations."

He does look young. "How old are you, fourteen?" He smiles with his perfect teeth. Doors have opened; he has developed a well-known endodontic device, good things have happened, great things that would not have unfolded as they unfolded had he made it into his dream school.

"Everything happens for a reason," he tells me.

I AM DRIVING along a country thoroughfare, past vineyards and almond orchards on a hot July morning, and I pass a sign on a farm that says FREE HORSE MANURE. This sign reminds me that today the bulls are running in Pamplona, and Brian and his friends Tony and Justin are in Spain, probably racing the animals through cobblestone streets. They are wearing white, with red bandannas knotted to one side. *I won't think about Brian running with the bulls. I won't. I won't think about "the craziest experience of all time," as he calls it.*

Maybe to equalize the universe, maybe because one son must never have trauma, another was born to defy it in gyms, parachuting from planes, barreling down the autobahn, and running with bulls. One son needs to navigate the world with supreme caution, while the other needs to take one leap of faith after another. *And both are equally brave.*

Maybe the pilots flying a single-engine Cessna around the world this month in a "Flight for a Cure" for FOP will look down to see Brian taking a bull by the horns and call out the side of their plane, *Your mother is a little worried . . .* I have just translated a press release for these pilots. This type of international publicity is

especially important, a fact driven home when I learn this month
that a fifteen-year-old in Buenos Aires diagnosed herself with FOP
after showing the first FOP article in a national Argentine paper
to her doctors.

These days I walk around feeling like I must keep from getting
jostled as we ready for the college departure, looking into medical
scooters, seeing an occupational therapist, finding an audiologist,
filling prescriptions. I can't fathom my son's leaving, and struggle
with a sinking sensation when I think of his soon-to-be Independence Day.

Of his own accord, Vincent has trekked with Celine in the
107-degree heat to a pet store across town to buy a land turtle for
Isabel's eighth birthday. He plans to keep the turtle in his room
tonight and slip it in a terrarium at breakfast. He has also brought
home a copy of *Turtles and Tortoises for Dummies*, confetti-colored
food pellets, and a rock dish for water.

Who will know which secret computer keys to press or which wires to
rewire when Vincent leaves?

)

IT IS JULY 23, 7:30 AM, and I wake with a headache and tooth-
grinding pain again. But none of that matters. I have had the most
redeeming dream of my life, and it is still with me. In the dream
Vincent is four years old, ages before FOP appeared. I see him so
clearly, his round face and soft brown hair and even baby teeth,
the striped shirt he used to wear with green shorts. His little body
is so active, *so free*, running, running, running, arms reaching high
over his head to swing, to grab monkey bars and ladders on slides.
He is smiling, giddy in the way of four-year-olds, and I feel so much
joy in the dream and so does Walt. *What if we can let him move on*
from this age? I say to Walt, because I know—in the dream—that
our son has gone back in time and will return to the present. *We*
have the meds now; we know about trauma, I reason. *We could prevent*
him from losing movement if we let him grow up from now. But even
in dream logic, I consider the confusion of this plan, how Vincent

would be younger than all his siblings and classmates, and what about his best friend, Peter? But then I think, *Who cares? We could win the race against time.*

My dream does not allow a decision because suddenly I am in an elevator, going up or down, I can't say. But none of that matters. What counts is the vision I have had and a glorious sense of redemption nothing can revoke.

)

WE ARE ON rounds to take care of things Vincent will need in preparation for his life away from home. Vincent and his sisters and I are at the PT office, where my friend and colleague from the university, Gary Lentell, has helped us over the years with exercises and experimental shoe inserts and encouragement. I am remembering when the girls sat patiently as we talked on our first visit, how Gary deferred to Vincent, with just the right amount of advising and pulling back. "You have to take ownership," said Gary. Then he asked Vincent to ambulate, noted how well he was walking, and brought out a plastic hip, with the sacrum and the femur attached on stretchy rubber; he showed us how Vincent was moving and how he could improve his motion. That was the first time a PT had given our son a visual aid. Vincent, the scientist, lost the detached, *I'm-not-really-here* look he can get in such facilities. And when Gary demonstrated the "hitchhiker" exercise, thumbs out, and the "drunken-sailor walk," swaying side to side, legs turned out, Vincent smiled.

Today we are here for the occupational therapist, a young woman with a Dutch accent, whom I didn't believe when she mentioned, offhanded, that she had another patient with FOP. "Charis Ramirez?" she says. I tell her how the family found us in *Newsweek.*

We are in a room full of green and yellow rubber balls and blue pads and exercise bicycles. A tiny boy with weak legs is wobbling on a walker toward the queen-size mat-bed. An athletic young man cruises past him and over to us on what looks like a motorized office chair.

"John rode in on one himself," exclaims our OT. John springs up from the conveyance to allow Vincent a seat. "I thought we should try one of these out first," she says.

Vincent was expecting a medical scooter. "Just keep an open mind," says the OT, trying to read his expression. *How many times has Vincent heard that lately?*

I'm not sure I like the contraption myself, but Vincent smiles, bemused at first, rotating the control stick on the armrest, and we all make jokes about being careful and not plowing into people. Isabel and Celine look on before turning to inspect a double rail of bars and bouncing a huge green rubber ball.

"Your insurance company says because he can walk it's not a medical necessity," the OT warns me.

"It will threaten his ability to walk if he doesn't have something to ride!" I protest. This corporate obtuseness keeps happening, it seems, in some form or another. The OT is sympathetic, and gives me a name at California Children's Services. As usual, Dr. Henrickson will write more letters.

We follow Vincent out of the building for a test drive. "Careful," calls the OT at every turn in a narrow hallway. Vincent navigates the Power Chair toward the parking lot, through a waiting room packed with parents standing against walls, children fidgeting, everyone watching us trail out. *It's like a parade*, says someone. *Move, it's a wheelchair coming*, says someone else.

Vincent has staunchly resisted adaptive equipment all these years. Once, during a leg flare-up, a company loaned us a medical scooter for a weekend trial. Vincent rode it up the block discreetly once and left it to his siblings to career around the neighborhood for as long as they liked. When our loyal high school vice principal tried driving a golf cart over to Vincent for rides on rainy days or when he had flare-ups, the boy would disappear around corners.

Vincent takes his test run. We order some adaptive tools from the company, and we drive home in silence. "I'll only ride a scooter," he pronounces, when I prompt.

"Fine," I say, "That's fine." Even though the OT has been repeating, *Keep an open mind*. She pointed out—sensibly—that a medical scooter would be harder on arms than a Power Chair. But the scooter is less hard on Vincent's faith in himself.

"You only need these things to keep you well," I say with energy. "Some people don't have a choice. Vincent, you're going to *Berkeley*! Nobody there cares how anyone else does anything! If you're feeling upset maybe you should—"

"Don't tell me what I'm feeling!" We ride the rest of the way not speaking.

At home Lucas picks up a shiny brochure on the kitchen table. It has photos of carefree grandparents on scooters riding past shops and posing on campuses. "Why is Vincent that way about it?" asks Lucas.

I know why. It's the same reason Walt's indomitable mother, who ran an olive ranch for decades, refused a cane until she had her knee surgery, and why my grandfather, the historian, never wore his hearing aid, preferring instead to be aloof and lofty.

LONG BEFORE FOP surfaced officially in our lives, it caused some mild hearing loss. Our first ear, nose, and throat (ENT) specialist told us a hearing aide was optional for our son; another said he might lose a little more audition over the years, though another specialist dismissed this notion. Yet another ENT warned that if we made no adjustments, the ability to hear words would wear away in the same fashion a lazy eye loses sight, telling Vincent to wear not one but two devices. Finally, Dr. Kaplan, who knows FOP's effect on the ears—and on the whole person—said: *Leave it up to him.* Vincent always preferred to sit in the front of the class anyway to earn his A's. And we left it at that.

But Berkeley will be different, with distant professors and strangers who may not repeat things and crowds that might require radar. And at Berkeley nobody will take any notice of an invisible piece of plastic.

I have made a random appointment with a large audiology center, not the best timing, because I have $125 in my bank account and the place expects half the costs of any device at the first visit. Walt's clients haven't paid him yet, and our insurance will not cover any of these fees, I already know. And California Children's Services, recommended by our OT, can help with nothing because of our income.

Vincent and I are in the audiology center's waiting room, and his name is called before I can pick up a magazine. And who has pronounced his name *out of all the audiologists in town*, but a friend of a friend. After tests in a soundproof booth, she reassures us that Vincent's word recognition is *excellent*, disproving several ENT theories. She shows us an illustration of a device that is virtually invisible, makes an impression, hands us a schedule. She also quotes frightening fees, and I confess we don't have even half of those sums lying around the house today.

As we leave, our audiologist whispers something to the receptionist, who makes our next appointment and then waves us off. We can pay when the device arrives.

"Your guardian angels are on the job," I say to Vincent as he pushes open the glass door for me. He looks back at me, puzzled.

At home we find long cardboard boxes stacked up on the porch swing. When the company that could not find us a scooter failed to order adaptive tools, Vincent located everything on his own via the Internet. The boxes contain a long-handled comb, a device to pull on socks, a mechanical reacher, slip-on running shoes. Years ago, a salesman came to our house to demonstrate similar items, and we bought a few, but they got stashed to oblivion in cupboards and drawers.

Brian returns home from Italy hale and well, if you don't count a long scab over his knee from a motorcycle going sideways in Venice or a scratch along an eyelid from a long story on a Greek bus. Isabel has colored him a homecoming sign in crayon, with rainbows, and I notice the Cal colors scrolling across a computer monitor: Celine has posted WELCOME HOME, BRIAN! in blue and gold.

It turns out it is not Brian running with the bulls in Pamplona I should have been worrying about, but rather Lucas at basketball practice, landing hard in the high school gym hugging his right leg.

MAGIC MOUNTAIN

Dear Carol,

*I hope Vincent's flare-up resolves with just prednisone.
If not, I hope the Zometa drip works. As for whether the
impromptu trip to the beach had anything to do with the
flare-up, I've come to believe that if a flare-up wants to
happen, it finds a way. FOP definitely doesn't care what
we think or want. Sometimes I'll still wonder if a particular
incident or something I did led to a flare-up, but mostly
I think that FOP just has a mind or power of its own. It
might just be coincidental timing. Of course, the reality is
that regardless of what I just said, I tend to be exceptionally
careful. But no matter how careful a person is, things still
happen.*

Hugs,
Sharon

—SHARON KANTANIE, thirty-five, diagnosed
at age three, Brentwood, Tennessee

ONE EVENING AT the dinner table, when he was thirteen and battling a chest-wall flare-up that threatened an arm, Vincent began railing at his earlier days of recess isolation. "They played games I couldn't play," he said, angry at the memory, his face flushed.

This old news was a revelation. I thought we had "fixed" that problem. "What about the adaptive PE games?" I asked. Vincent sat with his straight posture, tensed over a plate of half-finished spaghetti. Normally, while he was on prednisone, his appetite was better.

"They didn't want to play those," he said. I should have known: the novelties of adaptive PE games would eventually be supplanted by old standbys like ball tag or basketball. And Vincent never told us because—I knew this—he didn't want to call attention to himself at school.

"Didn't you ever play?" I asked. There were safe enough games with the rubbery old balls that were always bouncing over the school's wire fence. I was feeling something inside me bounce off-kilter.

"The last time I tried," said Vincent, rueful, "I tripped on the ball and they were all talking behind my back: 'He can't throw it, it takes him too long.' It was like they were glad I tripped and I couldn't play anymore." Who were "they"? *Let me at them.*

"At my school there was a boy who had polio, and he was always doing things with us on the playground," offered Walt. Our other kids ate in silence.

"Yeah, but he could get hit and I couldn't!" said Vincent, rising from his chair and violently slamming the back of it against the table before leaving the room.

We all sat in silence, stunned. "It's the prednisone," I said finally. Prednisone can affect moods—badly. "When he's off it, things will be better."

"Yeah, but he still feels it," said Lucas, who has always shared a room with Vincent. "The difference is the prednisone makes him say it."

Our eleven-year-old son Lucas understood what I still couldn't: that you can adapt and "fix" things for your child, but you can't fix the kids on the playground, and you can't fix certain feelings.

)

IT WAS IN August 1996 that I first met Dr. Fred Kaplan in person at an FOP fund-raiser. Vincent was ten years old and Isabel was a month old. It was in Santa Maria at the Elks Club lodge, and my first impression was of rows and rows of long tables with white linen and, at the head of the hall, Santa Maria dignitaries and the whole Snow family, including Stephanie, a tiny, vivacious blond. I remember Stephanie in a yellow dress, yellow as the sun, matching her hair (and if she wasn't in a yellow dress, then I guess that's just the color I remember her in). Stephanie seemed to dance with energy, with a verve and spark that ignored her stiff little shoulders and limited neck motion.

I remember Dr. Kaplan, poised to speak at the lectern set on the long white table, facing everyone from the front of the hall. He had a Fred Astaire look to him, energetic, eloquent, boyish in his enthusiasm. He thanked the rows and rows of families finishing a tri-tip dinner, and then the lamps were dimmed and the screen behind Dr. Kaplan shone with light for slides in a carousel projector. I watched as well as I could from the sidelines, from the very back, swaying my newborn in her striped baby sling side to side, like a pendulum, so she wouldn't cry, so I wouldn't cry. I wasn't sure if I could stand through the entire slide show. On the screen behind Dr. Kaplan, I saw a little child's back full of lumps; a young girl with her head permanently bowed; a multigenerational FOP family, the father with narrowed shoulders, listing like a tree in a storm, three young children, slightly stiff, the mother the only one standing at ease. I saw less frightening frames of scientific blots and DNA "Xerox" machines that copy the double helixes of our invisible molecules, and trays with tubes and messages in code, white on black, and lovely people in lab coats. I swayed side to side through the procession of images holding onto Isabel—and I stayed through the talk.

After the presentation, I motioned for Dr. Kaplan to join me outdoors, near one of the side entrances to the Elks Club lodge, as the throngs of wonderful, dear, kind people bid on gift baskets and jewelry and a day at the spa so the scientists in the photographs could look for the FOP gene, so they could find a cure for Stephanie, for FOP, for my own flesh and blood. Though I had made it through the slide show without bolting or fainting, I was agitated. I put my newborn's foot in Dr. Kaplan's palm, her soft new foot that had never felt anything hard, and he slid his thumb and forefinger along her baby shrimp toes. I had done that myself, a month back, but would not feel relief until I received official word. "Normal," said Dr. Kaplan. "Nice little feet!" The miniature bones in her big toe were all there. He smiled at the tiny girl in my arms and she smiled back.

And though Jeannie Peeper had reassured me, I also asked Dr. Kaplan about one of the most disturbing studies I had blocked out of my mind: deafness, baldness, mental retardation? The old studies were based on erroneous data, he told me, dispelling the last shadows of such worry.

And Walt and Dr. Kaplan and I and an infant Isabel met in the dark bar of the Elks Club, at a little table, the sky turning to night outside in Santa Maria and the ocean breezes cooling off what had been a warm, sunny day. And as we talked about whether you could still eat at McDonald's if you had FOP, and which pharmaceutical company was interested in testing a new drug, and how the immune system might be tied to FOP, Isabel obligingly slept. We were able to laugh about whatever struck us as funny with Dr. Kaplan, and the first time we met this Ivy League scientist, it was no different from running unexpectedly into an old friend from high school and finding out you could pick up exactly where you left off. This is the way Dr. Kaplan makes everyone feel.

When we left that FOP fund-raiser in Santa Maria, where, the first time, we had met another family facing the same disorder, I felt the ache of gratitude, something I have felt at every FOP gathering since.

)

IN NOVEMBER 2000, Walt, Vincent, and I traveled to Philadelphia for the Third International Symposium on FOP, planned and conducted by Jeannie Peeper, and indomitable FOP mother Amanda Cali, and their formidable crew. Vincent was fourteen years old, and though he had lived with FOP for five years and was ready to participate in an FOP gathering, we still fretted over his first encounter with those who suffer from advanced cases of his condition. As I stood in our hotel lobby, with its marble floors and distant ceiling, I recognized the children and young adults with FOP. The little ones played nimbly enough, near the elevators, ignoring upper-body stiffness, ignoring hovering hands. A few of the young adults ambled out of sheer effort. Others were frozen in stooped, standing, or sitting postures.

When a faulty gene strikes only one in two million, there are not many people in the world who understand exactly how you feel when you have to both seize the day and ward off disaster on a daily basis. Vincent made friends with an enthusiastic, stiff-shouldered Canadian boy who was also fourteen years old, and who ended every observation with that companionable "eh?" He met a handsome young Australian with a locked jaw who runs his own kennel and who told Vincent about his island's fairy penguins. He saw that the beautiful girl with a southern accent in charge of outings—who lost an arm when her FOP was mistaken for cancer—had a contagious self-confidence. Vincent was inspired by the indomitable leaders of our IFOPA support network, Jeannie Peeper and Sharon Kantanie, women who, with arms crossed and locked, have carried out monumental work in the world despite their physical limitations.

Walt and I began to look past the pain of FOP—something Vincent learned to do long before we could know. We recognized in all those who suffer from FOP the shining grace, the manifest spirit that sets our own son apart. Our communion with those there at the symposium in Philadelphia made up one of those times in my life when I have felt closest to seeing God's face.

I also felt God's hand: I met a small handful of physicians from around the globe who examined children from all over the world, late into the night; I talked to a biologist who had discovered how to convert adult blood cells into various tissue cells; I shook hands with an oncologist from Harvard who had regenerated a child's excised jawbone; I saw a scientist who had sent out an international plea for the rarest of the rare: ten multigenerational FOP families—parents and children with the condition—for vital DNA clues that would dramatically accelerate FOP research. And between scientific sessions, I heard a soprano from the Metropolitan Opera sing rock songs with a teenager locked in a permanent bow. And as I made friends with FOP parents from around the globe and helped translate for families from Argentina, Peru, and Chile, I felt that I was at a still point of this spinning world, at a sacred ground zero of solidarity.

AUGUST 2004

WE ARE IN Santa Maria again, eight years after our first visit, eight years from when I first met Dr. Kaplan. It is still the same small town full of light filtering cleanly over the coastal range and chaparral. We are on our way home after a family beach trip. This time, the annual fund-raiser is in honor of Stephanie Snow, who is now thirteen years old, and another young girl who lives near Santa Maria, fifteen-year-old Cassie Eckart, diagnosed with FOP a few years back.

We decided—last minute—to make our trip to Santa Maria for the fund-raiser, but also to see Dr. Kaplan, who will lecture after the dinner with research updates. Vincent started a hip flare-up at the beach and we need Dr. Kaplan to examine him.

We arrive in Santa Maria for a family barbecue on the eve of the fund-raiser, no hotel booked, operating on the assumption that little Santa Maria is little Santa Maria, not a tourist or business hub. As we exit the freeway, I call the Holiday Inn: booked solid. And no such thing as a Sheraton. So we pull into the Airport Radisson, which is, literally, a hotel airport, with little planes parked outside its rooms. I remember when Dr. Kaplan landed at the airstrip alongside the hotel and examined Vincent in his suite.

We all wait in the van as Walt disappears into the Radisson with my credit card to register. He comes back miffed. No rooms. "Some kind of church convention and a big wedding," he reports.

The front desk helped Walt call another hotel, a new one, with only a single king-sized bed per room, costing a king's ransom. Impossible for all of us.

"How about we just drive around and look?" I say. This is not a good idea, I realize, and the look on Walt's face says as much. We've been on the road for hours.

We decide we must skip the fund-raiser and just head to the barbecue at the Snows' tonight, see Dr. Kaplan, and drive home. I could kick myself for not booking on Expedia.

Everyone in the car is sad, especially Isabel, who loves hotels. And Vincent has been telling his sisters about fund-raisers and prizes, tri-tip and raffles.

"Give me my credit card," I say to my husband. "I'll try." A pleading mother might have better luck than an attorney, I figure. So I find the hotel lobby, an airy, open place with a skylight, ferns, and marble, flanking a restaurant where a man with a guitar is setting up his mike. I wait behind a grandmotherly woman in lilac who looks dressed for a wedding or a church convention. She checks in, pads off cozily to a room with two beds and a key card for which I might plead with her. I say a little prayer under my breath, and—*just in case*—call on whichever spirit it was that graduation party hostess said I had "with me": the nine- or ten-year-old boy with something wrong with his arm. *If you're there, help me get a room*, I add.

The receptionist at the front desk, a young woman with her hair swept back who has just beat my husband, a man who trounces State of California counsel teams in jury trials, looks at me and smiles pleasantly, as if I weren't feeling like an uninvited guest. The first thing it occurs to me to say is, "Has Dr. Fred Kaplan checked in?" She turns to her computer screen and I rattle on: "My son is one of his patients, and we weren't even going to be coming—it's kind of last-minute and—I wanted Dr. Kaplan to examine him. I know you don't have any rooms left, but I was hoping we could—" Sounding desperate, feeling desperate. Vincent is on his second day of prednisone, paying for a walk along the beach.

"You're with the FOP group?" she interrupts.

"Yes?"

"We have a room for you," she says cordially, looking up from her screen. "Are you from Foster City?"

"Fresno." I am tempted to say, *Yes, indeed, Foster City, Fantasyland, France, what you said.* But instead, I admit we don't want to take another FOP family's room.

"Oh, it's OK," she says, as if everything were all set, and all were right in the universe. "They saved a few extra for your group in case of an emergency." Now we can stay for Dr. Kaplan's lecture. Now we can have tri-tip and win prizes. "You're having your fund-raiser tomorrow!" she says, congratulating me. *Blessed little town of Santa Maria.*

I also bless Dr. Fred Kaplan's name. I ask again if he has checked in, but the young woman at the desk doesn't see him in her computer yet.

As I approach our car, I raise my plastic key card like a trophy, and the mood changes from glum to gleeful. Walt is amazed. Sometimes I can exert pressure on reality in ways my attorney can't.

"But Fred Kaplan hasn't checked in yet," I say.

"Maybe he couldn't make it," says Walt. The prospect is a downer, but in any event, we've got a clean, comfortable room.

Tiny, joyous, blond Stephanie and her family have long been joined in their efforts to raise support for a cure by the entire town of Santa Maria: the city has sent the mayor, official dignitaries, and news teams to eleven annual FOP fund-raisers at the Elks Club. Four years ago a Shell gas station manager, Clark Crandall, pledged 1 cent for every gallon to FOP research, battling city hall to hang on to a FILL 'ER UP FOR THE CURE sign. So far, he has raised $117,000—one penny, one gallon at a time. And a few years ago, when Cassie Eckart, freckle faced, clear eyed, and lovely, was diagnosed with FOP, Santa Maria adopted her, too. So now the Snows and Eckarts organize the annual Elks Club FOP dinner and other benefits together, just as other FOP families around the world carry on the desperate effort to fund the quest for a cure at the University of Pennsylvania's FOP Lab.

"Did Fred Kaplan make it?" is practically the first thing I say when we are met at the door by Stephanie's mother, Jennifer, who is lovely, blond, willowy, tireless. Jennifer leads us over the patio to a group in the grassy backyard by a brick barbecue, and there is Dr. Fred Kaplan, who greets us with his inimitable enthusiasm. He beams at Vincent, who is a head taller than his doctor now.

With the crowd of friends and relatives at the Snows, we

are lucky to find space at a table that includes Fred Kaplan and Stephanie's vibrant grandmother, Joann, a snowy-haired Ultimate Mom. Joann tucks my arm under hers and says, "Oh, how I wish you lived closer!"

We scoot and lift folding chairs and make room for us all at a round lawn table, where we set down plates of barbecued chicken and hot dogs and potato salad. I put a hand on Fred Kaplan's arm to say, "Thanks to your Open Sesame name we were able to get a hotel room." I also thank Joann Snow for reserving extra spaces at the Radisson.

Dr. Kaplan—Fred, as everyone now calls him—looks at me with a mix of humor and surprise. "I wish my name worked for *me* like that," he says. "Because I'm staying at the Holiday Inn!"

Joann is regarding me, wide-eyed through her glasses. "We couldn't get *any* rooms at the Radisson! They were all booked for a Pentecostal group and a wedding." She relates a litany of difficulties. "I had to get Fred a room at the Holiday Inn!"

I am probably more wide-eyed than Joann. "Are you sure?" I repeat to her several times. "*Really?*"

And then Fred Kaplan is smiling as he speculates—and he uses *my* expression, the one that came to me after a graduation party psychic said she saw a boy of nine or ten *with me*. "You must have hit some weird *time-space continuum* and gotten a room reserved for *last year*."

Joann is laughing. "Last year, we did book rooms at the Radisson." And last year, Fred Kaplan *did* land at the tiny airport near a suite set up to examine his patients.

We leave the barbecue on the eve of the Eleventh Annual Find a Cure Dinner, where Vincent will later be examined by a world-class specialist at an Elks Club lodge and we will learn about an experimental treatment with something called Zometa.

I discover later that someone else also said a prayer for a room while I was in the hotel lobby waiting in line under a skylight. It was a boy who had something wrong with an arm at ages nine and ten. And he was sitting in a minivan his summer before college in the Radisson Hotel parking lot.

15

SHAPES IN THE CLOUDS

AUGUST 2004

When I was pregnant, I was very panicky about the responsibilities before me, even though I had never yet heard of FOP. A psychologist told me that kids are not as breakable as I feared. She said the words I don't know and I'm sorry will go a long way to smoothing the road. I think that comment and those phrases have saved me. When I can't think of anything positive or hopeful to say to Daniel about something, I say, "I don't know." When I overreact or Daniel complains about FOP, I say, "I'm sorry." Those words have certainly come in handy.

—JERI LICHT, mother of Daniel, ten, diagnosed at age three, New Rochelle, New York

Three years ago, when Isabel was in kindergarten, her popular, veteran teacher with spun-silver hair, gold glasses, and a *Harry Potter* name—Mrs. Snavely—held Careers Week. During that time students heard from a nurse, an artist, a policeman, and a doctor: parents who visited to talk about their jobs. And on Career Day that week, the children were to dress for their chosen future professions. There would be a little girl in surgical greens, a boy firefighter with a red construction-paper helmet, and even a tiny clown, all sitting cross-legged in room K-1. I had done my best to steer Isabel in one of those directions, but her mind was very much set on her career choice: *queen*. "I want to be a queen, like Queen Isabel of Spain," she proclaimed.

I had suggested more realistic choices: astronaut, teacher, even movie star. Celine had picked movie star for her Career Day. But Isabel held firm. So I spent the morning clipping the hem of a pink satin costume Celine had worn a few Halloweens ago, and Isabel searched through her toy box and her Magic Chef kitchen for the *queen hat*, a plastic pink tiara from Target. Leaving for school in her satin robes that morning, she was frustrated as I buckled her into the booster seat, not having found the *queen hat*. But Celine ran up at the last minute with a silver princess cone trimmed with a white feather boa, and Isabel settled for the *cone hat*. "I'll just be a princess," she said, resigned.

Isabel went over some of the reasons I had given her as to why choosing royalty as a profession involved different steps from other careers: "So if I want to be a princess, I have to marry a prince? Is that how you do it?" she asked, a little doubtfully, as I helped her down from the minivan.

"That's pretty much it." But any objections I might have had to this future identity were no longer relevant, because when we arrived at K-1, Mrs. Snavely hugged my daughter and said, very matter-of-factly, "Isabel! So you're a queen!"

From kindergarten to college—as I see it these days—there is not much of a distance. We are preparing with Vincent, trying to steer him in the right direction with instructions and explanations, hoping he'll be seen as he wants to be seen when he gets to school. Like the preparations for Isabel's Career Day, we're getting ready the necessities for a new future, a new identity. And it is not much more complex than Career Day for Isabel was three years ago. And for Vincent, I remember kindergarten as the day before yesterday.

AUGUST 2004

TODAY IS THE day after the Santa Maria fund-raiser and Vincent and I are in the elevator going down to Rheumatology for Vincent's last checkup before college.

"You're late, Vincent!" A nurse in Rheumatology receives us with a pained look. It's my fault.

We are too late to be seen. Rheumatology is backed up and the doctor needs to leave in less time than he has to see patients. *And Dr. Kaplan told us to discuss with Dr. Henrickson the experimental treatment, the Zometa drip—in case Vincent's hip flare-up from the beach doesn't subside.*

The receptionist asks if we can return the next day, but I know I have a conflict, a physical for someone. *This is all my fault.* And then I say through the little glass window, "I feel like crying." And just saying it is enough and suddenly I am crying, right there in the little waiting room with a bin full of toys and the flags-of-the-world wallpaper around the corner.

I've never cried at Children's, not even when Vincent was diagnosed. And there he is sitting next to me, my stoical son. And the receptionist, a Latina with shorn hair and glasses, is studiously ignoring me, and the nurse, one of the best people in the world, is looking pained and busy behind the glass.

I want to punch the hospital walls decorated with the flags of the world, but instead I compose myself, set an appointment for the next day, write a note for our doctor about a drug called Zometa, which is related to the pamidronate we have not tried, but which—unlike pamidronate—can be given in a single intravenous session. I revise my message with little arrows until the note looks like scrap paper. I hand it to our nurse, who looks terribly sad.

I apologize to Vincent in the elevator for making us late, but really I have been crying because he will soon be away on his own without me there to make him late. "It's OK, Mom," says Vincent gently, and he pushes on the "1" button so it lights up and takes us where we are supposed to go.

)

It is a week later, and I am at Children's—again—wandering down a hall, lost. Vincent's last appointment before college with Dr. Henrickson is long gone—last week. Dr. Henrickson listened intently to our news about the experimental Zometa use, and we plotted its infusion for later, if needed. As usual, Dr. Henrickson will be Vincent's champion with hospital boards, pharmacies, and insurance coverage. Vincent was pronounced well, though with a little more restriction in the left leg, but we are hoping this is temporary, as it can be with FOP. "Good luck at Berkeley," Dr. Henrickson says to my son with pride and affection.

But today I am not at Children's for Vincent.

"I'm looking for my daughter," I say to a man in greens with a white mustache coming toward me in the hall. "She's having an X-ray."

"Do you know her name?" he asks cordially.

"Yes, I named her. She's my daughter: Celine." If I weren't so frazzled, I would find all this amusing, but I'm feeling haggard, so I wonder if the man in greens thinks I look too old to be the mother of someone in a children's hospital. (At least the guard at Security shot a glance at my legs.)

The man in greens motions me to an X-ray room, where I spy Celine standing against a long white pane. A nurse emerges. "We have to take it again," she says brightly. I hand the nurse a T-shirt I have brought for my daughter.

Now I'm getting nervous. Celine is only having a scoliosis series scan, but just waiting blithely goes against my grain. (Walt wants my theme song to be Stevie Wonder's "Don't You Worry 'Bout a Thing.") Last week, at a routine physical, our pediatrician had her touch her toes, and he and I both noticed something different in the curve of her back.

"It must have been kind of bad," says Celine after she has changed into her T-shirt and handed me the patterned gown with the little white ties. "Because the nurses didn't say anything."

"That's no way to tell." This is very true. I should know.

But as with Isabel's broken arm last summer, I don't need an X-ray to tell me what I see.

"Don't worry," I say—to both of us—as we join Walt, who has come in from his office and is in the waiting room filled with Mexican families giving each other moral support. Walt doesn't look worried at all. He's making marks on a yellow legal pad, and he looks just fine, so handsome in one of his dark suits, which I've always thought of as a sort of upholstery for the world. There is a solid, furniture-y quality about suits. Pablo Neruda has verses against suits, but if I were someone wrongfully terminated, I wouldn't want anyone but Walt in a suit between me and the void. *Things will work out, they always do,* Walt is always saying, and that sounds especially true when he says it in a suit.

But back in the car, as Celine and I drive away together, I can't help feeling that itch of maternal guilt: "You'd think I'd have noticed this at the pool, or when we took the X-ray when you broke your arm."

We are passing the peach-and-turquoise castle rising on our right, with farmland and nut orchards to our left. Celine looks at me with her sea-colored eyes and says, "Mom. Everything happens for a reason."

)

This is a strange month, a strange week. I am taking a left when I should be taking a right in a vast orthopedics complex, a building full of marble and stone tile and two-toned woods and X-ray rooms and rooms for surgeries and rooms for physical therapy and for braces and crutches. I am here for Lucas, who is in an MRI tunnel room getting his right knee scanned. This is the knee slammed at basketball.

I haven't been near an MRI in nine years. This time, I do not sit in a corner by a white tunnel, but down a hall, and this time—and this is good—I know what it is we are looking for.

We are in a room with a floor-to-ceiling window and an adult-size examining table. There is a knock, and in comes Lucas's young doctor, who looks like a football player with a *lost the game* look to his handsome face. He pulls the familiar dark acrylic from an oversize manila envelope, sets it up on the lighted panel.

"Here's a tear in the anterior cruciate ligament, the ACL," he says, tracing with a finger what is, to me, an invisible problem on the MRI's shadows. I've never heard *that* acronym. Lucas's face falls.

He knows, the orthopedist knows—I don't know, though—that this means no basketball for a year. This is a great blow to a fifteen-year-old athlete. Walt's face also falls, and Lucas presses his fingers to his eyes.

The doctor takes a plastic model of a knee with rubber bands for ligaments, manipulates it, and shows us what has snapped. "We can reconstruct the ACL with Lucas's own hamstring or with cadaver tissue," he explains. Both options sound equally appalling.

Lucas is scheduled for orthopedic surgery in September. At any rate, this is *fixable*.

I thought the only orthopedic ill in the world was FOP.

Brian gives Lucas a pep talk from Berkeley. "He said, 'Don't feel sorry for yourself,'" Lucas tells me. "And 'Don't be mad.' He says *he* wasn't mad when he got his jaw broken. He sure *looked* mad!"

On this same day I get a call from Children's Physical Therapy for Vincent. "Your child has an appointment on August twenty-sixth," says the receptionist amiably.

"Too late!" I tell her. "My *child* will be off in college." Something inside me tears like Lucas's anterior cruciate ligament. I give the poor receptionist a list of wrongdoings. It is not her fault that none of the adaptive devices my son chose will not make it here before he leaves for his new life. It is not her fault that nobody bothered telling us the medical scooter he picked is in a factory on another planet. It is not her fault that Vincent is my *child* in her office, but not in his new school, where parents are allowed no commerce unless he signs a legal waiver. It is not her fault that life will change drastically when he crosses a threshold that is invisible and abstract with a schedule and an address.

It is when you're grappling with big things that you can lose all control of little things, which, in turn, become big things, so this happens:

Celine has been asking for earrings for years, and the request has formed a point of contention between her Latin mother and her Irish father. If babies can be born with their ears pierced in Argentina and

Mexico, I see no reason why—right now, precisely—I can't distract my daughter from scoliosis with a pair of baubles.

We go to the mall, to a little boutique, with walls of fake silver and gold accessories. I sign a form and a young woman uses something like a staple gun to get costume jewelry through my daughter's earlobes. Celine wears two gold studs and I think she looks very Latin.

Walt, on the other hand, looks very furious. "I know it's cultural!" he says. "But you knew how I felt!" We argue, go around in circles, and slam doors, and I decide to be mad about this for a long, long time, months, years, forever, if necessary.

I am trying hard to read the silver linings, the lessons, the shapes in the clouds, the signs. But I can't anymore. The lessons seem invented—by me. I wonder if I've finally arrived at my breaking point. I wonder if others wonder, too. I find myself nattering on about Zometa and FOP and autografts and scoliosis until I see alarm flit over people's faces and they start to look as if I'm missing a front tooth or have a tic, but don't want to let on that they've noticed.

On day two of the earring war, after running errands, I arrive home to find Vincent making corn muffins. He puts his long fingers up to the right side of his chest and says, "It hurts here." This is the muscle connected to the arm.

Uh-oh.

He is still on prednisone, on it for over a week, and there is nothing more to be done but move on to the experimental IV drip if this doesn't go away. "Ice it," I say, and take off for the pharmacy, because we have run out of the meds we always have on hand.

I reach our pharmacy drive-thru. *Closed.* I sit in my car at its darkened window and think. No matter how much medicine we try, I know one of the discoveries since the diagnosis is that FOP is tied to the immune system. And I don't need a scientist to tell me emotion affects immunity. Of course, you can't help it with so much of this, but there is *something I can help*, for just today, at least . . .

I find a twenty-four-hour pharmacy. I buy more ice packs, the kind you smash to activate—for dorm use. I pick up Chinese takeout and make a decision: when I walk through our front door, I won't act happy, but I won't seethe.

How can you carry on a cold war over earrings?

And pretty soon we're all watching the Olympics, leaning forward as Michael Phelps launches into his blue lanes and the Hamm brothers make iron crosses. And we are taking bets and laughing, and Walt is bringing me a mug full of chocolate Dreyer's.

Why should I stay angry at the man who is my best friend, the love of my life—over earrings—when my son lies stiffly on a sofa with ice on his chest? I think that maybe laughter and peace might help fight FOP as well as anything I can get from the pharmacy.

FOP interrupted my plans to stay angry for the rest of my life.

"YOU'LL BE ABLE to hear the wind, the rustling of a newspaper, your fork on china," says our audiologist. "Sounds you might have forgotten, things that could distract you until they become routine."

Lucas, Celine, and Isabel appear at the office door, smiling craftily, trying to discern a device invisible enough to confound the nurse who will try to take Vincent's temperature in his ear this week.

Our audiologist has the siblings make noise, has me talk. She adjusts invisible waves of sound receptors, all via computer. Vincent is done getting ready for vast lecture halls and crowded sidewalks, and we thank this lovely person who has helped him prepare for life away at college.

We are back in the lobby, collecting forms to fill, and Vincent is like someone caught up in a first pair of glasses. Circling him, Lucas paces and stops, head down, in profile, like in the cell phone commercials. "Can you hear me now?" he asks. "Good." A man signing in at the receptionist desk guffaws.

This is a happy day, even as Vincent is still struggling with another cocktail of meds. At lunch I ask how he is feeling.

"Drugged," he says, looking groggy.

Lucas puts down his burrito, extends his reach across the table to

SHAPES IN THE CLOUDS

shake his brother's hand. "Congratulations! Acknowledgment is the first step on your road to recovery!" Vincent breaks into a laugh.

We still have no medical scooter. I grab the Yellow Pages, pick randomly, and dial. "We just happened to get a really nice one in," the owner tells me. Vincent and I make a trek in the heat down Clovis Avenue, past the old winery, over to a place called The Wheelchair Connection. We enter the neat, air-conditioned store with all manner of conveyances in rows, and there it is: an Elite XL, the *exact same scooter* Vincent wanted that was unavailable. This one is candy-apple red, fresh out of the box. And the owner, a former basketball coach, confirms that our insurance will cover it. *A miracle!* (Now, Children's PT gives business to The Wheelchair Connection. "You started a trend," our OT tells us.)

The new scooter, ready to go, just parked in our dining room, drives home the fact that Vincent will be moving on. I hear him on the piano, through the glass French doors. "Time to Say Good-bye" is what he plays.

How will it be when he leaves?

THE U-HAUL IS in our driveway with the red scooter and a knockoff Tempur-Pedic mattress in its plastic sleeve. Before we signed for it, I grilled the salesman on the bed's safety features, and Walt translated: "What she wants to know is, will it protect him from meteors?"

My father raises his camera and takes a snapshot of us all by the big orange truck. I will have puffy eyes in this picture, but today is a happy day, a glorious day.

It is still a glorious day when we arrive in Berkeley on an unseasonably warm afternoon, the San Francisco Bay flashing—we can see it from the front steps of Clark Kerr. Parents and students are pushing carts laden with boxes and bags and heaped with clothes. We find a stray metal conveyance to load and rattle past the Spanish courtyard and its fountain, where parent boosters welcome us from a little tent, with pamphlets and CAL PARENT pins. We move

down drab hallways to a big brown door with names tacked on in
little signs: Vincent, Travis, Tom.

"Wow!" I have to say as Vincent's key lets us into a big, sunny
suite with its own living room and kitchen. The bathroom even has
a tub, and down the hall is Vincent's single room with two windows.
I have never seen such luxury and space in a dorm. *Thank you,
Edward Malone, for giving me your card on Cal Day.*

Bags and boxes on couches and the little kitchen table tell us
the other roommates have come and gone. But while Brian and
Walt shoulder a mattress down the hallway, we meet Tom, a polite,
wiry kid with brown hair and an earring. His family trails him,
greets us cordially, and we go through parallel rituals, hanging up
clothes, filling drawers, pulling printers out of boxes. It is so warm
in Vincent's little room, I try to push open the old windows overlooking a construction site, but they are sealed shut. There is noise
and dust from below, even today, as tractors and men move debris
to quake-proof the cafeteria.

I hope we will not leave without meeting Vincent's other roommate. From his doorway, I have spied a photograph on his desk. It
is a portrait of an Asian boy with his arm around a girl with long,
fair hair. "You're going to be friends," I say to Vincent.

"How do you know?" There is something to the picture.

We hear a new voice in the suite and it belongs to a woman
introducing herself and her son in the next room, chatting, laughing. "I'm Geri Wong," we hear.

Geri, lovely and petite, resembles the fair-haired girl in the picture in the next room, and Travis is an earnest, nice-looking kid
with dark hair and glasses. He will major in science and math, and
played trumpet in his high school band, he tells us. At this, my son
brings out the blue instrument case from his new closet.

"How'd you get in the capped science classes?" asks Travis,
examining the silver trumpet appreciatively.

I seize this chance: "It's because of a disability. You get to sign
up first." For nine years FOP has trained me to inform. Now it will
be Vincent's turn, but I am in transition—as much as he is.

Most people would just nod politely, but Geri Wong asks, as if prompted by God, "What is your disability, so we can help?"

"Fibrodysplasia ossificans progressiva," says Vincent. Of course, Travis and his mother have never heard of it, and this is not the moment for scientific explanations.

"He can't have trauma," is all I say. "So no fistfights!" I tell Travis, who, with his math-and-science air, seems most unlikely to start hitting people. Geri laughs. I like her.

We say our good-byes, and Vincent follows us to the U-Haul yawning open at the end of his dorm's hallway. We are late in returning it. Brian is late for a reunion at Bowles.

But as I climb into the car we drove behind the U-Haul, and start to pull a seat belt across me, I feel uneasy, like when you aren't sure if you left the house with the oven on. The dorm and the university have all the FOP information, but will my son take up this baton overnight? "He's at the age where he can tell people about it himself," says Walt. He's right.

Is seventeen that age?

I have to do this—one last time—and if I'm not doing this for Vincent, I guess I'm doing it for me.

So when Walt and Brian are securing the U-Haul hatch, I unbuckle my seat belt. I have to answer that other mother. *Tell us, so we can help,* she said.

I rush back to the locked exit, opened by a young man emerging with an armful of empty boxes. I run down the hall and knock at the brown door with my son's name on it. Travis's mother greets me, surprised.

"My son hates when I do this," I begin. "But I just couldn't leave without answering you." And we both stand in the suite's entryway, where a ten-speed slants against the wall. I talk about FOP *as fast as I can*, about obstacles, treatments, emergency numbers, and Geri Wong promises to pass it all on. It isn't the most perfect way to do this, but under the circumstances, maybe the best way. Vincent finds us in the little hallway and raises his eyebrows.

"We're just talking mom stuff," Geri says. My son kisses me

good-bye again, and steps off lightly into his new life with his new roommates through his new front door.

"God bless you," says Geri, looking like an old friend as we hug good-bye. There is a knock at the big brown door: Walt, checking his watch. I've made us miss the U-Haul deadline.

"She's just being a mom," says Geri. "She's just being a mom." And as we leave her standing at the door watching us go, I have the illusion I am putting a lovely, capable mother in charge. At least for a few more moments.

16

STARRY NIGHT

*The Department of Vocational Rehabilitation helps me go to
college. DVR pays for my books, part of tuition, and a full-
time attendant. But DVR didn't help with summer school.
My family sprang into action. My dad drove me to school.
He is a professor at SPU, and he worked in his office where
I could call on him in case of emergency. My mom volun-
teered to be my attendant in lecture class and lab, and she
helped me study the textbook, which was too big and heavy
to handle. When my brother, Jonathan, got out of high
school for summer vacation, he took over as my attendant
and came with me to lecture and lab. Jonathan, Dad, and I
ate a picnic lunch on campus before we came home, where
Mom and I studied in the afternoons.*

—SARAH STEELE, twenty, diagnosed
at age two, Seattle, Washington

IN SEPTEMBER 1998, the month of our three boys' birthdays,
our good friends Jackie and Bruce Thornton planned Starry Night
with us. We sent out invitations to this FOP benefit with the photo of
Vincent holding a starfish, set against his vision of Starry Night, on
thousands of museum-caliber cards created by my dear *amiga* Susan
Early's company. Our event took place in the First Congregational
Church, an old Fresno landmark in the Tower District, also known
as the "Big Red Church" for its rust red walls. The pastor said a
blessing from the stage, and he and his family sold entrance passes
and raffle tickets; they carted in boxes of books and art and helped

serve food. There were Olympic-size trays of pasta from DiCicco's, wine courtesy of a friend who represented Gallo, Starbucks drinks and bags of coffee beans from the Forestiere family's store, and giant sheet cakes for Vincent's twelfth birthday by old Fresno bakeries, frosted with Vincent's version of Van Gogh's "Starry Night," which he painted it in Sister Paulina's class. The church and its garden courtyard were filled with friends from around the area and around the state, friends who were also Valley artists, musicians, poets, writers. There was Jemmy Bluestein under the stars, on his bluegrass guitar; Mas Masumoto being interviewed for the local news; Juan Serrano playing flamenco guitar onstage. So many blessed and talented people coming together for Vincent and the FOP battle. Dr. Kaplan flew out from Philadelphia and quoted a verse by one of the poets in his introduction. *Art in the service of science* was what Dr. Kaplan called Starry Night.

The art of Starry Night had more specific consequences than even Dr. Kaplan could have predicted the day of his lecture. They came about because a young nurse, Kelly Alexy, heard the highlights of Starry Night from her mother, a nurse, and her sister, Monica Carter, Vincent's old science teacher.

In the winter of 2003, I wrote to Kelly Alexy, a neonatal nurse-practitioner at the UCSF Medical Center's Intensive Care Nursery. By coincidence, Kelly worked under the direction of neonatologist Dr. Joseph Kitterman, whose grandson Matt was diagnosed with FOP in 2000. I asked Kelly if she could share with me the details of what Starry Night led to—in a twisty-path sort of way—a miraculous diagnosis that unfolded exactly four Septembers after the fund-raiser. So the sister of Vincent's favorite science teacher sent me a letter with her vivid account:

Dear Carol,

Of course I know who you are. I would be happy to share my story with you. Since it is truly due to your dedication in spreading the information that this child was diagnosed. . . .

My mother and Monica went to a dinner you had a few years ago. After that fund-raiser both my mother and Monica asked me if I had ever seen any babies with the disease. I told them I had never heard of it. They informed me of the symptoms of the disease from what they knew . . . and that was that.

Probably a year or two later I was at work and I heard Dr. Joe Kitterman discussing his grandson's disease. I told him I believed my sister taught a boy in her class who had the disease. He asked me where he lived and his name, and the connection was made.

Due to Joe Kitterman's interest in the disease, he invited Dr. Kaplan to come and speak at UCSF at the Pediatric Grand Rounds, in, I think, July of 2000. I went to listen to the lecture. I remember Dr. Kaplan discussing the disorder and reiterating what both my sister and mother had told me about the abnormal great-toe deformity. However, Dr. Kaplan's lecture discussed more of the specifics of the disease process.

Fast-forward to September 2002. I was on service in the newborn intensive care unit as the neonatal nurse-practitioner. Three times a week we go to the radiology department to look at MRIs, X-rays, and ultrasounds of the babies in the unit. Sometimes we have to wait while other departments look at studies of their patients. We were in the neuroradiology department waiting to look at head MRIs of our babies. We were waiting for the neuroradiologist to finish discussing a study that was done of a growth on the neck of what I knew to be a two-year-old. The patient was being followed by the hematology/oncology department.

The neuroradiologists were saying that they could not tell exactly what type of growth it was or exactly what tissue it was in. There was an open discussion within the group of doctors and suggestions regarding infections and asking if biopsies were made. The oncologist, Dr. Goldsby,

mentioned that a biopsy was done and was negative and
that the growth had migrated down the spine and the child
had decreased mobility where the growths were. I did not
say anything at first, but I mentioned to the neonatal
fellow that it sounded like it could be that disease Dr.
Kitterman's grandson has. He did not recall the disease
or the grand rounds that Dr. Kaplan had carried out.

Then a doctor in the room suggested it might be a
certain disease (the name I cannot remember off the top
of my head but I do recognize it as the disease that kids
with FOP get tested for by doing an open muscle biopsy).
Anyway, once the doctor had suggested that disease, all
the clues sort of added up.

I still was not going to say anything aloud to the whole
group of doctors, so when Dr. Goldsby was done and was
leaving the room I tapped him on the shoulder to see if I
could ask him a question regarding his patient.

He said sure and I asked if the child had normal toes.
With a slight look of surprise he said no, in fact, they
had just noticed that morning that the child had short
great toes.

He then eagerly asked me why I asked that. I told him
I knew of a very rare disease where children get swellings
that then ossify, which is really hard to diagnose. These
children are referred to oncologists and have biopsy after
biopsy and even get treated with chemotherapy. He asked
me the name of the disease.

He said that he was willing to investigate anything
because this child's condition was so perplexing. I said
it was called FOP. He then asked me what that stood
for and I said, "I can't remember, but my sister will
know and she gets out of chemistry class at 3:00 p.m.
I can call her." I also told him I would be able to find
it online because I would know it if I saw it. I had also
tried to get in touch with Dr. Kitterman while we were
in the neuroradiology department, but found out he

was on vacation. Dr. Goldsby gave me his card and the neonatal fellow and I went upstairs to do a literary search.

A funny thing was, while I was talking to Dr. Goldsby, he kept looking at my name identification tag, which was turned upside down, so eventually he said, "Please excuse me, but who are you?" I told him I was an NNP from the neonatal intensive care unit and said I knew about the disease and so did a doctor I work with.

We had no trouble finding it. The neonatal fellow was so excited and kept on saying, "That is amazing! You are right on!" At that time another fellow was in the unit and I asked if she recalled the name of the doctor from Philadelphia who came to UCSF to lecture on FOP. She gave me Dr. Kaplan's name and I called Dr. Goldsby and gave him the information. I also dropped Dr. Kitterman an e-mail while he was on vacation to let him know I gave his name to Dr. Goldsby and also what transpired that day in neuroradiology rounds.

The next morning at work, Dr. Kitterman called me on the phone to say he had received my e-mail and was going to call Dr. Goldsby. A few hours later he called me again to say X-rays were being sent to Philadelphia and they thought it most likely to be FOP.

Thank goodness the events happened as they did. It is quite a coincidence. I think my chances of winning the lottery are better than me walking in on a conversation of doctors discussing an undiagnosed child with FOP. I am so happy this child did not have to go through any more unnecessary testing. It makes you think sometimes you are put in a certain place for a certain reason. I often wonder if in my life there have been perfect strangers whose actions have changed the way my life is lived.

Take care,
Kelly

Dr. Kaplan responded to Kelly's story with a note of his own: "The bad news is that Hayden Pheif has FOP. The good news is that he has a guardian angel—Kelly Alexy."

SEPTEMBER 2004

IT WAS TWO years ago, on a day like today. Celine was ready for school in her plaid uniform, hair brushed and pulled back into a ponytail, pouring Lucky Charms into a bowl. Isabel was in the family room, getting ready for first grade and lamenting that time had passed, because life had been simpler in kindergarten when she could play longer with her good friend Sarah. "Hurry up!" I told her. "Pop's going to be back soon and he won't be happy to see you're not ready! He was already upset because he couldn't find his keys."

"Why was he upset about that?" asked Isabel.

"Because if he couldn't find his keys, he couldn't drive the car," Celine explained.

"Wouldn't you be mad if that happened to you?" I said.

"I'm a child," said Isabel. "And I don't drive."

It can get disorienting when you've gone through having your youngest enter kindergarten as your oldest is starting college. In the same week there is freshman orientation, where students file into a cafeteria pretending not to see the parent table, and a classroom where someone sits cross-legged on the floor wailing, "I want my mommy." There's probably nothing closer to cracking the time/space continuum than having lots of kids. I'm not talking about the typical confusion of saying, *Vincent, where's Lucas?* and getting told, *I'm Lucas.* I mean something like the day a young Lucas pointed to a picture of Brian as a toddler and said, "Celine can walk!" Celine, at the time, could barely pull herself up in her crib. And one night I looked at two-year-old Isabel, cherubic, arms raised for her fifteen-year-old brother, Brian. *You want to look back in time? That's you.*

But the time/space continuum is getting back at me for defying it. "It's like a whole bunch of people left when Vincent went away to college," says Celine sadly. Our twelve-year-old has said what I'm feeling. It is not just parents who miss kids when they leave home. Today, I am in Brian's room fishing out clothes, and I notice the computer screen saver keeps unscrolling a new gold and blue message: *Thanks for stopping by, Brian. Sarcastic thank-you.* Brian was gone for a year abroad, and then left early to line up an apartment on Martin Luther King Junior Way. Celine misses both her brothers.

Today I opened the fridge and saw cauliflower, a vegetable only Vincent will eat. I had to retreat to the laundry room, cry, and fling wet socks in the dryer. I have been having flashbacks of my second son as a very young child: the "circle head" baby, as Isabel called chubby infants; the kindergartner with Billy Goat Gruff headgear; the toddler dancing to salsa rhythms.

And all the little rituals that make up raising a child—when they're done, then what? "How do you deal with it when they leave?" a father asked a panel of parents at the CAL student orientation session. I've already had one son go away, and I still don't know, exactly. The mother of a sophomore on the panel answered, teary eyed, "She's been the light of our home." Another father called his freshman son every day for weeks until his wife made him stop.

I'm still here, but I'm the one who's homesick.

My mother cannot fathom how we can allow Vincent to go off, go away. "The family has been his support all these years!" she says. I like the Latin way better, too, after all: stay with your family—forever. But this is something Vincent wants to do, *needs to do.* How could we keep him, keep his gifts from a fabled place that is much more than a train ride away?

DR. GERARDI, WHO saved Isabel's arm last year and saved Vincent's leg years ago, is seeing Celine today for her spine.

We have with us, for Dr. Gerardi and his patients, one of the little bottles of Lourdes water Brian brought from the grotto in France. It is the small translucent statue of Mary with red roses and a blue crown. "For your most difficult cases," I say. He is pleased.

Dr. Gerardi has with him the familiar oversized manila envelope. "OK," he says reassuringly, setting X-rays up on the long lighted panel, this one a little larger than the screen that held Lucas's MRI films this week. "OK," he repeats, in the same kindly tone I remember from when he saw Isabel's buckled arm. I hang on to this "OK," because in black and white I can see my daughter's beautiful spine lit up like lightning on the X-ray.

Dr. Gerardi traces a bell curve for us on a piece of paper. "This is mild, moderate, severe," he lists, following the waved lines with his pen. He situates Celine's case along the rim of the bell: she has a considerable curvature, if invisible to the untrained eye, and she will be X-rayed periodically until her growth is done. He takes us down the hall, and we all stand in front of X-ray illustrations of spines.

"Those are Harrington rods," says Dr. Gerardi, pointing to white tracks with vertebrae running between them on the X-ray photos. I don't feel so good.

But current thinking is Celine will not need rods, not as long as the curvature stays in its range, so I start praying as we go back down the hall, over the speckled linoleum. From the window in our exam room, I see the green fields behind the smaller castle at Children's, Campus Pharmacy, where we pick up thalidomide.

"The good news is you're mostly done growing," says Dr. Gerardi to our daughter. Celine is near my height, five foot six. Growth could, conceivably, worsen the problem.

"I won't grow anymore?" Celine says, dismayed, when Dr. Gerardi steps out to get scoliosis literature.

"That's a good thing," Walt explains, trying to cheer Celine up. Our daughter is not convinced. She wants to play basketball.

"What if we had caught it earlier?" I ask Dr. Gerardi when he returns with some informational materials. *How could I have missed it? Me? Chicken Little?* Was I so busy trying to keep the sky from falling I didn't notice my own child's back? You have to catch these things *on time*.

"It's up too high for bracing to be effective," Dr. Gerardi says of the curvature. And this holds true for earlier stages, as well, he explains. *But how could we overlook it?* "It's like a tree in your yard. You see it every day, the same tree. But then someone comes to visit and notices changes." Usually a person outside the family first remarks the scoliosis, he tells us: a swim coach, a school nurse, a pediatrician. Dr. Gerardi has saved us again: this time, from parental guilt.

"It happens to healthy, happy kids," he says to Celine. He pats her on an arm, tells her she can play sports, swim, run, carry a backpack. He orders an MRI to rule out rare causes. "Most cases are idiopathic: nobody knows what causes them, but they can be hereditary. You might want to ask Dr. Kaplan if there's a genetic connection with FOP, see if there are any FOP siblings with scoliosis," he adds with curiosity. I wonder myself, and later hear from a mother in England whose daughter has FOP and whose two sisters have scoliosis. But there is, as yet, no known connection between FOP and scoliosis.

We mention Lucas's upcoming surgery: *How safe are allografts?* I've learned to say *allograft* instead of *cadaver tissue*, because the word *cadaver* sticks in my throat. Dr. Gerardi explains both types of grafts, reassures us: "Lucas is in great hands."

"This is orthopedics week," I say.

"You've certainly had more than your share," says Dr. Gerardi, shaking his head, looking down.

The next day, over fish tacos and salads at Rubio's, I tell Cherie that we've finally decided on an allograft—because it causes less pain, has a shorter surgery time, and leads to a quicker recovery. "The odds of getting a disease this way are something like one in a million," I say.

Cherie regards me in that skeptical-mother way she has, puts her hand over mine, and says, "But Carol, you have such unusual luck!"

Considering the odds of getting FOP to begin with are one in two million, and considering the odds of having an FOP hip flare-up, a torn ACL, and scoliosis intersecting in the same week, Cherie's words haunt me.

We choose the autograft, Lucas's own knee and hamstring tissue.

LUCAS IS IN the OR having his knee tissue reconstructed. Walt and I are in a waiting room at St. Agnes down the hall from the chapel. Walt is calm, reading legal briefs, and I am staring at student compositions. My cell's ditty goes off: *I'm lighting a candle for Lucas,* says my mother. It rings again: *How is everything going?* asks Candy, from LA. The ditty again: *I think the hip flare-up is back,* says Vincent. His call is as important as the next one, from the surgeon on the waiting room land line: *The surgery went great,* he announces.

Lucas is pale and groggy in the recovery room, but soon he is rolled out on a wheelchair, bound leg raised. He is prescribed a non-steroidal anti-inflammatory called Vioxx. I know of Vioxx because many FOP patients take it daily. But for Vincent, Dr. Henrickson preferred sulindac instead. Sulindac was in the Harvard study with thalidomide that Dr. Mitchell told me about one especially desperate afternoon.

At home, Lucas lies on the family room couch, on a passive-exercise machine lined with lamb's wool, strapped to his leg to flex the reconstructed joint. I am taking life twenty minutes at a time, like the ice packs I wrap on Lucas's thickly bound knee.

Twenty minutes of icing later, I contact Dr. Henrickson about Zometa, the experimental drug requiring an IV infusion we must have available if Vincent's hip flare-up fails to respond to our latest round of meds. Zometa's side effects can be potentially serious, though nausea and fever are its most common secondary effects.

"Zometa requires the approval of the Therapeutic Agents Committee," Dr. Henrickson tells me. Generally, this drug is not used in a children's hospital. "Realistically, the decision would likely take months to approve."

That doesn't sound good.

I am worried. Vincent is away at a new school, with a stubborn flare-up going on in a major joint.

How will we do all this?

Dr. Henrickson promises to look into other avenues, a home infusion for future use, if possible. This is new ground we're charting. "I hope the chaos settles down for you," he says kindly.

But before the chaos settles down, it gets worse. Vincent's medical scooter starts going in reverse for no reason. Then it stalls on a hill (a kind Dutch student pushes it). The Bay Area companies we call are no help. Celine wants to switch schools. Brian wants to switch countries (*I don't understand: he loved Berkeley so much at first,* I say to Lucas. *It was the freedom*, says Lucas. *You can get that at any college.*). And Lucas, always sunny, balanced Lucas, is angrily banging crutches around the house.

I wake up every morning feeling like I am about to take an exam. I am sobbing when I do laundry. I am having migraines with light shows.

My doctor prescribes medication, and I decide to try a natural remedy. So one night, at three in the morning, I am on the Internet, ordering an all-natural stress-relief product.

A FEW DAYS after Lucas's knee surgery there is breaking news on television, radio, Internet, newspapers. FOP patients write from all over the country and the world, wondering about a nonsteroidal anti-inflammatory and the surprise announcement about its serious cardiac risks. The University of Pennsylvania posts a message:

VIOXX RECALL—

This message is written in English, French, Spanish, Portuguese, Korean, Polish, Swedish, and Russian. Please scroll down to your language. Thank you from the IFOPA.

The sudden withdraw of Vioxx by Merck has caused much confusion and concern throughout the FOP community, especially for those taking the medication to prevent flare-ups and to reduce painful symptoms of FOP. Considering Merck has withdrawn the medication from the market, we have no other alternative but to recommend discontinuation.

Warmest Regards,
Drs. Glaser and Kaplan

I am grateful to Dr. Henrickson for choosing sulindac for Vincent these past years. But right now it is Lucas who is on Vioxx. Uh-oh.

"Things go wrong," I say in a line waiting for school forms. "But they get better." I am talking to another mother also having a terrible month. I can say this today because, strangely enough—suddenly— things *have* gotten better: the day after Vincent's medical scooter stalled on campus the owner of The Wheelchair Connection— himself—and a technician made a round-trip from Fresno to Berke- ley for repairs, carting along a backup ride. Then Dr. Henrickson engineered it so a vial of Zometa would be shipped to Children's, *covered by insurance.* We now have a $1,200 bottle of experimental treatment in our fridge, to take to any hospital in an emergency. And next door, our brand-new neighbors Corey and Wayne, par- ents of Isabel's friend Shelby, are a nurse and a doctor—and they have offered to set up a home infusion of Zometa should that ever be an option.

More often than not—and I must remind myself—the bad luck triggers the good, and good people appear like magic.

I TAKE LUCAS to physical therapy, to a large, busy facility where parents aren't allowed in for long. We are in a gym full of station- ary bikes and pulleys and athletes and elderly folks, with therapists pausing in assembly-line fashion by patients on padded tables. A construction worker with a bag of ice on his shoulder and a man in a cowboy hat on crutches flirt with Lucas's blond physical therapist. "Don't grow up like these guys," she warns.

"When you're done with that," the cowboy nods in sympathy to the knee brace Lucas is undoing, "you can use it to hit the dog." *We aren't in Children's anymore, Toto.*

While Lucas is pushing a foot with a towel under it against a wall, I run upstairs to request a non-Vioxx nonsteroidal anti-inflam- matory for him, the one Vincent takes.

"Have people been calling about Vioxx today?" I ask a reception- ist. Today is the day of the breaking news. She gives me a harried, *Oh, yeah* look.

17

WISH FLOWERS

OCTOBER 2004

*And to always look, every night at Hugo's back (the whole
body). It is getting better! Maybe it gets quiet for a while,
and BANG, two days later, a new big thing starting again!
It takes so much energy from us parents to worry over things
we can't do anything about. So for me, just one day, I just
stopped worrying.*

*And I read about all the things that can happen in the
future to be prepared for that day and for all things that
DO NOT happen to Hugo can I be happy for. Hugo is in a
quiet time, but not totally quiet—there are tiny FOP things
going on on his back; he has been like this for?? I don't really
remember . . . I think because when it gets more quiet we
have to deal with the normal children things . . . Say NO,
don't do that. Don't hurt your brother . . . Don't scream . . .
Eat your food. Try to put on your trousers by yourself . . .
blah, blah, blah . . .*

— MARIE HALBERT, mother of Hugo, six,
diagnosed at age four, Eskilstuna, Sweden

ONE SPRING AFTERNOON, when Isabel was about six years
old, she and I went for a skate walk. I walked, she skated. It
was a harrowing stroll, with Isabel trying out fancy moves that had
me lunging every few seconds. "This is nerve-racking," I said to a
mother watching us go by from her porch.

"It's harder on you, the mom," she said.

"You sure are trying some daring moves," I said to Isabel.

"What's 'daring'?"

"Taking a chance."

"That wasn't daring. *This* is daring!" she said, flailing her arms and legs in an even more alarming fashion.

Luckily, Isabel was distracted from her demonstration by something on the side of the road. "Wish flowers!" she said, trudging over a patch of rocky soil to pluck a dandelion. Under her helmet, her beautiful little face was reverent, her chestnut eyes serious as she blew on the nimbus, scattering sparkles in the air.

"What did you wish for?" I asked.

"I can't tell you or it won't come true," Isabel said, tossing the stem. She agreed to let me know when what she asked for came to pass. Then she held up a "flower" so I could make my own wish.

"You don't have to blow it all off," she advised, as I got light-headed puffing at the dander. "And this one's for a tiny wish," said Isabel, holding up a minuscule dandelion. She then picked one to take to her sister. But the wind blew away the "wishing stuff," so Isabel cupped her hands over another nimbus, and skated home slowly with the pretty weed, holding it as if in prayer.

On our porch, Celine held the dandelion with the same reverence, her sea-colored eyes looking fiercely inside for her wish. She blew. Nothing. The dandelion head was still intact. She blew again. Nothing. She puffed once more. Not a single filament budged.

"Here, I'll help you," said Isabel. "Do like this." She made spitting sounds. Celine made chugging locomotive sounds. A tiny bit of dander floated off.

"That's good! Now her wish will grow into a bigger wish!" pronounced Isabel.

"I'll never get my wish!" said Celine, and she started to tear at the white stuff with her fingers, plucking it all off. Holding just the stem, she had the face of a child with a popped balloon.

"The harder you work for your wish, the better its chances," I improvised.

I know we all wished for the same thing. And when it comes true we will be allowed to tell.

OCTOBER 2004

We have pulled into our driveway on a sunny fall afternoon. I have just heard from FOP activist Gary Whyte—the Whyte Knight, I call him—who has persuaded Arnold Schwarzenegger to declare October "Fibrodysplasia Ossificans Progressiva Month." I suppose seeing California's governor in a recent movie with his chest muscles showing is not so bad if he's going to help kids with a musculoskeletal disorder. This is good news, good news added to my kids telling me about A's in their hardest classes and new friends. Life is starting to normalize.

We lug backpacks out of the car. Lucas is moving faster these days, even with the heavy black brace that holds much of his right leg. To walk, he must hitch up from the hip, knee unbending, which makes for a wooden swinging motion.

I go to the mailbox and pull out a manila envelope with a return address in South Africa. It is from the natural products company I discovered on the Internet: my remedy for stress. Inside there is no vitamin bottle, no pamphlet of instructions or list of natural ingredients, only a Ziploc baggie with a white powder.

Huh.

"See Internet for dosing instructions," reads the baggie. It might as well say, *Drink Me*, à la *Alice in Wonderland*. Forget it. *I want my money back.* I take the package into the house and leave it in Brian's room, on his dresser, where no on will move it until I can get to the post office.

Then it hits me: white powder. U.S. mail. *Anthrax.*

Uh-oh.

Suddenly I'm having a *major stress reaction, major.* I run into our master bedroom and call the police.

"Just wait for the sheriff to arrive, ma'am," says a male dispatcher. "And don't transport the package."

If this is anthrax, I can't just leave it on Brian's dresser. I have no choice but to transport the package—somewhere. I rush back into my son's room, tweeze a corner of the envelope, and race it out of the house, past Lucas, who is busy employing a rubber stretching device for his physical therapy exercises, using our foosball table as a bar. "Don't be alarmed when you see the police," I call to him, running past. "I just need them to check something I ordered for stress." Lucas continues calmly with his leg lifts.

I throw the manila envelope on the front porch, away from the porch swing. When our doorbell rings, there is a young policewoman, dark-haired and fit. Her K-9 unit is parked in the driveway, and it has a German shepherd in the backseat. I point to the envelope and hand her a copy of Internet information on the product. "It's for stress," I say. "From South Africa." She and I read that the Zulu warriors use this product.

I feel ridiculous.

The policewoman, a deputy sheriff, pulls on latex gloves, picks up the envelope, and takes out the Ziploc baggie. "Doesn't look like anthrax," she says, studying the contents. "Anthrax is more powdery," she explains. "Like baking soda. This looks more like crystals." She turns the product over and notices a gold sticker with a Las Vegas address. Now everything looks even more suspicious, considering the Internet ad's mention of Zulu warriors. Maybe they mean a cabaret act.

I make the mistake of asking if the white powder could possibly be cocaine and the deputy sheriff glances at me a little sharply. Luckily, the drug dog is watching us idly through the backseat window. After a few moments, she tosses the package into her car's trunk and begins to take her leave.

"Will you test it in a lab?" I ask.

"It's just disposed of—as toxic waste."

"But we don't know what it *is*. Couldn't I pay a lab to find out?" I explain we have five kids, one who had surgery, one with a genetic condition.

She thinks for a moment, seems to weigh something. "Would you like me to call Environmental Health to examine the powder?" she asks. *I would, of course, indeed.*

I phone Walt at work so he won't wonder what happened if he pulls into our driveway before the authorities take off. (Neighbors have called to ask if everything is OK.) I offer the young deputy a

Canada Dry, figuring (correctly) that she won't accept the drink—
under the circumstances. So I just boil water for spaghetti and wait
until Environmental Health rings the doorbell.

The Environmental Health specialist who arrives on our doorstep
is a tall, dark, kind man in civilian clothes. He hands me his card
with a beautiful Nigerian name on it, and smiles at my apologies as
he turns the baggie over. "We'll test it and get back to you in forty-
eight hours," he tells me.

How unusual is it that an African Environmental Health specialist arrives at our doorstep to check a remedy I ordered from South
Africa (via Las Vegas)?

It is Lucas who sums it all up: "You order something to relieve
stress and you have to call the police when it gets here. Pretty
ironic."

)

"I DON'T KNOW anything about FOP," a San Francisco doctor
is telling me cordially. "And I'm not accepting new patients." This
isn't going very well.

Our dear friend Dr. Joe Kitterman, UCSF neonatologist and an
FOP grandfather, has been hunting all day for a colleague to help
us on short notice. Vincent's left hip is worse, and I am trying to
set up an IV with the Zometa vial we have in our fridge. So I am
on a cell phone pulling a red velvet dress over Isabel's head in a fit-
ting room, talking to a rheumatologist. We're getting ready for my
mother's birthday in the Bay Area, where we will see Vincent and
Brian—if we aren't seeing them at a hospital infusion center.

The San Francisco doctor does say that one of his residents
will take Vincent's case. A *resident*. "But we can't order an IV this
weekend," he stresses. Our son must be established as a patient. We
argue politely. I lose.

I turn to pull up the zipper of a blue moiré dress Celine is wearing. With her gold hair and aqua eyes, she is a Renaissance beauty.
"I don't like it," she says, looking pained. Seventh grader that she
is, Celine wants to be invisible; she is displeased with herself before
mirrors. I am displeased with *myself* right now, mirror or no mirror,

and it is all I can do not to run into the next pastel-toned stall and cry. My reflection looks undone as it is: next to two young beauties in blue silk and red velvet is a woman with fried highlights and bruised-looking eyes. I look like a "before" picture.

How could I have thought there was more time to find a Bay Area specialist? But all these years we've managed flare-ups over the phone with doctors who are like family, and it is *so hard* to entrust my son to someone who has never seen a case of FOP, whom I might have to warn, as I warned the UCSF residents that June, *Don't push his limbs past capacity or I'll kill you.*

So right now we have the $1,200 vial of Zometa in our refrigerator, and no one to administer it to increase the chances that my son's leg will stay mobile.

I am on the Internet in the dark morning hours, not to order anything (though the natural remedy powder turned out to be starch based—harmless), but to conjure the Web's telepathic powers to save my son. I e-mail a young man with FOP in the Bay Area for his doctor's name; I ask for the same from Megan Pheif, mother of little Hayden, diagnosed by Kelly Alexy. I appeal to an old high school classmate at UCSF and even contact a rheumatologist at that Other School. Finally, I write to a friend with FOP, Sharon Kantanie, in Tennessee, to cry on her shoulder.

I feel William Butler Yeats's words of catastrophic force: *Things fall apart; the centre cannot hold.*

It is a *dark night of the soul*, darker than San Juan de la Cruz could ever say.

)

I AM IN a powder room of marble and mirrors trying to fix my hair with my fingers. I am worried about Vincent's latest flare-up. *Will it resolve? Will he need an experimental infusion? Will it be safe?* I have arrived in such a state at my mother's birthday party, Saturday night, with all the stars behind the Santa Cruz hills, Latin luminaries here, and a bagpipe-playing doctor. My mother is out there, glamorous as ever in flowing finery, gesturing, exuberant, by the round tables of fine linen and white china waiting for salmon and radicchio salads. She looks much younger than her age, younger and much better than her daughter, in fact, whom I see in the mirror right now—who is still a "before" picture, even in a burnt-orange jacket that is *me* according to a saleswoman. No help for it. *Is there?*

I pull from my purse a sleek bottle marked Enlighten, and slap enough Skin Enhancing Makeup on myself to correct the bruised look under my eyes. The bottle is not misnamed. It *makes up* for me, at least on my surfaces.

Can you have a moment of truth in a powder room? I always tell students about the optional *punto decisivo* in a story, optional because characters aren't always given to choose a path or make a clear-cut decision that will lead to a resolution. But maybe, right now, I can choose my own *punto decisivo*, a go-this-way, go-that-way—

What is my choice? Do I have one?

The powder room door swings open and a large woman in jogging togs smiles at me absently. I don't know her. Is she a sign? A deus ex machina? She disappears into one of the lattice-door stalls, snaps the lock. Probably not.

I take out my little red pencil to bring my eyes into focus. There. There I still am—barely—in the mirror, under the French bangs, the highlights I fluff over worry lines.

I look spooked.

A crowd applauds somewhere or a toilet flushes, I can't tell which. The woman in jogging togs is making unlatching noises from her stall. Since I can't stand looking in the mirror next to a stranger, I give myself one last glance: roots too dark, highlights too—*something*. But I do feel slightly *enhanced* by the Enlighten . . .

I'll decide on a decision—later.

Outside, in the clubhouse of white wood and little chandeliers and rock floors, I catch up with my college kids. Brian has driven with Vincent over from Berkeley. It is Brian who took practice runs to campus with Vincent riding his medical scooter; Brian who introduced his brother to friends and facilities and made late-night pharmacy runs. And when a chemistry TA (called GSIs there now) lost a lab report and told Vincent he could redo it for 40 percent credit, only a brother like Brian could intercede. I ask how he trumped Berkeley bureaucracy.

"I told him I was bigger than he was." Even in a sports coat, my good-looking son has his considerably muscled arms out, like a wrestler.

"That's not funny."

"What I said was, 'If my brother says he turned it in, I believe him, because he's really meticulous.' And I explained about Vincent overcoming FOP."

The TA relented, with full credit. "I had to redo it, though," says Vincent, so handsome in the formal attire my mother insisted her grandsons wear, no sign of his recent trials. Despite FOP and chronic pain, and leg mobility threatened, and campus hills and absentminded TAs and arrogant professors, and vast lecture halls, Vincent is getting A's in inorganic chemistry and calculus, brutal classes meant to weed out people on their way to medical school.

"The GSI told me he had a brother with a disability, too," says Brian.

At this moment, that story alone begins to explain the reason Stanford did not take Vincent. Up until now, FOP placed my sons in the separate worlds of athletics and music. For a year they will share the same world. It won't exactly be easy for either one. But something important will come of it—it already has.

Vincent seems better from his hip flare-up, so we plot: if he continues to improve for eight days on prednisone, he does not return soon to the Valley for an experimental infusion. Dr. Kaplan took the urgency out of my hunt for a Bay Area specialist when he stressed that an experimental treatment should take place at our own hospital with Vincent's longtime rheumatologist. "Don't change more than one variable at a time," he warned. "Safety first."

Please, dear Jesus, let my son stay well. I also call on my grand-mother's favorite saint for intercession: Saint Anthony, San Antonio: the patron saint of lost things never fails (even though Celine once protested the wait: *He takes too long; he takes two weeks!* But Saint Anthony found my friend Verena's cat, missing for just a few days in New York City). *Please, find a cure, Saint Anthony, find a way for Vincent to stay well.* Walt tells me you can't create loopholes that way, you can't ask a saint in charge of Lost and Found to work on other problems by rephrasing petitions—but that's just because he's an attorney. The laws are different in heaven—they have to be.

Lucas's leg is improving after his knee surgery. And I've learned a few tricks from taking him to physical therapy. There is, for example, an ingenious icing device: a blue gel "sleeve" that zips up around a limb. You keep it in the freezer, and inflate it with a little bicycle pump to surround a joint.

With FOP I've considered myself an expert vis-à-vis the experts, but with Lucas's recovery, I see how little I know about the normal rules of motion. It's a strange feeling, *a relief*, to be taught by health professionals. In Physical Therapy—the PT palace, I call it—the damage from trauma can be reversed, the mechanics of bones and muscles and pain are not so mysterious, and people can learn to move normally again.

The other strange thing I learn at the PT palace is that Lucas *must* exercise through discomfort. "Push through the pain," say all the athletic young therapists. Pain is not a sign of impending catastrophe here, and he must feel it to regain mobility. "You'll have *lots* of pain after exercising," a pretty blond PT tells him—and Lucas does, grateful for the frozen gel sleeve zipped up along his leg. And this dynamic, in and of itself, is also a strange relief, because in the FOP universe, pain is *bad, bad, bad. It is a relief to know that pain is an ally.*

Down the hall from where Lucas learns how to do leg lifts, I find a wood-and-bronze plaque across from the warm-water pool. On the plaque is a coach's quotation: "Courage is not measured by the heights one has achieved, but by the obstacles one has overcome." I write down this quotation to give to someone I will meet later on.

This month, Walt and I will go to his Stanford class reunion, and I would like to sit in on a lecture by the dean of admission.

"RACHEL SAYS SAVE MART has Dino Chicken," Isabel is telling me as we rush into the market to buy dinner before Lucas finishes his PT.

"What's Dino Chicken?" I want to know. Isabel has been talking about this item for weeks now, searching for it in markets without success. But today she marches purposefully down the frozen foods aisle, Catholic school jumper bouncing, and returns, triumphant, with an orange box. Dino Chicken. The box has a stamp of some kind of authority pronouncing it healthy for kids. That's good enough for me—breaded chicken breasts in the shapes of dinosaurs. I toss the box in our cart.

"How about we get a whole chicken in the meat section?" I say to my eight-year-old. I've never cooked a whole chicken in Isabel's lifetime, I realize—only parts. Isabel consents, enchanted by the idea of choosing chicken that looks like an actual chicken. We pick out a plump Foster Farms three-pounder as deliberately as if it were a Thanksgiving turkey. "Let's cook it tonight," I say optimistically, checking my watch.

Isabel and I make it through the registers and rush to the car, both of us trotting, cart rattling through the parking lot. We are late to pick up Lucas and late for Isabel's soccer practice. As we pull into the PT palace for Lucas, who waits behind the bank of glass doors, black brace locking his leg rigid, Isabel calls out, "Lucas! Mom bought a whole chicken! A real whole chicken! With wings and everything!"

Hi, Dr. Kaplan,

I have a small swelling above my left shoulder blade. It is right about where my shoulder meets my neck. It is right on top of where I already have a bone growth on my back. Brian took a look at it tonight and said it felt a little swollen. It starts to bother me when I put pressure on it, like when I lie down on my back. Sometimes it causes a little pain when I take in a deep breath. When this happens, I would say the pain scale is about a 5, but otherwise it is only about a 1 or a 2. . . . My leg is doing better now—it only bothers me when I sit down for a long period of time—but I was just wondering if you think that I should get a Zometa infusion this weekend. The only problem is that I have a chemistry midterm on Tuesday. Should you feel I need this infusion, I am probably going to need a medical note to give to my chemistry professor.

Thanks again, for all your help.

Vincent

Vincent copies me his first patient-to-doctor e-mail, his first communication with his doctor as an adult. This note is my sign, my marching orders: I can choose to worry over whether my grown son's leg will stay well or not, whether the swelling on the left shoulder blade will go up or down. Or I can choose to *not worry.*

I hereby choose: *not.*

Here is my breakthrough, my punto decisivo: I've worried enough to stay up into the morning of the day of my mother's birthday, hunting for help. There's nothing more for me to do. So I solemnly resolve, *once and for all,* as Vincent has reached his eighteenth birthday, to take the advice I have been giving myself all along, to trust that everything, no matter how worrisome, will—somehow—work out.

Maybe deciding not to worry is not a once-and-for-all thing. For people like me with an optimism deficiency, swearing off worry should probably be more like making sure to take a regular vitamin supplement.

18

FIELD OF DREAMS

Dear Carol,

*I am extremely proud of Vincent, and I am keeping Lucas in
my thoughts and most sincere prayers as well. I will continue
to pray for Vincent, as I always have and still do. I think of
Vincent as my FOP younger brother. I know he will excel,
and do well in everything he attempts to do, he just needs
to approach it all carefully . . . I heard about Dr. Kaplan
asking Vincent to work in the FOP Lab. . . . Way to go,
Vincent. Just think: my little FOP brother just may be the
one who finds a cure for me and him, and all the others who
suffer from FOP.*

*Anyway . . . just trust that everything will be just fine,
relax your mind, relax your body, take some deep breaths,
know that there are many, many people praying and rooting
for you . . .*

With love and prayers,
Robin

—ROBIN RICE, thirty-four, diagnosed
at age two, Porterville, California

IT WAS A warm October evening in 2002, and we were watching
our red and blue high school marching band line up on the edge
of the field, waiting patiently for the football players to jog away
and the cheerleaders to hop off their stands. The digital billboard

marked halftime, the flag girls finally advanced, and we heard the vigorous drums, the white tuba, and the endearing flat notes from the brass section. Vincent was a junior, and he looked intense on his trumpet, concentrating on choreography. Lucas was a freshman in his first field show. He had most of his attention on the saxophone he had just learned to play.

Some of the teenage boys parading along the bleachers called out to our younger son, " Lucas Whelan! Lucas Whelan!" The salutation was some good-natured joking, partly because Lucas didn't exactly know how to play the saxophone, partly because he is such a gregarious soul, but mainly because in the hierar- chies of high school, the "cool" people are not usually in band. But Lucas, a natural athlete, joined the band for a while to join Vincent.

When the field show came to a close and the musicians made it back to the bleachers, a group of boys went up to Lucas with sly smiles and took him away in a teenage-boy pack to look for food. Vincent went off on his own to the snack bar after the girls and Walt and I exclaimed over his performance.

My heart ached at that moment for my second son because he looked—*to my worried mother's eyes*—a little lonely. And I wished right there that Vincent might be more outgoing, as outgoing as Lucas, as gregarious as Brian. This wistfulness lifted a little when I ran into other mothers who asked how Brian—in his element at Berkeley—liked school. But as we said our good-byes, I thought of Vincent standing in a line alone.

I knew that our son has the best of friends, like Peter and com- pany. But at that moment I wanted him surrounded—exactly like his brothers—his reserve dispelled, his genetic condition dismissed in the fraternities of youth. His solitude that night reminded me that my beloved boy had been singled out with a catastrophically disabling condition so rare it hits one in two million.

As I made my way along the perimeter of the football field, hold- ing my two girls' hands, I noticed Vincent's trigonometry teacher, a beautiful woman with golden Pre-Raphaelite hair, standing at the edge of the field. I introduced myself to her as Vincent and Lucas's mother. I was meant to see her at that moment. "Did Vincent tell you what happened the other day in class?" she asked. No, I said, he hadn't.

"It's amazing how he works things out in his head," she told me. I agreed: Vincent has always been gifted in math (*he doesn't get that from me*). The teacher went on: "I was writing a problem on the board, going through a good deal of calculation, and Vincent raised his hand and said, 'Ms. Franklin, do we have to take all those steps?'"

Ms. Franklin asked Vincent if he knew a faster way to finish the proof because she sure didn't. He did; he had already worked through the problem, an extensive one, without using a pencil, and explained it in three steps. When he was done speaking, one of the students in the room began to clap, and the entire class broke into applause.

I had tears in my eyes from Ms. Franklin's story, and have never left a football field so elated. I realized that we often fret more than we should about our children, and that our dreams for them are sometimes irrelevant. I realized that God sends our children to the world equipped with the exact talents they need in this life, and that all we have to do is love them.

OCTOBER–NOVEMBER 2004

IT IS NOT long after my Internet quest on that dark October morning before my mother's birthday that I receive a response from my St. Francis classmate at UCSF, Jeff Lotz, a PhD in bioengineering who works with orthopedists. He puts me in touch with a UCSF specialist, Dr. Sigurd Berven, who knows of FOP and Dr. Kaplan from his days at Oxford. "I will be happy to see Vincent here," Dr. Berven tells me.

And my friend in Tennessee, Sharon Kantanie, found me Dr. Jeff Tabas, a former researcher in the FOP Lab who authored a seminal paper on FOP with Dr. Kaplan. Dr. Tabas is now at a San Francisco hospital and is affiliated with UCSF. He offers to help

Vincent and promises to ask his ER director about emergency Zometa infusions.

I also hear from our UCSF lifeline Dr. Kitterman, who forwards me a note from Dr. Robert Goldsby, the pediatric oncologist who cared for Hayden Pheif and listened to nurse Kelly Alexy about FOP. He is also the specialist who offered to mentor Vincent in San Francisco last summer when the UCSF high school internship fell through. Dr. Goldsby has received news of a student at Berkeley with FOP through the head of UCSF Orthopedics, Dr. Mohammed Diab—who was contacted independently by Dr. Sigurd Berven. Dr. Goldsby will be happy to oversee Vincent's care.

Now we have not one, but three qualified doctors for our son in the Bay Area.

After my dark night of the soul, a golden circle of e-mails has worked its way around San Francisco.

And there is more good news from Dr. Kaplan in Pennsylvania: because the current FOP flare-up site is dorsal and Vincent's leg continues to do well, no experimental infusion is necessary—anywhere. Not yet.

)

WE ARE ALL in Berkeley for Homecoming. We drive past the shabby mansions of frat row, past young men in sweats and jeans lounging on porches or setting up kegs. The campus's narrow streets are teeming with people of all ages, in cars, on foot, in the different shades of blue and gold for the Cal Bears or the UCLA Bruins. There are security guards in golf carts, mothers and children, young fathers with babies riding their shoulders, grandparents, fans of all sizes mixing with students.

There is the usual stalling at the gates since Vincent is required to use the remote student entrance, separate from ours. But of course, I can't go into a medical history with the gray-haired woman in a blue and gold parka taking tickets who insists that Vincent is at the wrong gate. "He has a disability," I say. Sometimes that's enough.

"He has to swipe his card at the other gate," says the woman, unimpressed.

"It's too far!"

"He still has to go swipe it at the other gate." *Berkeley bureaucracy.*

"I'll go swipe it!" *I'll swallow it whole.*

The poor woman hesitates, then vaguely throws up her hands and waves us through. This is the kind of thing Vincent will have to learn to do on his own. (*I learned it.*) And right now, we are not just conscious of Vincent in the crowd, but also of Lucas, who wears the leg brace under waterproof jogging pants—insurance against the heavy gray skies. Walt is protecting them both as Lucas stiffly negotiates his way up bleachers, hitching his right leg up from the hip. "I almost fell," he reports. *Good thing I missed that particular miracle.*

This game, between Bears and Bruins, is festive and relatively civilized, but I am not one to recite scores or plays. Suffice it to say the event is loud and colorful, and there is crowd surfing, and one of the teams wins. Nothing like the rivalry with that Other School across the Bay: there are no T-shirt expletives, no young men yelling, "Go home!" no student section chanting the words on their T-shirts, no frat boy at an exit, palm raised, calling, "God bless, God bless," to alums in red. And in the bathrooms at the UCLA–Cal game there are no existential disagreements over where the line begins or ends.

Vincent's mission dorm overlooking the Bay still has its peaceful air, none of the simmering mischief you sense on frat row or in Bowles Hall down the street. Brian is complaining that the Bowles men are now prohibited from duct-taping each other to chairs and sandwiching themselves between mattresses dragged up the hill. "It's a seventy-five-year-old tradition!" Brian insists, his brown eyes shining. Walt smiles and shakes his head.

We are having burritos on a picnic table at a little eatery close to campus. "And they won't let you do any of that anymore!" says our oldest. He looks for commiseration from Vincent and his quiet roommate Travis (whose desk photo I saw of "him" with a fair-haired girl was, in fact, a portrait of his parents). They don't seem to share Brian's sense of indignation at the new rules.

When we are back in Vincent's suite, I notice shoes in the hall, an exotic woodwind instrument, a backpack, towels, books, strewn *recklessly* across the floor. My son, it seems, has said little to his other roommate about obstacles and FOP. "Let Vincent take care of it," Walt tells me. He's right. *But only in principle.* So when Vincent takes the girls for a spin on his scooter through the Spanish courtyard, I compose a note: "Hi, Tom. This is Vincent's mom—" *No, strike it, sounds like elementary school.* Again: "Hi, Tom, I hope your college experience is going great." *That's ridiculous. Scratch that.* Then, "Tom, sorry to bug you, but—" Of course anything from a roommate's mother is going to bug you. I finally just write, "Tom, can you please keep the floor clear? Trauma bad for Vincent." I leave the note as visible as possible on a heap of bills.

Vincent is back, and he reports a twinge that comes and goes with the medical scooter on the knotty city terrain. My brother, Martín, a social worker who has just come back from Argentina, tanned and youthful, has visited Vincent and says the doctors have told him to just watch things. I pray it means muscles getting used to moving with a scooter—like riding a horse. I don't want to have to come back with asphalt and repave Berkeley myself.

There is one last behind-the-scenes item to take care of before our drive home. In my wallet is a little white emergency card with doctors' numbers and medical warnings. In this megalopolis of students, I can't just assume a resident assistant has gotten all the necessary information. So while Vincent and Walt take baskets of clothes to the first-floor laundry, I slip off with the FOP card, following signs that say SANDY RA!

I knock on the RA's door. Nobody answers. I drop the laminated card in a designated envelope tacked on a nearby wall. But I cannot just take off without leaving instructions on a dry erase board. It takes me fifteen minutes and one of my own pens to get this message right, and when I try to erase, I see I have used indelible ink. *So there we have it, a permanent announcement from MOM.* (Uh-oh.)

I am trying to rub out "MOM" with the hem of my yellow Cal sweatshirt when the RA door flies open. A bewildered girl with curly brown hair is looking at me. "I've written a—message—that won't erase—" I say. This is the type of thing that happens when MOM can't let go.

I've since found out rubbing alcohol wipes out indelible marks. Next time I go to Berkeley, I'm taking rubbing alcohol and asphalt.

THE WEEKEND AFTER our trip to Berkeley, I am with my husband at his twenty-fifth reunion at that Other School. I am here to attend a lecture entitled "On Our Side of the Desk," given by Stanford University's dean of admission.

The dean of admission is a nice-looking woman with shorn blond hair and a brilliant smile, standing before a blackboard. Prospective parents and alums are seated around a long, polished table, leaning by windows, or doing their best to fit into student desks along the walls. A slender, dark-haired woman, is drawing diagrams on a blackboard, outlining the mechanics of admissions.

After a question-and-answer session, I shake hands with the dean of admission, and tell her a little about my son. She refers me to the director of admission, who has been the one at the blackboard, as she herself will not be returning to Stanford. I do not read the dean my quotation about courage and obstacles, but—who could blame me?—I decide to give a little bit of advice to the director, who turns to me cordially after greeting a young man in a red cap. "Stanford should eliminate its deferred decision for Early Action applicants," I tell her. "A clean yes or no in December would have been better for my son, who has a disability." She takes this in and hands me her card, because there are other parents in our semi-circle. But I cannot seem to leave. "And I have some feedback for you on the rejection letter."

"We don't call it rejection," says the director. "We call it—"

"Well, we do," I say. "A rose by any other name . . ." She smiles.

I point out which paragraph in the letter Stanford should strike out. "It's patronizing," I say. The director of undergraduate admission at Stanford thanks me and shakes my hand, gracious and—I think—puzzled. She may be used to this, but how many FOP mothers has she met?

Walt and I leave through the stone arches of the mission building that has held the lecture. "I don't think the dean's serious hair matches her voice," is all I say. "Do you?" Walt laughs and puts an arm around me as we walk off. The sky is low over the country club campus, over the drive lined with palms, and there is a light drizzle, but the air is mild.

We leave Stanford early for an FOP fund-raiser, the Second Annual Hayden's Hope. It is at the Sausalito Women's Club in an elegant neighborhood overlooking the Bay. The club is all wood paneling inside, lighted everywhere with candles and old Spanish chandeliers. Its architecture is that of an upscale barn with a little stage. I've never seen so many beautiful young people in one place in my life; it's like walking into a Hollywood bash or a movie set: the men are all athletes in suits and every woman is gorgeous in tailored jeans. "I'm just having a good time looking at all these pretty girls," says a man buying chances for a trip to Paris.

There are stuffed mushrooms and silver trays with mounds of chocolate truffles I grab in handfuls, and there are crystal glasses and more candles and red and white wines. At the last Hayden's Hope, says Megan Pheif, Hayden's mother, a brilliant young blond, the family raised $120,000. This year they are sure to make more, as I hear someone bidding $21,000 for a single weekend in Lake Tahoe. I meet Hayden, a towheaded preschooler with a cherub's face, hanging tight to his mother's leg. He is heartbreakingly lovely, and I recognize FOP in his stiff little neck and shoulders. His father, John, whom Hayden seems to resemble, remembers his hospitalization last fall with an FOP flare-up from a flu vaccine.

Kelly Alexy is here, and so is Dr. Joe Kitterman, who has brought with him two UCSF physicians who took part in the e-mail chain forged from a dark night. I meet Dr. Jeff Tabas, who worked in the FOP Lab. I meet Dr. Rob Goldsby, the pediatric oncologist who diagnosed FOP with Kelly Alexy that day in Neuroradiology. And there, in the center, is Dr. Fred Kaplan. I feel like Dorothy in *The Wizard of Oz*, waking up from catastrophe and recognizing the real people behind a dream. It is a glorious sort of awakening at this fund-raiser for little Hayden and Vincent and Matt, Dr. Kitterman's grandson, who is seated at one of the cocktail tables. Matt has the same profound *something* in his eyes that my own son has. *Maybe it is the look of the spirit that takes up spaces suffering leaves behind.*

Matt rises to join Vincent, and I see that Matt cannot straighten from the waist.

And then something happens. Dr. Kitterman holds up his wine glass as if to make a toast. Instead of a toast, he makes an announcement, one I could never have predicted at the start of October: "We're going to start an FOP Consultation Center at UCSF," he says.

The doctors around Joe Kitterman all smile. And his declaration charges the air: this brilliant advance, the first FOP center outside the University of Pennsylvania, where an orphan disease was first "adopted," is what Joe Kitterman will make happen. (On May 31, 2005, the *San Francisco Chronicle* will run a front-page story subtitled, "UCSF starting world's 2nd center on rare disorder that causes crippling bone growth.")

My dark night of the soul and Starry Night set us on a path that led to this vantage point of Hayden's Hope. And from all the windows, over the dark shimmer of the bay, I can see San Francisco sparkling through the fog, from this place where we are illuminated with candles—and with much more than candlelight.

Five years after Starry Night, we meet the little boy diagnosed in time because of Vincent, because of Matt, and because the designs of Providence are what we help forge. So we have convened exactly here, exactly now, for scheduled and unscheduled miracles.

Dr. Kaplan announces from the stage that Vincent will work one summer at the FOP Lab at the University of Pennsylvania, and after, Dr. Goldsby asks, "Vincent, would you like to intern in my department, too?" So now our son has almost as many medical internship offers as he has summers before medical school.

And while Dr. Kaplan is onstage to speak to the crowd, he

announces that Vincent is a freshman at UC Berkeley, and there are cheers, and beautiful young women call out, "You go, Vincent, honey!" Our son smiles broadly as Walt and I watch him, shoulder to shoulder, and my eyes sting, and glory is what I feel.

"Half of us here went to Cal," John Pheif tells us. And the local doctors present tonight are all affiliated with UCSF, affiliated with Berkeley. I cannot help but think: *This is the reason—one of them—that the dean at Stanford decided Vincent's FOP did not count.* And when the young Armenian predicted, "Doors will open for him at Berkeley that would not have at Stanford," he could not have known that his words were only half a prophecy. Doors have opened for Vincent, but his presence at Berkeley will have helped open doors for others, doors to the future.

"GET ME A pen, please," says Isabel. "I need to write something. I need to write it on your hand." Everyone has seen me jotting notes on my palm, though no one has offered to do it for me until now. I extend my hand.

The pen won't write, and Isabel starts running the ballpoint up and down on my palm to get the ink going. "What is it you need?" I ask, pulling my hand away.

"You'll just forget," she says, exasperated. "*I* have to write it."

"You can dictate." She sighs, hands me the pen, but still won't tell me what she wants, understanding somehow that words work better if they're recorded, and even better if you can record them yourself.

"What is it you need me to write?"

"Buy shirt for Isabel."

I print large blue letters and raise my hand as proof. She seems satisfied, and we go to feed Oliver, the turtle Vincent got as her birthday gift, the pet whose cage Walt and the boys built one Saturday morning. We feed Oliver broccoli, and splash water into the rock bowl.

"My left leg, in the middle of the thigh, hurts." It is Vincent from Berkeley. I am at a red light by Lucas's high school.

"What's the pain on the scale?"

"A six."

I start to call Rheumatology to see if we will need the experimental Zometa treatment, but my phone goes off again: friends calling with directions. "First you get on the freeway, north on 41," says Vittorio, restaurateur extraordinaire, who knows I get lost. "Go twenty-one miles. Then make a U-turn at the black rock." This isn't helping.

Now I have a call waiting: my life-saving Late Club friends, Mira and Kathy, offering to pick up Isabel.

I dial Rheumatology again, waiting for Lucas at the curb. Students stroll past the mission buildings in pairs or groups, their red, white, or blue shirts untucked over khakis. I honk at one of them poking his head inside a station wagon window. Parents, a basketball coach, Lucas's friends Dimitri and the seven-foot-tall Lopez twins all turn. I hope I haven't honked at the wrong tall, brown-haired kid in a uniform. But this kid looks up, limps over.

Today Lucas will skip physical therapy: we are going to *The Incredibles*.

I am worried that I will be talking to our doctor on my cell in a dark, noisy theater. But Dr. Henrickson calls back promptly, just as we find parking by Borders, around the corner from the art deco temple of Edwards 21. "I'm so sorry, bothering you again," I tell Dr. Henrickson as I fish out sweaters, lock doors, send Lucas ahead with kids. There have been too many flare-ups since Vincent started college, too many questions and decisions. "You know I worry a lot," I apologize.

And as I move toward the marquee Dr. Henrickson says something I will carry with me for the rest of my life, a kind of absolution: "It's because you worry," he says, "that you've jumped on this so quickly, and it's because of that, that he's doing so well, and will learn to take action fast."

I will never take credit for a rogue gene's random about-faces or retreats. But with Dr. Henrickson's words, *for the first time* I begin to accept that my most dogged deficiency, *worry*, my vice since kindergarten, might sometimes have its place.

A PHYSICAL THERAPIST assembles a jazzy new brace, metallic green, on Lucas's leg, and tells him to start walking. Lucas returns to his stiff-legged gait, and all the therapists surround him and say, "Bend your knee, man! You can bend it now!" Lucas suddenly loses the wooden upward hitch as he walks back and forth almost naturally. *And the look on his face!*

Celine and Isabel trail their brother out, Lucas slapping his other leg, shouting, "Joy!" We pass the front desk and I call to the young Latina receptionist, who is smiling with us: "He's cured!"

One day, I know, we will walk out of a medical building with Vincent and those same words.

IT WAS FOUR Septembers ago, the day of Vincent's fourteenth birthday, September 10, which was a Sunday: he was suffering from a leg flare-up, and I was worried. We were late to Mass that day, but arrived in time for the First Reading of the 23rd Sunday in Ordinary Time. My mother was there, and she silently pointed to the middle of the page in my missal. The words there, dated September 10, were a gift for the mother of a boy born fourteen years to that day with a catastrophic disorder that would not reveal itself until later. These were the prophet Isaiah's words:

> Thus says the Lord: Say to those whose hearts are frightened: Be strong, fear not! Here is your God. He comes with vindication; with divine recompense he comes to save you. Then will the eyes of the blind be opened, the ears of the deaf be cleared, then will the lame leap like a stag, then the tongue of the mute will sing.

And then I knew on the date of my son's birth, a day I especially feared the curse of FOP, that divine recompense is also here and now, with its own hidden schedules. And I understood that vindication comes when we allow ourselves to see and hear the miracles that attend us in suffering. And then a "curse" is turned into a blessing.

Seven years ago when I spoke to the Filipina healer, guilty over whatever my role in our son's suffering might be, I was told a curse, a sin from an ancestor, was responsible. This theory jibed with the Tibetan monks' explanation to an FOP father of past life transgression and his daughter's disease.

Of course, those past lives, those ancestors in question, can only have been Adam and Eve, parents of the human condition.

And I know with all my heart that Vincent will one day *leap like a stag*, because he already does. And it is with a tongue loosed from fear that I can give voice to what I keep discovering: that on this steep course tracing the path of FOP, life is a magic mountain rising over fields of dreams for as far as our eyes will see. And it is never too late to have such vision. And with it I will never be lost.

My mom says that I am the detail man in the family, and when we built a house this summer, she put me in charge of telling the construction company about every imperfection in the walls, the doors, and every chipped piece of tile: I was the one in the family who noticed those details. I think this kind of vision will serve me in the medical world, where you learn to pay attention to the small things that go wrong to help people with the big things, like good health.

—Vincent Whelan, seventeen years old,
college essay/personal statement

EPILOGUE

Dear Carol,

*I wanted you to tell Vincent to keep up the good work; he is
so brave to go off to college away from home. I think about
him often and you also. Please tell Vincent that he is an
awesome role model for Cody, my son.*

Love,
Jen

> —JEN DENNINGS, mother of Cody,
> eleven, diagnosed at age nine, Texas

VINCENT WEATHERED THE FOP flare-ups at Berkeley all through
his first semester, excelling academically but struggling with medications and campus hills and distances. In January 2005, Walt drove
him home for a Zometa infusion at Children's Hospital. That same
week, Walt's mother survived a freeway accident and was making a
miracle recovery with her five children on vigil in ICU shifts.

We needed another miracle, and I asked the sisters at our parochial school to pray for one on the Friday morning Dr. Henrickson
ordered our experimental treatment. The back of Vincent's hand
took in the silver drip of the Zometa as he relaxed on a recliner,

watching movies on the monitor in a little room with flags-of-the-world wallpaper. Walt, exhausted from recent events, fell asleep in a wooden rocking chair.

The Zometa infusion took less than an hour, and it was uneventful, no sign of the fever or nausea common to this treatment. But that evening, after Walt had left for an L.A. hospital to continue keeping vigil over his mother, and my own mother arrived from the Bay Area take her grandchildren to a prime-rib dinner, Vincent announced suddenly, "My ears are numb." And there were pins and needles up and down one side of his face.

I rushed to my room to make calls and reached Dr. Kaplan first. "Give him a glass of milk," he instructed. Zometa, a bisphosphonate, can radically deplete serum calcium and produce the symptoms Vincent was reporting.

With a few glasses of milk and calcium carbonate tablets, the alarming side effects vanished before dinner. The FOP itself, however, played hide-and-seek for weeks before it gradually loosed its hold on Vincent's leg, but it had not robbed mobility. On Vincent's next visit home he arrived pain free, to sit next to his grandfather in auditoriums and watch his brother Lucas ad-lib a coach in *Footloose* and his sister Celine shine in a zany *Sleeping Beauty*. We cannot know for certain, not clinically, but it is possible Zometa beat back the FOP. (Still, it is a big gun with big-gun risks, not to be used more than two or three times a year.)

Should Vincent ever need a future Zometa treatment in the Bay Area, he will be able to have one at the UCSF FOP Consultation Center, where he has established himself as a patient. At UCSF he saw the specialist recommended by my high school classmate, Dr. Sigurd Berven, who diagnosed a case of FOP in South Africa two weeks before our visit. That visit was documented by a *USA Today* photographer for an article about Vincent and the center's founder-director, Dr. Joseph Kitterman, and his grandson Matt. The *USA Today* piece drew messages to Dr. Kaplan at the University of Pennsylvania from physicians around the country.

With the Zometa infusion I believed we had tricked FOP. Vincent continued well enough, able to manage flare-ups with his usual medications. But I learned, not long ago, that FOP had attacked in a different way—without the usual red flags.

As we were leaving his last ophthalmologist's checkup, I asked Vincent why he hadn't worn contacts in a long time. He had alternated between wire-rimmed glasses and the soft lenses since high school.

"My right hand won't reach all the way to my eye," he said, without fanfare.

"How's that?" I was bewildered.

My son demonstrated, his right hand reaching just shy of his brow. He had lost that ground months ago, at Berkeley, but never made mention of it through the time he played in pep band, granted interviews to the *Daily Cal* and the *San Francisco Chronicle*, sold green FOP Awareness bracelets with Travis, or asked students to write Congress because twelve-year-old Whitney Weldon spoke on Capitol Hill Day to seek funds for research on her FOP. (Whitney's family founded the FOP Awareness green-bracelet campaign. Our kids, their teachers, and FOP families and friends across the world have distributed the bands.)

"Did you have a flare-up in your arm?" I asked Vincent, thinking back on the past months. Vincent shook his head no. FOP can also do its work in stealth.

"It's OK, Mom," Vincent said, unruffled. "I didn't like contacts, anyway."

Vincent's news left me, once again, astonished at his capacity to adapt. But it also drove home the brutal reminder that FOP—this rogue gene—may retreat, hide, and even capitulate, but it is *always there*.

IN THE FALL of 2005 Walt and I made a pilgrimage to Philadelphia to see Brian in his first year of law school, to tour the FOP Lab, and to meet a dedicated Latin American doctor, Patricia Delai, planning an FOP dental-care center for South American patients. We did not meet Patricia Delai, because we missed our plane from Fresno (it finally happened . . .). But we made it to Penn to visit the FOP Laboratory. The little lab I remembered had changed and grown, and had been renamed the Center for Research in FOP and Related Disorders at the University of Pennsylvania School of Medicine—this through the efforts of FOP families and friends around the world.

Dr. Paul Billings, a molecular cell biologist who came to Penn via Harvard, gave us a tour of the facilities on a day when Dr. Kaplan and his other researchers were away at a conference. When we first saw Dr. Billings, fair and Nordic looking, in white lab coat and running shoes, he was at his workstation, peering through a glass panel hood to protect against bacteria and dust, holding a large syringe, and injecting a mysterious fluid into receptacles. Near him were bottles of reagents, one of them labeled "Modified Eagle Medium." I memorized that name, because it made me think of those currents over the mountains that the great birds use to fly, their shadows sliding across the snow.

Dr. Billings pulled off a latex glove to shake our hands and ushered us into a closet-size space with the fat frozen nitrogen tanks that keep cell cultures alive; he opened a cupboard to reveal rows of plastic receptacles in different shapes, used for blood cells kept in solutions. He had us squint through a microscope at the irregular outlines of pulp cells from baby teeth lost by children with and without FOP, mixed with reagents to make the cells clump. (I took a picture to prove to Isabel that I had, in fact, found the Tooth Fairy's repository.)

Along one wall of the larger room in the lab, we saw a row of what looked like dorm-room refrigerators, little appliances kept at body temperature, near 36.5 degrees Celsius, to incubate FOP cell cultures. Dr. Billings also led us down the hall into a workshop of shelves and bottles holding reagents in crystals and powders, some like the silicon beads in packets with DO NOT EAT warnings. Walt and I stood reverently, as if in a museum, while Dr. Billings took up and set down arcane objects with familiarity, updating us on research on BMP4, FOP's bone-making protein, and cell lines and all the rest of the Greek-god terminology of extreme science he tried very hard to break down for us mortals.

We had brought a little gift for Dr. Kaplan and the lab, and left it on Dr. Kaplan's desk in his office, where every available surface of wall and filing cabinet space was taken by children's art and photographs of his FOP patients and their families. I saw, under one window, two Christmas seasons of our kids, and a photo of Vincent in this same office as a boy, with young Tiffany Linker, both of them smiling, raising lollipops, Dr. Fred in between. I asked Kay Ray, Dr. Kaplan's right hand at Penn, to open the little white box we had brought. Kay reached in to unwind white tissue and then exclaimed over the treasure Isabel and Celine found at Kris Kringle & Co.: a gold fortune cookie. Kay unclasped it, pulled out the little slip of paper, and began laughing.

Kay had not forgotten Stephanie Snow's injunction to Dr. Kaplan at an early Santa Maria fund-raiser. She reread the gold fortune cookie message in her sweet Scottish voice: YOU WILL FIND THE CURE FOR FOP AND IT WILL BE CHERRY FLAVORED.

In solidarity with the quest for a cure, Isabel founded a Best Friends Forever FOP Club with her friends Sarah Dick, Rachel Chen, and Shelby Arioto to raise research funds. The club's Isabel's Rules were read to an enthusiastic reception at the last University of Pennsylvania School of Medicine FOP Lab meeting, and, next to a photo of our five children, they will hang in the laboratory. They state: I: 1. IDEAS ARE POWERFUL THINGS; 2. IDEAS ARE LIKE INVENTIONS; 3. SHARE YOUR IDEAS; II:. I. PAY ATTENTION; 2. RESPECT OTHER PEOPLE'S IDEAS; 3. FEEL FREE TO ASK ANY QUESTIONS OR SHARE ANY IDEAS; 4. LISTEN TO OTHER PEOPLE'S QUESTIONS; 5. BE CREATIVE; 6. WAIT 'TILL IT'S YOUR TURN. (These are rules forged through trial and error by five glorious kids.)

On the same trip east to the lab, I reunited with two soul sisters, friends who have lived through the FOP battle with us, but whom I had not seen since the 2000 symposium: Connie Green and Verena Dobnik. Verena Dobnik is the AP journalist who wrote the first internationally distributed FOP newspaper piece, and afterward became a family friend of Connie Green, a soprano in the Metropolitan Opera Chorus. Connie has sung "Songs for Sophia" for her nine-year-old, Sophia, who bravely battles FOP, and she has lent her voice to the cause with Plácido Domingo, Stephanie Blythe, Heidi Grant Murphy, and Bryn Terfel, the latter three onstage in *Falstaff*. We all saw *Falstaff* that fall night in New York City, with Brian,

Walt's sister Jennifer, our brother-in-law Ken, and nieces Nicole and Natalie. I witnessed opera as I had never before, with colors and voices as vivid as dreams, with the thrill of finding my friend in Elizabethan costume on a stage with a real unicorn and Zeffirelli fairies and trees in an aqua-colored forest. And when the elegant musicians of the orchestra had filed off with flutes and trumpets and violins through the shadows under the stage, Connie led us to diva Stephanie Blythe, who had sung for the FOP effort, so we could thank her. And at that moment Dr. Kaplan's words echoed through me: *FOP is a hell of a way to make friends. But what friends! What blessed, blessed friends* . . .

Two weeks after looking into the orchestra pit at the Met, we were in an orchestra's audience at the oldest college in California, to which Vincent transferred his sophomore year, deciding that FOP might give him some peace on a small campus with no hills. (And this has proven mostly true.) We were in a grand terra cotta mission church of polished brick floors and sky blues and a gilded altar washed in sepia light, honoring the Italian saint whose name was given to a university, a name that signifies illumination: Santa Clara.

And there I was, raising the video camera, listening for the silver trumpet tuning itself to the other instruments, so full of pride it took me a moment to get my bearings, to hear the A of the oboe in the woodwinds and the brass and the silence before the strings, to aim a viewfinder at my tall, handsome son in black tie rising for an opening bow from the last row, Saint Anthony in a painting over his shoulder extending his arms to the Christ Child.

There we all were, along with Walt's sister June, and uncle Tony and cousin Joe, feeling the rivers of flutes and violins and the silver current of one trumpet. And after the gold of the opened tabernacle had reflected every note; after the applause and hugs and the flash of a bouquet of red roses; after Vincent had zipped his trumpet into the blue fabric case so light it seemed empty to him one Christmas, Isabel pointed to a faded saint's statue by Our Lady of Guadalupe. And she told us something I know each one of our five glorious children would believe possible: "I saw a twinkle in her eye."

AFTERWORD
By Michael Henrickson, MD

VINCENT AND HIS family inspire me. Their story reaches out to us for a satisfying conclusion. However, you have simply read his prologue; for this is neither a story of limitation nor of life spent adjusting to impairment. An encounter with Vincent or his parents does not leave you feeling powerless. I have had the extraordinary privilege to share their journey for a decade, marveling at their resilience. Indeed, I have learned many essentials of the human experience along with them. Courage, adaptability, resourcefulness, perseverance, redefinition during crisis, and enduring love are characteristics that you witness in this book and their journey. It is metaphorical that while Vincent's illness has increasingly attempted to embody rigidity, he has adapted by becoming increasingly flexible in his attitude, imagination, and planning. Vincent's quiet resolve drives him to confront tasks of daily routine while allowing creative spiritual and mental escape from the confines of a body that cannot be willed to do more than flesh allows. By any measure of success, Vincent has flourished. This is the reason his story needs to be told.

I expect there have been dark, unbearable moments of doubt for Vincent and his parents. In such gifted people, these periods forge a steely character, preparing them for challenges. Here, true growth begins. Such collective strength of character will allow them to succeed in managing many unforeseeable future uncertainties. Vincent is a stirring model of the indomitable energy such trials produce when tempered by initiative and the grit required to never accept "no" as a satisfactory option. However, Vincent and his family do not operate under a romantic assumption that his recovery depends upon garnering sufficient willpower. They are fully aware of the imminent dangers Vincent faces. In the mercurial fashion of FOP, loss of an important musculoskeletal function may occur overnight; restricted chest-wall movement may escalate a cold into pneumonia. Their curiosity about scientific advances and their advocacy rapidly linked them to an international community. Ultimately, they are confident the medical community will identify a successful treatment strategy after unraveling the molecular biology of FOP.

The parallel here to a broad diversity of chronic diseases is how individuals choose to prevail while shouldering their illness. If confronted with such an unrelenting foe as FOP, we hope we would have Vincent's courage. His tenacious will is as much an inherited trait from Vincent's parents as the affliction that besets him. He has had the full measure of support from his family, with parents who have never, ever flinched from the grade of the hill they have had to climb with Vincent. Carol and Walter have demonstrated for Vincent and his siblings how to tackle seemingly insurmountable odds, finding not simply a way to cope, but an avenue of success through this adversity. I invite you to learn from the lessons patterned in this brilliant story of life lived fully, to find ways to overcome the hardships in your own life, and, if that cannot be, then to adapt innovatively where possible.

MICHAEL HENRICKSON, MD, Past Medical Director of the Division of Rheumatology, Children's Hospital Central California, and Assistant Professor (Clinical), UCSF; currently Clinical Director, Section of Rheumatology, the Children's Hospital at University of Oklahoma Medical Center, Clinical Associate Professor, the University of Oklahoma Health Sciences Center, Oklahoma City, Oklahoma.

THE FOP LABORATORY

Aiming for Answers Amid the Peaks—
from the Valleys

By Verena Dobnik

DR. FREDERICK KAPLAN describes the unusual challenges in his life: scaling mountain peaks, facing a terrorist, and even venturing deep inside the bodies of mice and men.

He's really speaking about only one thing: his life's quest to conquer an illness whose Latin name is as convoluted as the extra bone it leaves in a human body—fibrodysplasia ossificans progressiva, or FOP.

"While climbing mountains in Alaska some years ago, one of us scrambled to a ledge with a stunning view of the highest peak in the range—or so it seemed," Kaplan wrote in the annual report on the progress of his FOP research team at the University of Pennsylvania. "Only by climbing farther did the realization occur that the perceived summit was only one of many smaller peaks that obscured the real summit deeply shrouded in clouds. So, too, it is with FOP research."

The battle against the genetic disease he calls "a bioterrorist" that attacks children's bodies is being waged in a Philadelphia laboratory that I first visited in 2000, as a journalist for The Associated Press reporting on FOP.

"Fred"—as everyone calls him, including his tiniest patients—is a doctor whose laughter and brilliant spirit are fueling a fight against FOP that has taken up 15 years of his 53-year life, and counting.

Inside a lineup of drab lab rooms off a long corridor, the whirring sound of scientific machinery creates a 24-hour soundtrack for the team of about a dozen scientists. Led by Eileen Shore, who has a PhD in molecular biology, the team includes Dr. David Glaser, an orthopedist, and Dr. Robert Pignolo, a clinical bone specialist, as well as interns headed for careers in science.

Kaplan, who ties the research to his hands-on encounters with patients, has a title as daunting as FOP: the Isaac & Rose Nassau Professor of Orthopaedic Molecular Medicine, and Chief Division of Metabolic Bone Diseases and Molecular Medicine in the Department of Orthopaedic Surgery at the University of Pennsylvania School of Medicine.

Privately, he sums up his role in far fewer words: "To lead the expedition to the summit."

That means finding an effective FOP treatment and, eventually, a cure.

In the lab, the white refrigeration boxes, rows of glass test tubes, and centrifuges that spin genes from human cells are sterile and still, offering no healing warmth. The air-conditioning is cranked up to keep both cell specimens and scientists cool. The researchers move from task to task, their faces often expressionless as they focus silently.

But behind these high-tech contraptions, plastic countertops, and poker faces are flesh-and-warm-blood human beings with an unflagging sense of purpose: cracking the mystery of FOP, however long it might take.

Occasionally, a real victory is scored—a major one recently.

It came as the researchers struggled to pinpoint the exact gene that triggers the disease, while zeroing in on the most crucial question: Which path in the human body does the mutant gene take to turn soft human cells into extra bone?

FOP sends its signals "like the game of telephone, in which one bit of information is passed on to the next person, with genetic errors transmitted along the way," says Shore. "If we can block that signal before bone starts to grow, that's a great target for therapies and treatment."

The latest victory came from the lab results of Jennifer Fiori, a 27-year-old University of Pennsylvania PhD candidate in molecular biology.

With Shore and Kaplan guiding her, Fiori reached a major breakthrough in FOP research: In an experiment using a lab incubator and FOP cells, she drew the first real "roadmap" of the renegade bone forming pathway, tracing what was in fact healthy bone-building protein as it streams through human tissue toward its target pathway. What she discovered was that one pathway, a kind of receptive "door" that should lock when enough of the protein has passed through, fails to stop the remaining bone-making force. That fatal, flawed encounter helps produce FOP, the researchers believe.

This new knowledge of where, and with what exaggerated energy, FOP surges through human molecules will now allow scientists to create a drug that blocks the bone-making protein from advancing through the key pathway.

Kaplan and his researchers will test various antibodies, aiming for one result: to stop the bone growth in its tracks.

"It's really exciting," says Fiori, who was deeply moved when she first saw children and adults living with FOP in several documentary films—before she started working in the FOP lab three years earlier.

But there's no instant gratification in this work, which requires the patience of Job from the researchers.

It will take years to develop an antibody that can be used by humans. A pharmaceutical firm must first agree to test and manufacture such a drug, which would then be subjected to fierce government scrutiny before it's approved for human beings. Drug companies might agree to invest the tens of millions of dollars needed to develop such a drug, says Kaplan, once they know that an antibody effective against FOP could also be used to control the extra bone growth that's a typical side-effect of hip surgery, as well as traumatic head injuries in accidents, heart valve replacements and spinal injuries. That would make investing in a drug for a rare condition like FOP cost-effective—a prime factor in the competitive pharmaceutical industry.

Along with Fiori's discovery, there have been other recent findings on FOP that Kaplan says could well be called "Of Mice and Men"—not the title of the John Steinbeck novel, but two real discoveries, one involving a man with FOP, the other a mouse.

The man had received a bone marrow transplant for an unrelated condition. Observing him closely "told us more about FOP in one hour in the clinic than one-quarter century of experiments could possibly have revealed," Kaplan wrote in the annual report.

The discovery in a mouse came out of a Chicago lab—one of a handful in the United States and Europe that also do FOP-linked research, often collaborating with the Penn team. Neuroscientists in Chicago studying brain development had engineered a mouse to overproduce a certain protein, which turned out to be a similar protein that kick-starts the renegade bone growth in a child. They observed a pattern that could be used to probe such bone explosions in a person.

Members of Penn's FOP team often are awakened in the middle of the night by emergency calls from all over the world—anguished appeals from parents whose children experience a sudden flare-up that precedes another bout of irreversible bone growth.

"Seeing FOP progress in a person without having the ability to do anything right now is the hardest thing in our work," says Shore. "I know that we're doing whatever we can and I know it's a slow process, but you just want to stop it—you want to stop it right now!"

The energy to never stop working comes from the hope that bursts through the tough shell of scientific precision.

"One of the terrors of suffering from a rare disease is that there might be no interest in it, and there's nobody working on it," says Kaplan. "But the fact that every FOP patient around the world can go to sleep at night and wake up in the morning knowing that there are teams of scientists and collaborators who are thinking about this every day—I think that does bring great hope."

Kaplan and his colleagues often stay at the lab during off-hours, nurturing experiments that continue past sundown through the night and into the next day—work involving hour after hour of drudgery, with no immediate result.

"It very often isn't like a Eureka moment," says Shore.

Kaplan works six, sometimes seven, days a week—including visits with patients who come to see him so he can run his fingers across the bulges of bone, playing and giggling with the kids while his pained eyes examine what he shares with parents about living with FOP. Kaplan also visits patients in Germany, England, France, South America and all around the United States. He sometimes participates in fund-raisers for the research, which is supported through private donations and by the National Institutes of Health in Bethesda, Maryland.

In the end, it comes down to the human touch.

The scientists at the FOP lab exude a burning sense of mission that mirrors the Hippocratic Oath, created by the Greek physician who is considered the father of modern medicine. Part of the ancient Greek text reads, in modern translation: "I will not put personal profit or advancement above my duty to patients."

The FOP team is driven by the dream, Kaplan wrote in the annual report, that "some day, a child with FOP will be born and everything about this daunting mountain range of FOP will be known—its genetic basis, its molecular origin, the nature of its pathways, the identity of its receptive cells and their downstream targets, the drugs to prevent it, and the therapies to cure it.

"That day is not yet at hand, but the journey and the climb towards the real summit continues unimpeded and uninterrupted."

A FURTHER NOTE FROM
CAROL ZAPATA-WHELAN

On April 23, 2006, at 1:00 PM EST, days before this book went to the press, Drs. Frederick Kaplan and Eileen Shore made an announcement on behalf of their colleagues at The Center for Research in FOP and Related Disorders at The University of Pennsylvania and their collaborators in the International FOP Research Consortium. Drs. Kaplan and Shore announced their discovery of the FOP gene, ACVR1. Verena Dobnik's Associated Press article on this monumental advance—fifteen years in the making—was run by newspapers around the nation and around the world. The discovery of the FOP gene can help lead us to the next horizon: effective treatment for FOP, for conditions such as osteoporisis and arthritis—and, we hope and pray: a cure.

ACKNOWLEDGMENTS

*We have had FOP our entire lives. We know our FOP may
get worse, but our joy in life is not affected by this fact. . . .
As we have grown older, our needs have increased. . . .
All along, our mother has been there for us, to help us and
to help make our lives better. One day, I said to Christine,
"Our mother deserves a medal for all she does for us every
day. It is important, at least once, to say thank you to our
mother in a very public way. There are millions of people
who live in Germany, but our family is unique. We are the
only multigenerational family with FOP in all of Germany.
. . . So I wrote to the President and I told him the story of
our family. . . . I told him that our mother deserved a medal
for all she did for us every day . . . and I also described
how she looked after our father as well, who also had FOP.
The President was convinced, and he decided to award
this historic medal to our mother. A letter arrived one day
in the mail from Berlin, and I, the mailman, delivered
the news to our mother. The letter said that our mother
would be awarded the highest civilian honor of the German
government. . . . We all attended a beautiful ceremony
at a castle in Bavaria, where the Secretary of State . . .
presented the medal to our mother.*

—Norbert and Christine Seidl, thirty-
three and thirty-one, son and daughter of Franziska
Seidl, Freyung, Germany, as told to Dr. Fred Kaplan
in March 2005 (*The FOP Connection* 18)

ALL OTHER FOP mothers are infinitely more worthy of having their efforts in the FOP battle committed to paper than I. Every family's battle with FOP is unique and terribly inspiring; I only hope that I have been able to communicate some of what we all face to draw attention to such a rare disorder, and in the process share my son's courage.

These acknowledgments will read like the list of credits after a movie, because this book would have been impossible without all the people in it and behind it.

My deepest gratitude goes to my beloved husband, Walt, and my glorious children, Brian, Vincent, Lucas, Celine, and Isabel, for *being them*, for allowing me to share their lives in writing in the service of a greater good. I thank my beloved parents for what could never fit into the most infinite book by Borges, as well as Walt's miracle-maker mother, June, and our kids' third devoted grandfather, Roland Hamilton; my brother, Martín, my Mexican sister, Elia, my UCLA sister Candy, my whole family, all of it—everywhere—in the United States and in Argentina: Zapata Mercader (Jorge, Juan Antonio, Aída, Federico, and families; Roberto Carlos and all); Correas Leal (Raúl, Margarita, my godparents, Jorge and Susana, and families; cousin Adrián Calise and all); Whelan (June, Tony, Joe, Chris, Linda, Jennifer, Ken, Nicole, Natalie, Joan, Robert, Blaise, Bianca, Bede; uncles Don, Tom, Eddie, aunts Marjorie and Donna, and all), as well as our FOP family around the world. I also write in memory of my children's grandfather Walter, my grandparents Edmundo and Carolita Correas; Juan Antonio and Aída Zapata. We are forever grateful for the love of: Sor Paulina, Sor Isabel, Sor Pilar, Sor Gloria, Sor Olvido, Sor Esperanza, Sor María, Sor Angeles, and all the Immaculate Conception sisters in the United States and Spain, who have prayed steadfastly through the years for Vincent and our family. They are the miracle facilitators.

We thank Father Raúl Sánchez, Father Ray Dreilling, Father Gregory Beaumont, the late Father Chuck and all of Vincent's parochial school teachers, particularly Cyndi Clopton (who sold green bracelets) and Monica Carter. We are especially indebted to the support of families and every single one of our children's teachers at all their schools, particularly for special support and attention from Father Vincent López, John Eckman, Dennis DuPertuis, Shawn Carey, Stevan Fabela, Ranay Franklin, Nyla Zender, David Warmerdam, Sharon Cook, Marvin Enns, Michael Martin, Joan Johnson, Bruce Garabedian, Kate Fourchy, Tom Skypeck, Lisa Cameron, Lisa Jones, Jean West, Michelle Fox, Cathy Frye, Michael Danks-Ferguson, who had all of his classes write to Congress to help raise funds for FOP research.

We thank every single one of the hundreds of relations and friends, colleagues and businesses who have boosted FOP research in Vincent's name through the years, and we never forget the special efforts of our friends: Bruce, Jackie, Isaac, and Cole Thornton and friends; Blanche Nosworthy and her family; Mimi Cott, Patricia Oren, Roberta Palomino, and friends; the Lonjers and Yosifov families and friends; Viviana Schwarzbein and friends; Roberta Shelby, Pascual Gargiulo, MD; Audrey Schwarzbein, MD; Diana Schwarzbein, MD; Phyllis Preciado, MD; Gary Singh; Zoe Scott and friends; Caitlyn Shreve, and every single soul praying for and supporting this effort.

We have been blessed with the best health professionals in the world: Horst Weinberg, MD; Brad Sumrell, MD; Michael Henrickson, MD; Dowain Wright, MD, PhD; Alfred Peters, MD; Joseph Gerardi, OD; Anthony Molina, MD; Plamen Yosifov, MD; Rob Lonjers, MD; Thomas Larson, DDS; William Asbury, DDS; Roger Lambert & David Wright, DDS; Gary Waters, MD; Gail Bernthal, MSPA; Salma Simjee, MD; Davis Baldwin, MD; Steven Thaxter, MD; Gary Lentell, MS; at the new UCSF FOP Consultation Center: Director, founder Joseph A. Kitterman, MD; Mohammed Diab, MD; Kelly Alexy, NNP; Robert Goldsby, MD; Sigurd Berven, MD (and my St. Francis classmate, Jeff Lotz, PhD); Hanmin Lee, MD; Jeffrey Tabas, MD; Kersten Morehead, MD; Emily Von Scheven, MD; at the Center for FOP and Related Diseases at the University of Pennsylvania: Directors Frederick S. Kaplan, MD and Eileen Shore, PhD; David Glaser, MD; Michael Zasloff, MD; Paul Billings, PhD; Meiqi Xu, PhD; Kamlesh Rai and every single present and past precious researcher at the FOP Lab; and related: Diana Mitchell, MD; Thomas Jefferson University Hospital in Philadelphia and Burt Nussbaum, DDS; Zvi Grunwald,

MD, Colleen Vernick MD; Eileen Kilmartin, MD; Robert Decidue, DMD, MD; Daniel Taumb, DMD, MD; Kathleen Herb, DMD, MD for supreme generosity with Latin American FOP patients.

Profound thanks go to our lifelines: all the expert, warm, lovely nurses and staff at Peachwood Pediatrics, especially: Laura Lee Brown, RN; Leta Hering, FNP; Kelly Silipigni, Dawn Mezco, and Valerie Pérez; in Rheumatology at Children's Hospital Central California: Barbara Pagluighi, RN; Paula Lyman, ACT; Sally Flores, RN; Charlotte Nason.

Special thanks to my life-saving friends: Candy Candelaria, Julie Olguín Molina, Cherie Lonjers, Kathy Yosifov, Mira Dick, Kathy Chen, Sandy DiCicco, Viviana Schwarzbein, Carmen Díaz Flores, Corey Arioto, Cate Casa, Monica Carter, Fran Palomo, Lisa O'Neill, Kathryn Henry-Clay, Moira Gordillo, Theresa Ellison, and Doris D'Annibale, for *everything*. Thanks to my soul sisters on the East Coast, Connie Green and Verena Dobnik, for the same.

Special gratitude goes to Edward Malone, Cathy Jay, Marco Ruffini, Aurâlie Vialette, Geri and Travis Wong—for everything at UC Berkeley; at Santa Clara University extra thanks go to Ann Ravenscroft and Valerie Sarma. Nearer home, we are grateful for Paul Chen, CPA extraordinaire, who computes that 1.3 billion people will buy this book.

I am forever grateful for the painstaking editing and lifesaving of my dear, dear *amiga* Susan Early (and her Dumont Printing), and indebted now and from forever for the literary support of my mother, Dr. Celia Correas Zapata, and of Isabel Allende, Malcolm Margolin, Elba Peralta, Roland and Paul Hamilton, Marta Schwarzbein, Charlie Ericksen, Ginger McDonald, Isabel Valdez, Jaime Correas, Luisa Hansen, María Elena Ratinoff, Mas Masumoto, Peggy Preciado, Susan Sánchez Casal, Ericka Lutz, Tamara Kaye Sellman, Hugo Moser, MD, Anne Lamott, Martha Beck, Margarita Cota-Cárdenas, Gerard Jones, and Margarita Engle.

Very special gratitude goes to the music and moral support of tenor José Carreras and Antonio García Prat at the Carreras Foundation in Barcelona, Spain, and Fresno Philharmonic violinist Arthur Howansky.

Great thanks to Michael Blunt, for his aesthetic expertise, to Sandy Wendland for all her hard work with ink and paper, to Destrie and Michele for Rubio's, to all at Chico's for beauty and kindnesses, to Meggin and Juanita for sunny mornings; to Paul for all the help; to Ronnie, for his example; to Mr. Cool for air; to Ralph Hudson and Don King of the Wheelchair Connection/Scooter Warehouse for their kind, amazing assistance.

Thanks and admiration to every single past and present officer and member of the IFOPA, specifically to those friends and their families around the world with whom we have personally intersected in this effort: the inspirational Jeannie Peeper, Amanda Cali, Jeri Licht, Joe and Kathy Kitterman and the Horrick family, Gary Whyte, Linda Daugherty, Eyal Goldshmid; the Snow, Eckart, and Danzer families; the town of Santa Maria; Susan and Shay Williams; Marilyn Hair and Sarah Steele and family; Charis Ramirez and family; Robin Rice; Holly Pullano; Jen Dennings; RoJeanne and Jasmin Floyd; Hillary and Whitney Weldon; Carol and Ashley Kurpiel; Lori and Nick Maher; the Heyn family; Lori Henrotay; Teresa Caruso; the Pheif family; Amie Darnell; Lakshmi Natarajan (India), Julie Hopwood (England), Marie Halbert (Sweden), Martine LeTartre (Belgium), Melody Del Val (Spain), and Norbert Seidl (Germany); with particular gratitude to my dear friend Sharon Kantanie for her work, counsel, and writings. I offer profound thanks to Nancy Sando, in memory of Andy Sando and Mary Kay Weber. Thanks to Claudio Toro and family in Chile; Ricardo Díaz and family in Argentina; Moira Liljesthröm in Buenos Aires, who brilliantly heads FOPlatinoamérica; Mari Fuentes Barrantes in Boston; and to Patricia Delai, MD, in São Paulo, for her inspiring and devoted work through Latin America. Special gratitude and blessings to Teresa and Reynaldo Tejada, in special memory of beloved little María Claudia, in whose name the FOP effort will progress in Peru and in the world.

I am grateful to my colleagues and friends, from CSUF, UCLA, and Stanford for their kindnesses and special support through time: Bruce Thornton, Victor Davis Hanson, Steve Yarbrough, Ross Shideler, Kathleen Komar, Michael Predmore, the late Fernando Alegría, Rubén Benítez, Gerardo Luzuriaga, Luis Costa, Paul Priebe, José

Elgorriaga, Juan Serrano, Jacinta Amaral, Ron Freeman, Maurice Gendron, Cosme Zaragoza, John Barta, David Ross, Saúl Jiménez-Sandoval, Barbara Birch, Elsa Castillo, Diane Hazeltine, Dianna Meyer, and Karen Streatch—and the late Ara Hairabedian, iconic CSUF swim coach, who included FOP in his kinesiology exams.

I thank my beloved CSUF students, especially those who buoyed me through the writing of this story: Olivia Becerra, Lourdes Estrada, Janet Gusukuma-Hamilton, Yadira Solorio, Susana Días, Anita Gutiérrez, Ana Ponce-Jiménez, Julia Palacios, Lilia, María, and Teresita Rubio, María Elvira Hernández, María Arteaga, Georgina Betancourt, Francisco Alvarez, Felicitas Carrillo, Luz Cervantes, Ken Cox, Susana Curiel, John Furtado, Alicia García, Oscar Hernández, Rubén Hernández, Rubén Landeros, Nereida López, Luis Martínez, Yulma Martínez, Gerardo Mendoza, José Morales, Dianne Pickin, Griselda Islas, Rosa Rodríguez, Lorena Sánchez, Lauren Scott, Maritere Vásquez, Teresa Zamora, Lourdes Arellano, Miriam Balderas, Yanet Castro, José De La Torre, Sol De La Torre, Sagrario Díaz, Rosa García, Imelda Hernández, Efraín Huizar, Juan Ibarra, Mireya Jiménez, Everardo Mayorga, Ricardo Ortega, Edgardo Pacheco, Ariel Quezada, Yaneth Ramírez, Rosa Rubio, Sandra Vallejo, Antonio Vera, Delia Villanueva, Gabrielle Waters, José Alvarez, Every Argueta, Noemi Benavides, Mayra Cerna, Jamie Farley, Margarita Hernández, Claudia Robles, Jesse Ruvalcaba, Mayra Santana, Olivia Torres, Omar Naftaji, Grisel Ruiz, Rosa Quevedo, Rosa Soltani, and Lee Wilson. *Gracias.*

I would like to thank *Newsweek* (Pam Hamer, especially), *Literary Mama*, *The Rotarian*, *El Andar*, Hispanic Link News Service, *Chicken Soup for the Latino Soul*, *Diario Uno*, *Mindprints: A Literary Journal*, *The Philosophical Mother*, *The FOP Connection*, *The Simple Pleasures of Friendship*, and *Angel Over My Shoulder* for publishing versions of a few passages in this book.

For their invaluable journalistic contributions to our own effort, we thank Verena Dobnik of the Associated Press; Pat Yollin of the *San Francisco Chronicle*; David Kelly and Suzanne Leigh of *USA Today*; Andrea Hernandez and Julie Hime of UC Berkeley's the *Daily Californian*; María Eraña and Samuel Orozco of Radio

Bilingüe; Eddie Hughes of the *Clovis Independent*; Kathy Barberich of the *Fresno Bee*; National Public Radio; Fresno affiliates of ABC, NBC, and CBS.

For the April 23, 2006 announcement of the discovery of the FOP gene, ACVR1, we express profound and eternal gratitude to Drs. Fred Kaplan, Eileen Shore, David Glaser, their past and present colleagues at The Center for Research in FOP and Related Disorders at The University of Pennsylvania and their collaborators in the International FOP Research Consortium.

Great gratitude goes to my wonderful and receptive publisher, Matthew Lore, and his colleagues, Peter Jacoby, Vincent Kunkemueller, and Donna Stonecipher, for caring, for allowing me the promise of miracles that this story represents.

Gracias, gracias, gracias a Dios.